LET

CLARA SCHUMANN

AND

JOHANNES BRAHMS
1853-1896

EDITED BY
DR. BERTHOLD LITZMANN

IN TWO VOLUMES
VOL. II

VIENNA HOUSE
New York

*This Vienna House edition,
first published in 1973,
is an unabridged republication of
the work originally published by
Longmans, Green and Co., New York, in 1927.*

*International Standard Book Number: 0-8443-0054-3
(Volume I)
International Standard Book Number: 0-8443-0055-1
(Volume II)
International Standard Book Number: 0-8443-0056-X
(Set of Volumes I & II)
Library of Congress Catalog Card Number: 77-163792*

Printed in the United States of America

1877

Clara *to* Brahms.

BERLIN, *Jan.* 7.

DEAREST JOHANNES,

Once more I write to you on your own account! Can't you put off the decision about Düsseldorf until we have discussed it in Leipsic? All the best people in Düsseldorf long for you to come, including, of course, Fräulein Leser, but she is calm and thoughtful about it, and keeps on writing to me that, much as she wants it, nobody could desire it for your sake, provided they meant well by you, as the orchestra is miserably poor and you would have to reorganize the choir from top to toe, etc., etc. If only we could discuss it by word of mouth! The Bendemanns wrote to me to-day that I must not be over-hasty in my decision.[1] They very much want me to go there, but they begged me to remember how limited my opportunities would be in the little town, both as regards pupils and other things. As to the pupils, I confess I had been thinking about obtaining them only from a distance, but I quite realize that the matter requires very serious thought. And yet where am I to go? I certainly do not want to end my days here.

. . . Many thanks for your letter. But how bitter the separation from friends is, particularly when vital matters have to be discussed, as in your case now. That is why it is indeed a comfort to me to know that I shall see you soon, and then we can go over all the pros and cons and weigh them.

Good-bye for to-day. Now that I have written I feel relieved. A thousand hearty greetings from Your CLARA.

[1] This seems to refer to some appointment she had been offered at Leipsic, about which Brahms writes to her in the next letter.—TR.

BRAHMS *to* CLARA.

VIENNA, *January.*

DEAREST CLARA,

Just one word—I have refused the Düsseldorf post. This is quite between ourselves, as I must await the answer.

The performance in Breslau was very fine.[1] The introduction to the finale, just as I like it, that is to say different from what it was in Leipsic. Unfortunately I am inclined to allow such important matters to slide. But it was most beautiful in Leipsic—this was not due to my fair hostess,[2] but above all because you were there ! Think well over Leipsic. If you move there, I should certainly spend some more winters there ! There are many, a great many, nice people there, and music of every kind, so that one can gladly do without other things.

N.B.—Röntgen's Serenade was quite exquisite and wholly delightful.[3] It is enchantingly fresh, thoughtful and profound. I have heard nothing of his which is as good. Besides, he is such a frank and hearty young man, that one cannot help being pleased about it. But I travelled all night and wrote, among others, to Bitter !

Hearty greetings to the children and discuss Leipsic thoroughly over breakfast !

With love, from JOHANNES.

CLARA *to* BRAHMS.

DÜSSELDORF, *Feb.* 6.

I could not answer your letter before ; I received it just as I was going away, and during the first days here could not find a moment to write. As regards Hanslick, I am horrified ; as I did not think he would dream of writing about my husband's years of illness ;[4] I could not bring myself to give him a helping hand in this. The more I think over it the less am I able to grasp Hanslick's idea and your agree-

---

[1] C minor Symphony.

[2] Elisabeth von Herzogenberg.

[3] Julius Röntgen, subsequently Musical Director at Rotterdam and Amsterdam.

[4] Cf. Hanslick's later essay, " Robert Schumann in Endenich " in *Am Ende des Jahrhunderts*, Berlin, 2nd Ed., 1899.

ment with it. People know Robert Schumann none too well
as he was in his days of good health, and now I am expected
to acquiesce in a description of his years of illness ! Quite
apart from every other consideration, this might be extremely
painful to us all. His illness can anyhow only be of interest
to doctors, and if a biography of Schumann were written, it
would surely be more fitting and more reverent to deal very
briefly with these latter years. I am sure that when you have
thought over the matter calmly you will agree with me. If
you had explained the matter to me as clearly in Leipsic as
you have now, I should not find myself in the present painful
position with regard to Hanslick. But I feel sure that you
will lay all this before him and support me. I must dictate
the rest, as writing is too much of an effort for me.

I found everybody here very much excited over your refusal,
and Bitter is said to be doubly vexed by your hesitation,
particularly as he heard three weeks ago from other sources
that you were going to decline. They tried to persuade me
to write to you further about the matter, but I begged Stein-
metz to do it, for to try to influence you further would be a
responsibility which I would not willingly undertake. But I
may as well tell you that all idea of a school dependent upon
the Ministry has been abandoned, for the subsidy would not
be paid, as was originally supposed, by the *Bergischen Schul-
fond* but out of the Kaiser's privy purse, and only if you
accepted, not for anybody else. Schöne [1] confided this to me
when he came to see me about this matter a little while ago.

I will end now so that I may post this letter, and spare
myself until I have a few hours of peace at Utrecht, where I
go the day after to-morrow. . . . So farewell for to-day, and
heartiest greetings from Your CLARA.

CLARA *to* BRAHMS.
                                    UTRECHT, *Feb.* 12.
. . . Thank you for your letter. It came just as I was
with Frau Engelmann at the piano practising your Handel
Variations, which from the technical point of view she plays
very well. We were overjoyed that your letter should happen

---

[1] Alfred Schöne at that time the authority in charge of Art matters
in the Ministry of Education.

to come then. I feel so much annoyed about the Hanslick business, but I cannot help it. You may take my word for it that none of us had understood that Hanslick intended to write only about the years in Endenich. On the contrary, it never occurred to us that this period would be referred to except quite cursorily, though we certainly thought that the years immediately preceding his illness, about which Wasielewski has given such a misleading account, required treating in greater detail. It would, of course, be out of the question for me, in order to promote Hanslick's object, to hand over letters which my husband wrote to me. When you spoke to me about it, I did not realize what it all meant, and was preoccupied with other things, but now I see clearly that it cannot be. Try to persuade Hanslick to write a brief account of Robert's life as a healthy man ; he would do this very well, as he was so friendly with Robert. Tell him he must forgive me and try to put himself in our place. It would surely be impossible for me to promote such an object. As I said only a little while ago, written by a doctor for doctors it might be of real interest, for others it is mere sensationalism. I should like to hear that you think or acknowledge that I am right. I spoke to Bendemann and Engelmann about it also, but they both agreed with what I wrote to you the other day. . . .

You have not told me what you actually replied to Düsseldorf. But let me urge you most emphatically not to keep them waiting too long again, they find that less easy to forgive than anything else. . . .

With fond love, Your CLARA.

BRAHMS *to* CLARA.

VIENNA, *April* 24.

Even if this letter should be unusually long, it will not take you more than a quarter of an hour to read ! But in a few days I will write you one which I should like you to think over for an hour or two ! I want to publish my songs and should be so very much obliged if you could play them through beforehand and give me a word of advice about them. What I should like most of all would be to do this at your side— but I could not come to Düsseldorf, and Berlin also has its disadvantages. Simrock is waiting anxiously. If necessary, in case you do not like so much sweet stuff all at once, send him the songs one by one. They are numbered. For instance Op. 69, 1–9, and if he behaves himself, he will get Op. 70 the next day. But write and tell me which of them pleases you and whether you dislike any of them. Particularly in regard to the last I might accept your criticism and thank you ! But don't be too ready to think them crude. Read the words through again if you don't like them, for instance the *Mädchen-fluch*, which may horrify you. Forgive me. I am only afraid of being scolded.

After the above sweet stuffs you can refresh yourself with an *Étude*,[1] which I enclose. I think it is a jolly one to prac-tise, but difficult ! Please tell Simrock not to send any money. I wanted to ask you whether you would kindly deposit the money for me in the National or some other bank in Berlin. I should also like the money that I have lying with Levi Brothers in Mannheim to be deposited in Berlin. Don't you think that would be better ? I shall not tell you to-day what I am getting for the songs and for the Symphony. It gives such an inadequate idea of their value that it would inevitably create a prejudice against them. But give me your advice !

I am very glad to hear that Felix is going to Zürich. I am also thinking a good deal about Zürich and about my rooms there in Ruschlikon. Surely you would come there too ? As a matter of fact the neighbourhood is full of charming places to live in, Bochren near Horgen for instance (on the Lake), etc. Then I propose to spend a few lovely weeks in the autumn at Baden ! But I must be off. I hope the letter I shall get to-morrow will not be too hard ! If possible write me a short comment on each. You need only give the opus or the num-ber ; for instance, Op. X, 5, bad ; 6, outrageous ; 7, ridiculous, and so on.

Affectionate greetings, Your JOHANNES.

CLARA *to* BRAHMS.

BERLIN, *May* 2.

What a wonderful surprise ! And how glorious the songs are ! I have spent a great deal of time over them during the

---

[1] Presto after J. S. Bach. Published in the *Pianoforte Studies* (without any Opus number).

last few days. If only I could have had a really good singer
to go through them with me ! As it was I had to hum them
in my own hoarse voice. And now you want to have my
opinion about them. I hope you won't be angry with me if
I ask you, or rather beg you, to publish the best of them in
two books, and omit the few unimportant ones altogether.

I will start at the beginning and tell you what struck me.
I may be wrong occasionally, but you must be indulgent with
me.

Op. 69, 1. *Klage* does not appeal to me much ; the accom-
paniment is rather strained, and I don't think the melody
flows smoothly.

No. 2. *Klage* is a characteristic folk-song. I like it very
much.

No. 3. *Abschied* is altogether unsympathetic to me, though
the introduction is beautiful as well as the progressions in the
middle.

No. 4. *Der Liebsten Schwur* is one of my favourites, and
must sound delightful if it is sung lightly and with humour.

No. 5. *Tambourlied*, I do not like, and the Introduction is
too reminiscent of Schubert.

No. 6. *Vom Strande*, I adore the beginning and the end,
but the melody in the middle is not sufficiently interesting.

No. 7. *Über die See* is one of those I should like to omit,
also

No. 8. *Salome.*

No. 9. *Mädchenfluch* is one of my favourites, the music is
so full of swing and interesting from beginning to end, which
makes me forget the ugliness of the words.

Op. 70, 1. *Im Garten am Seegestade* is glorious, it takes one
into dreamland.

No. 2. *Lerchengesang*, the feeling is beautiful but I don't
care so much for the melody.

No. 3. *Serenade* does not please me, it does not seem to
flow naturally, and the prolongation of the text at the end
makes it stiff.

No. 4. *Abendregen*, the text seems to me bombastic, the
whole lacks spontaneity and is laboured. A text like this is
utterly uninspiring.

Op. 71, 1. *Es liebt sich so lieblich* I like very much, only I wish the semi-quavers at the end had been left out, they destroy the feeling for me.

No. 2. *An den Mond* is a great favourite, the end is wonderfully delicate and beautiful.

No. 3. *Geheimnis*, another glorious song, the second half is enchanting.

No. 4. *Willst Du, dass ich gehe* I don't care for much, I don't like the text either, it seems to me too cut and dried. All the same I should like to hear a good singer sing it some time.

No. 5. *Minnelied* opens well, but towards the end the melody becomes insignificant.

Op. 72, 1. *Alte Liebe* is indeed an old love of mine. How glorious it is ! And

No. 2. *Sommerfäden* is beautiful ! But the word *Fetzen* (rags) jars upon me. Can't you find some other word ?

No. 3. *Oh kühler Wald*, wonderful !—

Nos. 4 and 5, great favourites. What swing and passion there are in No. 4, *Verzagen*, and how absolutely original the last song is. (I knew that one too before.)

Now that I have done as you asked me, are you angry with me or not ? You know very well I cannot work myself up to a pitch of enthusiasm when I am not irresistibly stirred.

The songs, which I do not consider worthy of your name, make one book ; I think it is far better to have two books containing only important songs, rather than three interspersed with unimportant ones. I have not yet told Simrock that I have got the songs, as I should like to keep them a few days longer. I am expecting the Herzogenbergs on a visit to-morrow, and we should like to spend a few pleasant hours over them together. I have not the least idea what you are getting for the songs, round about 100 louis ? [£80.] For the Symphony I heard you were getting 18,000 marks [£900]. Is that true ?

Bach's *Presto* will be a hard nut for me to crack for some time to come, but it is a pet hobby of mine to study a piece like this until it goes at a great speed. But the things that come from your mind ! Many thanks ! above all for the gift of songs. I spoke to Mendelssohn some time ago about your money, but could not do so just now, because he has been away for about a fortnight. His advice was to put it in the Bank. . . . I shall tell Simrock that for the time being he is to hold the money for you, don't you agree ? Or shall I ask Mendelssohn to invest it for you straight away ? I can write no more to-day, my hand is hurting me. I will write more later.

With affectionate greetings, Your CLARA.

CLARA *to* BRAHMS.

BERLIN, *May* 19.

Yesterday for the first time I was able to have a quarter of an hour's quiet conversation with Herr Mendelssohn. He told me that he would be very pleased to deposit your papers in the Bank and also buy Prussian State Bonds with the money from Simrock. He strongly advises the latter if you don't want a higher rate of interest ; they are now 95, but pay only $4\frac{1}{4}\%$. The arrangements with the Bank are simple. They will send you a form which you must sign, you must also tell them who has your power of attorney so that interest and other communications can be received on your behalf, as the Bank does not correspond with Austria. If you like Ferdinand could do this for you, for he is exceedingly conscientious, understands the matter thoroughly, and would save you all worry. I haven't spoken to him yet, but I am sure he would undertake to do it. . . . Write to me soon about this, as I only have three weeks longer to stay here and would be glad if I could settle it all for you.

But now I must trouble you with some business of my own and beg you to advise me quite frankly. I think I told you that Härtels asked me some time ago whether I would undertake the revision of Robert's works at some future date. But they did not make any definite arrangement with me. Now I have received a letter from Novello begging me to prepare a revision of the pianoforte pieces at once, and offering me 1,000 thalers [£150] for the job. Thinking this would not clash with Härtels' interests, particularly as they only intended publishing the complete edition in about nine to twelve years from now, I entertained the proposal, in the first place because I was anxious to substitute a correct edition for the very bad English editions which are now in circulation, and secondly, because the fee is naturally not one I could afford to refuse. But now I have received a letter from Novello in which he tells me that he agrees to pay the sum of 1,000 thalers, but insists upon securing the copyright in all countries.

I could not agree to this without consulting Härtels, and wrote to Raimund to ask him whether they could not get into communication with Novello and persuade him not to insist on this condition. In this case Härtels could pay me a portion of the fee offered by Novello and include the English Edition, which only consists of pianoforte solo pieces, in their own production. Whereupon I got the enclosed letter from Raimund, and yesterday received a visit from Dr. Hase,[1] who came to discuss the matter with me. He said the English edition would not prejudice theirs, but begged me to try to persuade Novello to give up his demand for the sole rights. The arrangement would then be that he would hold the copyright for all countries, but that Härtel would be excepted, and the two firms would share the rights and pay me compensation for any losses I might incur by the arrangement. But is it not strange that he should not have said to me, " Prepare the edition for us only and we will give you the same fee " ? Then I should have done it and with greater pleasure for Härtels. But Hase never once inquired what I was to get out of it, he merely made it quite clear that they could not hope to compete with the English firm, as the latter enjoyed greater advantages as publishers than any German concern. In any case he added that if Novello agreed to this that they would immediately acquire the rights in all works not hitherto published and publish them simultaneously with Novello. If Novello agrees to share the rights with Härtels, all will be well; but—my feelings ! ! ! I have been arguing with Marie a good deal about all this and I must confess that she is right when she says that the German publishers, in this case Härtels, have never treated me very well. Even now they are not doing so, for, if they had liked, now that they have such a costly edition in preparation, they might have spent 1,000 thalers more on it and asked me to do it only for them. For the truth remains that if I followed my own feelings, which would incline me to do this work only for a German publisher, I

[1] Dr. Oskar von Hase, of the firm of Breitkopf & Härtel.

should suffer a great loss—a loss which, in spite of the fact that I am not without means, I could ill afford to incur, for I am still dependent to some extent upon what I earn annually. What shall I do now ?   Am I in any way committed to Härtels ?   While we were reading some old letters (to Robert) the other day, we found some from Härtels which showed how horribly they had beaten him down over details.   Marie was quite beside herself with fury over it, and she says that it would be ridiculous for me to have any consideration for Härtels in this matter.   (It certainly was peculiar that although I told Hase that if I had known that they wished to produce a complete edition so soon I should much have preferred to do the revision for them, he did not respond, but on the contrary changed the subject as if they were afraid of being involved in too heavy expenses.)   I don't know what I ought to do and am very much upset.   I might ask Joachim, but I do not trust him as much as I trust you.

I beg and pray you to write to me at once about this, for both Novello and Härtels are waiting for my answer, and my feelings hover in a constant struggle between sentiment and duty. . . .

Felix is now in Zürich and has changed over to Philology. I am very pleased about it, because how can one wish anybody to choose for his career a calling into which he cannot put himself heart and soul ?   He never had a vocation for Law ; I knew that long ago. . . .

And now good-bye for to-day. Excuse this hurried note, but I am frantically busy, particularly with pupils, so much so that I am hardly able to attend even to the most pressing duties.   Many thanks in advance, and with affectionate greetings from Marie and myself (Eugenie is still in Meran and very well), Your old friend CLARA.

BRAHMS *to* CLARA.

VIENNA, *May.*

In the first place let me tell you most emphatically that in such matters there is no hurry.   Never and under no circumstances allow yourself to be harassed, worried or pressed. Deliberate calmly over every aspect of it that concerns yourself and then reflect and consider to your heart's content in peace. So do not put yourself out, and even if they wrote to you at once as if the matter were of the utmost urgency, don't hesitate to keep them waiting for an answer for a month if necessary. Let Novello wait; let Härtel wait! And give up all "hovering in a constant struggle between sentiment and duty." You can sit quite comfortably on both sentiment and duty and act accordingly. Supposing you had reasons to be in a hurry, do you imagine that the other parties would care if it didn't suit them, and they required time for reflection?

Secondly, let me implore you never to think of anything or anybody other than the matter in hand and yourself. Thirdly, and incidentally, trust nobody, particularly an interested party.

You rightly desire that Härtels should publish a complete edition. But in my opinion all offers coming from other quarters should be used to help you to define your position with Härtels, particularly on the financial side. Offers, such as that made to you by Novello—I am quite positive about this —ought to have no other importance in your eyes. At least certainly not now and in its present form. If you should quarrel with Härtels, which I hope and trust will not happen, you can always turn with the same proposal to another large publisher (Simrock, for instance).

I certainly think that you would do yourself harm, even financially, if you were to consider too many offers. You are far more likely to get the best possible terms from one. From two you will certainly not get so much, whether they share the spoils in anger or in amity. So, for the time being, let Novello go hang! You will not find it so easy to come to a decision. You must think it over quietly and in any case enjoy your summer holiday first. Their concluding reference to "copyright in all countries" is of course astute in the highest degree and ought to make you extremely cautious!! As for Härtels, open serious negotiations with them, but go slowly and warily. The fact that they pay those who work for them badly and are over-anxious and suspicious in their dealings with them, we have all known from time immemorial. But they are, after all, a fine firm, and there is an imposing atmosphere about the whole concern. But don't expect nobility, and take care not to give away too much to them. In my opinion Härtels ought to ascertain how many plates would be required for Schumann's complete works. (Remember always to write to them as if you were merely interested in the work itself and as if you were concerned about what you should do and how you should do it.) If you have the record of the plates you can at your leisure work out your demands accordingly. Then you can compare them with what was paid for the editing of Mozart's and Beethoven's works (per plate).

I could go on chatting for some time longer, but my object would remain always the same. All I wish to do is to induce you to think over and dispatch the business calmly. Keep only one thing in your mind (a really complete edition of the works), and pursue this object single-mindedly and without haste. Meanwhile, however, do not throw overboard considerations which do not embarrass you and which may prove useful in some way. But in reality nothing else should have any weight with you. I find it impossible to believe that you would ever come to satisfactory terms with several publishers. It would be sure to lead to trouble from every point of view.

And now just a word about my money affairs. Faber here, and Lindeck of Mannheim, each have charge of half my money.

Lindeck has a steel box containing my papers, and every New Year he sends me an account, which I sign, without, of course, reading or understanding a syllable. Faber does the same. But what I maintain is that in such matters one must never trust even one's best friend or brother.

I would rather not make use of Mendelssohn, or Ferdinand. I am thinking of simply handing the whole matter over to Simrock, but it will be a bitter letter for Lindeck when I inform him that his custodianship is at an end. Or do you think I ought to let the matter alone ? Was your relation to Wendelstadt any different ? Was he not simply in charge of your papers ? Did you allow him to do business with your money ? I have nothing against Lindeck, etc., but I should very much dislike to wake up one fine day and discover that something had happened. But I think I should do better to invest my present receipts in the shares we have mentioned and to let

Simrock deposit them in that Bank. (I have nothing to do with the firm of Ladenburg. Lindeck does the business privately as a favour.) . . . I don't know whether I shall be in Zürich soon or not. I think I shall perhaps go first to the Wörthersee in Carinthia to see a new part of the world. But now farewell. I hope you will see my good-will through all my chatter. Remembrances to Marie, and don't forget Your affectionate friend JOHANNES.

BRAHMS *to* CLARA.

VIENNA, *May.*

The other day I forgot to explain to you the incomprehensible passage in Härtel's letter. And so the letter was thrust aside. What Härtels say is that they cannot secure to themselves the rights in critical work, but that anybody can use or reprint it. This is perfectly true, and in their last undertaking (Beethoven, Mozart, etc.) was much to be deplored. Nevertheless, in this case I think it's rather mean of them to remind you of this, as they naturally do so with an eye to your fee. But so far as I can see at present in the case of Schumann's works even the most thorough and scholarly man could not find much that is new or worth mentioning. Everything is there perfectly correct and complete. Even the English edition of Novello is by no means bad, at least as far as I have been able to judge, for I scarcely ever play Schumann except by heart. But nobody can say that this edition has not been carefully and conscientiously prepared.

Your name is valuable to Härtels for their edition, and they can pay for it just as well as anybody else. This is an advantage which they will not fail to estimate at its proper value, etc. The account with the number of pages is surely superfluous. I don't know what you think, but if Novello is offering 1,000 thalers for the pianoforte pieces, the fee for the complete works ought to be at least 2,000 or 3,000 thalers. I still feel certain that you cannot give your name to a whole number of people (offers might come from St. Petersburg and Paris). But after you have quietly thought over the matter for some time just calmly ask Härtels for a sum not less than 2,000 thalers. Send me a line to let me know what is passing through your mind. Marie need not be disgusted by Härtel's old letters. If she wants a pick-me-up let her read the correspondence between Schiller and Cotta.

Lienau of Berlin have just sent me two fat volumes of Strauss's Waltzes! Surely I knew quite enough about this stuff before, as you are well aware! At last summer has come. It is really beautiful here at this time of year, but the heat rather makes one wish to be off. I am thinking soon of going to see what the Wörthersee looks like.

With most affectionate greetings, Your JOHANNES.

CLARA *to* BRAHMS.

BERLIN, *June* 6.

I don't want any longer to delay answering your two last letters, and thanking you for them. And that is why I am dictating to-day, otherwise I should have to put it off still longer, and my debt of thanks lies heavily on my conscience. When I received your first letter I thought as I read each sentence—now I know what he means! But lo! the very next sentence always contained the opposite of what you had said before. So that in the end I really did not know where I was. But the second letter made me see more clearly, and now, as, after all, I am to some extent bound to Novello, I have not broken off negotiations with him altogether, but have told him that I can only continue to entertain his proposals if he will be satisfied with the copyright for England alone. I really never thought of doing anything else and I told him that I had long ago promised Härtels my services for their complete edition. The other day Härtels sent me their Dr. Hase, and he thought that I ought to give Novello the copyright in all countries, making an exception of his firm. I could not quite understand this, and so wrote to Novello as I have described. I must remind you that the latter is only concerned about publishing a pianoforte-solo edition. I cannot entirely withdraw now, but he may not agree to my condition. I expect his answer any day and hope that the whole thing will fall through. My reason for trying to get the matter settled now is that the summer is the only time that I can do this kind of work, whereas you seem to think I can do it in the winter as well.

As to any other offers from St. Petersburg or Paris, I would naturally take no notice of them. I have had enough worry and trouble about this last business. Regarding Härtels I shall be guided by your last letter. . . .

Now I must appeal to you about a trouble of my own, in case you should be going to Zürich. You will find Felix there. His present mood, to judge from his letters, really makes me feel quite desperate. I told you that he had changed his calling and that he is now studying History and Modern Languages, and is, moreover, very anxious to go in for literature himself. I wrote to him the other day that if he did this he must write under a pseudonym at first, in order to spare us any unpleasantnesses in case his attempts should prove unsuccessful, particularly as with his name people would expect more from him than from Tom, Dick and Harry. This seems to have upset him very much, as have other things about which I cannot tell you in writing ; and now he writes to me such unkind and, I must confess, cold letters, that I am quite miserable about it. If you get a word with him, couldn't you try to influence him a little regarding his aims in life, about which he will certainly tell you. Couldn't you point out to him how fantastic they are and try to revive his sense of duty towards his family ? If you are going to Zürich, I will send you his last letters, in which case I trust you will do me the kindness to deal with this matter which is causing me so much anxiety.

The other day I was looking for something and came across your A major Serenade (arrangement for two hands), and I now play it with great pleasure. I am still studying the Bach *Presto* very hard, and can play it fairly well, but cannot yet manage the part built on the inversion [of the theme ?] It is a hard nut to crack but the kernel makes it well worth while. The way you develop it is interesting and astonishes me every time. Bach himself could not have done it more beautifully ! Now farewell for to-day, with renewed thanks, Your affectionate old friend CLARA.

Eugenie came back looking very much better, but she cannot endure the climate here, which is a source of constant worry to me.

BRAHMS *to* CLARA.

PÖRTSCHACH, *June.*

I don't suppose I have ever sent you anything as amusing as what I am sending you to-day,[1] provided your fingers can survive the pleasure ! The *Chaconne* is in my opinion one of the most wonderful and most incomprehensible pieces of music. Using the technique adapted to a small instrument the man writes a whole world of the deepest thoughts and most powerful feelings. If I could picture myself writing, or even conceiving, such a piece, I am certain that the extreme excitement and emotional tension would have driven me mad. If one has no supremely great violinist at hand, the most exquisite of joys is probably simply to let the *Chaconne* ring in one's mind. But the piece certainly inspires one to occupy oneself with it somehow. One does not always want to hear music actually played, and in any case Joachim is not always there, so one tries it otherwise. But whether I try it with an orchestra or piano, the pleasure is always spoilt for me. There is only one way in which I can secure undiluted joy from the piece, though on a small and only approximate scale, and that is when I play it with the left hand alone. And then at times I cannot help thinking of Columbus's egg ! The same difficulty, the nature of the technique, the rendering of the *arpeggios,* everything conspires to make me—feel like a violinist !

You try it yourself. I only wrote it for you. But do not overstrain your hand ; it requires so much resonance and strength. Play it for a while *mezza voce.* Also make the fingering easy and convenient. If it does not exert you too much—which is what I am afraid of—you ought to get great fun out of it. Greet the beautiful Baltic for me and also your dear secretary and dictate to him soon again for YOUR JOHANNES.

CLARA *to* BRAHMS.

KIEL, *July* 6.

It was indeed a most wonderful surprise I found awaiting me here ! Just think, wasn't it strange, on the day after my arrival here, when I was opening a drawer I strained a muscle in my right hand, so you may imagine what a glorious refuge

[1] Arrangement of Bach's *Chaconne* for the left hand (*Pianoforte Studies,* No. 5).

your *Chaconne* has been to me ?   You alone could have accomplished such a thing, and what seems to me most extraordinary about it is the way in which you so faithfully reproduce the sound of the violin.   However you came to think of it amazes me.   It is true my fingers do not altogether master it ; they always get paralysed over the passage which goes,

and my right hand itches to join in.   But for this, I do not find the difficulties insuperable, and the pleasure I get is enormous.

My hand alone is responsible for my not having thanked you before.   It has been all right now for two days but I did not want to strain it, and my secretary is not with me.   I am alone here ; Mary and Eugenie are in Baden.   As our house is empty, I strongly urged them to spend their time in Baden rather than in Berlin.   Let me thank you then most heartily for the joy you have given me.   It was really most kind of you. . . .

And now let me thank you once again for your second letter about the Härtels business, which was much clearer to me than the first.   But oh ! even so I don't know what to do in order to clear matters up with them.   I wrote to Novello saying that I never intended giving them the copyright for all countries and that unless they chose to drop this condition, I must close negotiations with them, as I had already bound myself to Härtels.   To my unbounded relief I received no reply to this. I have certainly forfeited a substantial addition to my income ; but I am easier in my mind at not having two people to deal with.   I thought of writing to Härtels to tell them that the episode with Novello was closed and that I had allowed it to be closed out of consideration for them, but that I should now be glad to know what they thought of the matter and what they proposed to pay me for my revision.   What do you say to that ?   Please tell me ; for this beating about the bush is very irksome.   Surely they must make some definite offer now ! Or shall I let the whole thing rest until I hear from them again ? I suppose I ought to write to them in any case and tell them that Novello is off. . . .

I am longing to hear from you and to know how you are,

how you have settled down and what you are working at. May one ask this question ? My thoughts are often with you, more often than you know, and when you are elsewhere than in Vienna my thoughts go astray about you, which is most unpleasant. . . .

With most affectionate greetings, my dear friend, from Your loving CLARA.

BRAHMS *to* CLARA.

PÖRTSCHACH, *July*.

Let me thank you again for your kind letter.   I am delighted that the *Chaconne* was not merely a childish freak, and that it gave you pleasure and everything. . . .

I have owed Härtel a letter for some time and I also wanted to write to you about the matter, but I don't seem to be able to do anything.   All I ask is that you should not write anything to England and certainly nothing definite to H.   Leave everything vague and keep yourself perfectly free.   I, however, being bold and independent, have written to H. quite casually to-day as follows.   If you don't like what I have said you can turn me down by writing and telling them that you cannot have anything to do with what I have said, and that in any case it is all wrong.

" Regarding the Schumann business I hardly know what to say without being very frank and perhaps giving you offence. The English episode arose simply through a chance offer which Frau Schumann had every reason to consider seriously.   What I cannot understand is why you do not proceed in the same simple way and make an offer which will put the other one out of court.   I and many others are very anxious to see the German edition of Schumann's works appear under the joint names of R. and Cl.   The great respect which one feels for this couple can only increase with the years and knit their two names ever more closely together.   They were united in life just as closely as they were in art, and this noble bond should be consecrated in regard to both spheres by some outward sign.

" I need hardly point out to a publisher how glad everybody would be to possess the pianoforte pieces and the songs in such an edition.   It would make the publication precious and, at the same time, lend it a unique character. The English without stipulating for the exclusive use of the name have offered 1,000 thalers for the pianoforte pieces alone. If the songs and everything else are included, it seems to me that 3,000 thalers is quite a modest fee. Generally in such cases you run some risk, but in this instance I doubt whether you run any risk whatsoever. No other publisher is in a position to enjoy the advantage which the combination of these two names would give him. The whole world will always feel more love and reverence for those two names when they are together, and I need hardly discuss how this will affect the commercial aspects of the undertaking.

" You are well aware of Frau Schumann's delicacy in all matters connected with money ; but you also know her circumstances which force her to consider the financial side. If, therefore, like Frau Schumann, you refuse to speak, it is impossible to say what the outcome will be. Besides yourselves there are perhaps two other German publishers whom I might like to consider. But I will be perfectly frank and tell you that if there were the remotest possibility of Frau Schumann deriving the smallest advantage from so doing, I would spare no pains in urging her to allow the proposed edition (particularly her own pieces and songs) to be published in London, Paris and St. Petersburg, and thus to erect to the German nation a monument which, in this case, as in the case of many another of their great men, they have often enough deserved.

" Incidentally I may say I am quite disinterested in putting myself entirely at your own and Frau Schumann's disposal in this matter. Frau Schumann knows nothing whatever about this letter, but I am writing to-day to tell her the attitude I have adopted both towards you and her. I can only beg you both to forgive me, if I have unintentionally done anything to cause either of you any distress."

I shall now copy this practically as it stands. As a matter of fact you need not trouble about it. But in any case don't be in too great a hurry, and send me a line to let me know whether you are angry. If I had waited to consult you first there would have been no end to it. So for to-day, with most affectionate greetings, YOUR JOH.

CLARA *to* BRAHMS.

BADEN-BADEN, *July* 22.

In the first place heartiest thanks for your kind letter. How glad I am that you have let yourself go about the matter ! It is essential to take a high hand with Härtels. You could not seriously have thought that I should be angry ! How could I regard your letter otherwise than as a sign of deep friendship to me ? But I am certainly curious to see what Härtels will answer.

I can find no peace for writing to-day, but I must thank you and tell you of a joyful event which has been causing us some excitement for the last few days. When I arrived at Büdesheim to see Elise, I found her very happy, as she had just become engaged to a very charming and excellent young American named Louis Sommerhoff. He has a good position as a business man in his own country and hopes to be able to settle down in Europe in a few years. They have been attracted to each other for the last year and the fact that he has learnt to know and love her fine qualities, her general capacity and her loyal nature, seems to me a guarantee of her happiness. . . .

Another pleasant feature of the engagement is that his family, as well as Frau Berna,[1] whose cousin he is, have long desired the match, as they took a great fancy to Elise some time ago. So one could not wish for anything better except that they will have to go to America. That is hard lines, particularly for Frau Berna, who is heartbroken at the thought of losing Elise, although she has done everything in her power to throw the young people together. She loved Elise like a sister, and in her difficult position as a solitary woman with landed property she used to find Elise's firmness a great comfort. Have you by any chance come across his family in Zürich—Frau Sommerhoff, his mother, and Frau Bertuch, his sister, etc. ? We are going to Zürich to-day to see Felix and the new relatives. Under different circumstances this would probably have been most unpleasant for me ; but, during the last few days, we have been under the same roof and I have got to like him so well that I shall be glad to make the acquaint-

---

[1] Afterwards Countess Oriola, a friend of Elise, with whom she had been staying for some time at this period.

ance of his people, of whom everybody thinks very highly. The wedding is to take place in November, when he is to come and fetch her. He is now going back to America to attend to his business there and settle everything. Thus another joy has fallen to our lot. May God bless them both! But you can easily imagine with what qualms I look to the future, for I cannot help thinking of poor Julie's unhappy fate, and this makes me anxious about Elise. Your ever loving CLARA.

CLARA *to* BRAHMS.
SPINABAD BEI DAVOS, GRAUBÜNDEN, *July* 29.
Here is Härtel's answer.[1] What do you say about it ? I think I will undertake the job, but I must first ask you to promise me to take over all the orchestral and ensemble-works and to accept at least half of the fee. Please answer me at once so that I may let H. know, and if you should think of any stipulations I ought to make, I should like to know what they are, as I am quite ignorant about the requirements of such an edition. But I hope I may rely on you for help even in other matters, otherwise I shall be in constant dread that I am not doing the work properly. . . .

Please let me have an answer soon and return the enclosed letter in a registered envelope. With our affectionate greetings and a hearty shake of the hand, Your CLARA.

BRAHMS *to* CLARA.
PÖRTSCHACH AM SEE, *August.*
I do not think you need trouble yourself to think about any further conditions. You can take the postscript in Härtels' letter quite seriously.[2] They will keep their word if ever you should express any wish about any particular point later on. I also have no experience of this sort of work. It sounds rather ridiculous but I believe that had it not been for my

[1] In this letter Härtels offered Clara 10,000 marks (£500) for the exclusive rights in her edition of Robert Schumann's works. The letter is given only in the German edition of Clara's *Life*, Vol. III, p. 359.—TR.

[2] Härtels' postscript was to the following effect : " Please be perfectly frank with us and let us know if you feel any doubt about the above conditions. We want you to be satisfied with the arrangement so that this great enterprise may be brought to a successful issue."—TR.

letter, this great enterprise would never have been undertaken.

I know how serious you are about your proposal to share the fee, but unfortunately I have neither the wish nor the patience to reply to it seriously and in detail. Let it stand over until we can have a talk. You surely know that it is a habit of which I am childishly fond to pocket thousand mark notes ; but for the time being do try to accustom yourself a little to the idea that towards your husband and yourself I am, so to speak, and under all circumstances, and as it were, and in every respect— ! etc., and then exercise your ingenuity a little in order not to appropriate all the kind feelings to yourself, but to allow others some small share.

One supremely important condition is that Härtels should pay you the money before putting the edition in hand. You ought to have at least half this year on starting the work. The second half you can have any time. This you ought to discuss with a man of business. Your part of the work will be finished before publication and in any case it will prevent you from earning money in other directions. If you were to do only the work required for the edition, the fee would be a good one ; but you will do much more work than is necessary and much more than would be adequately remunerated at 10,000 thalers ! ! ! As to the orchestral and choral pieces, I cannot say at present how much editorial work they will require. The most difficult things are the first pianoforte pieces, particularly those which your husband published twice.

I have just been on a walking tour for two days in the Ampezzo valley with Wüllner and Iwan Knorr, a young Russian who has written some most excellent variations for orchestra. Nothing could have been more beautiful than this walk ! You would be enchanted with the Ampezzo valley, above all with the mountains (the Dolomites, with all their strange shapes and shades which one never grows tired of looking at), the lakes, the flowers, the magnificent highways and everything. I enjoyed Wüllner's visit very much, but I cannot write to you about the business which brought him to me. Let me congratulate you once more most heartily about Elise, and I send my most affectionate greetings to you all.

Let me remind you once again about stipulating for payment to begin at once. You need not allow yourself to be worried by any scruples. . . .

Let me hear from you soon, Your JOHANNES.

CLARA *to* BRAHMS.

SPINABAD, *Aug.* 20.

I have been unwell for some days and this has prevented me from writing to you sooner to say that I had received your packet with its precious contents, and to tell you how much I enjoyed the ballad.[1] The words are horrible, but your setting is wonderful. In spite of the many repetitions of the motif it is always interesting. It recurs in such a variety of ways in accordance with each change of feeling, and every time it strikes one as new. I cannot tell you how often we have played it together (Volkland [2] and I). Oh, if only we had had a couple of singers such as Vogel and Brandt with us ! The piece reminded me of them all the time. You want the ballad back, so I am sending it to you to-morrow morning. I should like to keep it, but do not want to appear ungrateful by abusing your kindness.

With the piece I am sending you a few of Felix's poems and would like to know what you think of them. He has not polished them up yet and seems as if he wanted to wait a bit before doing so. In spite of the fact that, as you know, I have always taken his poetical powers rather coldly, and have always been afraid of over-estimating the intellectual gifts of Robert's children, I must say that much in these verses has surprised me. They seem to me to be full of subtle poetic feeling, and the language is often beautiful and sometimes quite musical. Do tell me, dear Johannes, what you think of them. Felix wants to have them printed, and that alarms me. As soon as I get them back from you he wants to send them to some authority, either Heyse or Grimm. Please send them to me as soon as you have read them. We shall leave here on the 30th or 31st. It is magnificent here. The weather is beautiful and the air refreshing in spite of the heat. But I long for Baden.

As to Härtels, the die is now cast, though my answer lay

[1] *Edward*, Op. 75, 1.
[2] Alfred Volkland, musical director at Bâle.

unposted for three weeks. Following your advice I wrote saying that I should like them to pay me half my fee on New Year's Day 1878, and the other half on the completion of the whole work. But as an extra precaution I am sending you a draft of the agreement. Please read it and tell me whether I may sign it and send it back. I have not done so yet, because I don't want to be rash. You have taken my interests so much to heart from the very beginning in this business that you must not be angry if I hesitate to do anything without your concurrence. Härtels have asked me what I would like to begin with. Surely this depends on what they wish to publish first ? According to the contract they intend to start publication as early as 1878. Just fancy, after having concluded from Novello's ten weeks' silence that on the receipt of my letter they had decided to drop the matter, I had a letter a week ago saying that they were prepared to meet all my wishes and to surrender the exclusive rights for all countries if only I would undertake the work. I then wrote saying that, as I had gathered from their long silence that they wished to regard the matter as ended, I had now come to an agreement with Härtels, and was not free to do the work for any other publisher. Whereupon a letter arrived to-day according to which they appear to be very much perturbed and say that I had no right to come to any such agreement with Härtels without letting them know, and that they never dreamt I was in such a hurry about the business. What dilatory people they are ! I will enclose their letter in the parcel I am sending you. Perhaps you will think it advisable for me to say something to Härtels about it. Regarding the wish expressed by Novello, ought I to write to H. and put in a word for the English firm ?

I am aghast at all I am asking you to do, but you know how incompetent I am in these matters ! . . .

But now your patience must be at an end. Please be so kind as to write to me here at once about my business questions. With affectionate greetings from us all, Your ever loving CLARA.

Once more hearty thanks for the musical treats with which you have beguiled my exile here.

CLARA *to* BRAHMS.

BERLIN, *Dec.* 24.

Even if Christmas is nothing to you, I cannot help sending you my heartiest greetings for the occasion. If only I could think of some gift that would be really useful to you, I would send it at once ! But what can a poor creature find to give in return for the pleasures that you can bestow ?

I received the Symphony for four hands [1] with the greatest joy. If only I could keep it written as it is by your own hand, what a magnificent possession it would be ! But remember that all I can do at present is to look longingly into it, for to-day I can find nobody who can play it with me. The children cannot read manuscript music at sight. We are not all musicians ! During the holidays I will try to conjure up someone and then will write immediately. My heart and thoughts will be with you on the 30th. With a thousand greetings for to-day and heartiest thanks, dearest Johannes, Your old friend CLARA.

We have received a telegram saying that Elise arrived in New York yesterday.

CLARA *to* BRAHMS.

BERLIN, *Dec.* 30.

I am overjoyed at the telegram just received.[2] How splendid that the Symphony should have had such a brilliant reception ! Oh, if only I could have been there ! These words of joy and of thanks for the telegram (which was probably sent at your instigation) are intended to welcome you in Leipsic to-morrow. Oh, if only I could do so myself ! I am seized with melancholy at this thought. What a lovely conclusion to the old year for you, and for me through you. My kindest thoughts will be with you for the passing of the year. Your ever affectionate old friend CLARA.

[1] The Second Symphony.

[2] This was from Billroth about the great success of the Second Symphony in Vienna on December 30.

1878

CLARA *to* BRAHMS.

BERLIN, *Jan*. 25.

DEAR JOHANNES,

. . . As regards the Leipsic affair, my old luck has pursued me once more. Once when I was talking to you about the Schumann evening, you mentioned to me that they wanted to pay me a delicate compliment by this means. But nothing more occurred to my mind, not even the obvious fact that the matter could not remain a secret, and that the public must ultimately take its part in the proceedings. It was only when I read the announcement in various copies of the *Signal* that I grew frightened and wrote at once. So premature a celebration as this would only have made me look ridiculous, and would therefore have been very painful to me.[1] It was well meant, but tactless. They ought first to have inquired of you or of Livia (or someone who was intimate with me) whether it would please me. No one who knew me could be in any doubt about the matter. Thank God I did not go there ! . . . I am very sorry to hear that you were not pleased with Hamburg.[2] With your letter came one from Avé and Friedchen. It was funny to compare them. The latter writes about endless applause but says that the composer took a long time to appear on the platform and adds that the conducting was magnificent. Apparently the orchestra did not come off so well after all. I am curious to hear what they gave you as a fee. Are you performing your first symphony in Utrecht ?[3] And with the

---

[1] This refers to her Jubilee in celebration of fifty years of artistic work. She had made her first public appearance in the *Gewandhaus* on October 20, 1828, when she had played with Emilie Reichold a portion of Kalk Brenner's Variations, Op. 94.

[2] In connection with the performance of the C minor Symphony on January 18.

[3] On January 26.

orchestra ? How happy you must all be together now ! I hope that all of you will often think of me, for somehow I believe that when you do I ought unconsciously to feel more cheerful. Greetings and thanks to both.

My arm gives me a great deal of trouble. I only hope it will not stop my playing altogether. It would be such a great loss to me. I have already had to sacrifice 1,000 marks in Leipsic owing to the fatal business. I was to play in Amsterdam and The Hague on the 4th and 6th of February, but it fell through, as I could only accept for one town, because I must have a week's rest between each of the concerts. My only regret is that I shall not see the Engelmanns, and, now that you are there, I feel it all the more. Thus does ill luck dog my footsteps. Let me have a word from you soon, dearest Johannes. You know how glad I always am to be able to follow you in the spirit. So now, farewell ! My arm bids me stop, but I did so much want to write to you myself. They are all at the rehearsal of the 9th, so I have been alone and undisturbed, but also perhaps a little " unreasonable " ? Show that you are not angry with me by answering promptly. Yours,
CLARA.

BRAHMS *to* CLARA.

AMSTERDAM, BROCK'S DOELEN-HOTEL, *Jan.*

DEAREST CLARA,

It is a crying shame that you did not accept the engagement here. Everything is so pleasant and beautiful, and the Symphony will go splendidly. The orchestra and everybody else are highly delighted with it. On the 4th and the 8th (*Felix meritis*) it will be performed here, and on the 6th at The Hague. I am particularly pleased with Holland, and I am most comfortable here. I like Verhulst very much ; he reminds me of your husband. On the 4th he is performing the Overture, Scherzo and Finale.[1] It goes none too well. But it is the greatest joy to me to see how enthusiastically he practises it. I get more pleasure from it than from a more perfect rendering.

In Utrecht it was also very pleasant—wreaths, an honorary membership and good photographs into the bargain. A small choir sang my new love songs in quite exemplary fashion, and

[1] Schumann, Op. 52.

repeated them two days later. The Engelmanns are all well
and the little lady will probably come here for the Symphony.
I am glad that the *Feuerzauber* will not prevent you from going
to Dresden.[1]   But do write to me if you change your mind, as
I am only going there on your account, and would otherwise
stay at home.   In Utrecht we certainly had the first Symphony ; but the resources are limited (a few Amsterdam folk
added their numbers to the rest).   But little Hol [2] did his work
so well and had practised the piece so splendidly that one could
not help enjoying it.

By-the-bye, what you call your " old luck " seems to be a
good guide to you, for it is so now in the matter of the celebration at Leipsic and also in regard to the Zauber at Dresden,
from which I felt sure you would suffer the most dreadful
effects.   I am thinking that Joachim will have a great success
with the 9th in Berlin, and I am happy at the thought of it for
his sake.   My arm would allow me to go on writing for very
much longer, but time fails me.   So content yourself with this
greeting and, if possible, give me the pleasure of another letter
however short.   On the 9th I am leaving for home.   I long
for it.   One can't stand gadding about for long.

With most affectionate greetings, Your JOHANNES.

BRAHMS *to* CLARA.

Feb., 1878.

Levi writes saying that you may come to Munich for a concert on the 12th of March.   Let me have a line at once, for if
that is so I will of course come and perform the 2nd.   What a
pleasant conclusion it was to my journey to see you and hear
you in Cologne, the hearing was particularly so.   I sometimes
dread hearing intimate friends in public.   But if I should do so
my pleasure is all the greater when the friend plays as you did
the other day, better than I ever thought you could. . . .
What about March ?   Shall I begin to think about hotels ?

Your Elise has written me a charming letter,[3] and if so many

---

[1] In a previous letter she had said that although his Symphony
lured her to Dresden, she was terrified of the *Feuerzauber* and did not
want to hear it.—TR.

[2] Musical Director in Utrecht.

[3] Thanking Brahms for his wedding present—an alarm clock which
played a melody, " *Guten Abend, gute Nacht.*"

people were not waiting for answers from me I would write to New York. Now I have to go to the rehearsal of Rubenstein's *Makkabäer*. After the performance Billroth, thank God, has arranged for supper at Sacher's. That will do us good! Let me hear about Munich. . . . Your JOHANNES.

BRAHMS *to* CLARA.

March, 1878.

I don't know whether I shall be able to answer your two kind letters in greater detail, or to look over the *Carnaval*. But I must beg you to let me know immediately whether you are thinking of going to Baden in the spring. At this time of year my thoughts wander every day away from here. I am offered very nice quarters in Pörtschach, but Baden tempts me more, and how much more if you are thinking of going there too. So please let me have a word.

As to Frankfort, I don't know what to say.[1] In my opinion you need not feel any anxiety about it. The salary and the hours of work seem to me to be all right, as well as everything else, and all I can do is to wish you luck and to hope that you will all be happy there. I certainly think Czerny's large pianoforte course is worthy of study, particularly in regard to what he says about Beethoven and the performance of his works, for he was a diligent and attentive pupil. You ought also to read Hummel's course. But it is a terrible undertaking. Is Marie going to shoulder that load? Czerny's fingering is particularly worthy of attention. In fact I think that people to-day ought to have more respect for this excellent man.

I don't think Rietz would have given the C major Symphony away.[2] It is the heirs that I suspect of having stowed things away to prevent them from coming under the auctioneer's hammer. I have a positive proof that this does happen. A very keen dealer in M.S.S. in this place has an unprinted Symphony, written by Mendelssohn in his youth, as well as

---

[1] While she was in Frankfort at the end of February Clara was offered a post in the new Hoch Conservatoire.

[2] This refers to the MS. of the C major Symphony by Robert Schumann, which Clara gave to Rietz after a very fine performance of the Symphony which he conducted.

letters from M. to Rietz ! Can't you appeal to the heirs direct ? The things I have mentioned were only sold by them here quite recently to Kafka. I have looked over the *Carnaval* again. What a joy you will have when your edition is completed and it will stare you in the face with all its new and old faults ! But I must now close. With heartiest greetings to everybody, and begging you to let me know about Baden. Yours affectionately, JOHANNES.

CLARA *to* BRAHMS. [1]

BERLIN, *March* 21.

I have kept you waiting a long time for your answer, but it has not been my fault, I have so many pressing things to do. Last week I had my third concert here with Frau Joachim, to which the Herzogenbergs paid a surprise visit. They stayed on with us till yesterday, which was a great joy to all. Of course I had to give up every free minute I had to them. Now I shall have a few days' rest, then go to Hamburg again for a concert with Frau Joachim. Avé is making all the arrangements, but he is causing us much annoyance because he is giving away heaps of complimentary tickets, which of course we don't like, for we don't go there to give concerts for our own pleasure.

In the first place I have to thank you for your prompt reply regarding Raff.[2] I replied immediately telling them of certain conditions which I must insist upon, and they answered by return saying that the Committee were prepared to meet me on all points and that Raff would call upon me to settle the whole business. So it seems as though the die were cast ! I undertook to give one and a half hours of teaching a day, said that I would require four months' holiday and the right to go away for short periods without asking permission, provided I did not neglect my pupils. Finally, I stipulated that the lessons should be given in my house and that my salary should be 2,000 thalers [£300]. Do you think this is all right ? I have also said that I should like to have an assistant teacher, either a man or a woman, who would help me by giving lessons on my

---

[1] Dictated.

[2] This refers to the proposed appointment of Clara at the Hoch Conservatoire of which Raff was the Director.

own methods.[1]   If anything of importance to me should occur
to you in connection with the drafting of the contract, please
let me know.   I need hardly tell you that the whole business
is causing me a good deal of anxiety.   As you know Wüllner
wrote to me the other day about a post in Dresden, but I
declined without further ado.   When you mentioned the matter
to him you surely were not thinking of my family there ! ! !

Stockhausen's post in F. is not yet settled.   I have put in
the corrections you were kind enough to send me, but this new
edition is a terrible business.   I have compared all the pieces
sent me by Härtel with my husband's books, and there is
hardly a copy which is right.   Herzogenberg is going to be
good enough to do his utmost to find some of the old editions in
Leipsic.   I was very much surprised that you came to Dresden
after all, but bitterly disappointed that you did not yourself
conduct, for when you do the orchestra has such a different
swing about it.   Thank you for your trouble about the C major
Symphony.   I suppose we may take it for granted that Rietz
sold it long ago.   But there is no doubt about the fact that I
gave it to him, for I even remember the words I wrote at the
end of it.   I suppose you received the D major Symphony for
four hands ?   I sent it as soon as I got your letter.   And now
with most affectionate greetings dear Johannes, Your Clara.[2]

Clara *to* Brahms.

Berlin, *April* 5.

I have been wanting to dictate a letter to you for some days,
but my secretary has never been here.   So to-day I prefer to
write to you with my own hand than to dictate nothing.   In
the first place then let me send you all good wishes for the journey, which I have longed for you to take for years.[3]   How you
will revel in it all !   And in such pleasant company too !   I
wish that, some time, I might get to know Billroth a little better.
It must be so stimulating and profitable to see a great deal of
such people, and how educating for folk like ourselves !   But

---

[1] In answer to this Raff proposed that Clara should have her daughters to help her in this way ; to which Clara agreed and chose Marie, who
had recently been giving her much assistance with her private pupils.

[2] These last ten words were written with her own hand.

[3] This refers to Brahms' visit to Italy with Billroth and Goldmark.

please be careful about typhoid fever, particularly in Rome. The climate is frightfully dangerous for foreigners who always want to see as much as they possibly can in the time, and who often do themselves a lot of harm, particularly in the cold galleries. For you all this is twice as dangerous as for anybody else, because you never think of what can harm you. So here's luck, and may you have a delightful journey. Felix's address is, Acé Reale, Hotel des Bains, Sicily. But please do not encourage him in any extravagance, as I have very bad news of him and am much upset by it. He sent us a few poems yesterday and begged us to copy out the best and send them to you. If you do not leave before the 10th they will have time to reach you. I was so overjoyed at your plan that I could not wait to write to you about it. The people here are desperate about my going and they are making me feel very miserable, for I should never have thought that I could have inspired so much love as is now being shown me. They have only just come from the Hochschule and are crying out about my not staying here, and protesting that after all I belong here ! ! !

Thank you for further corrections, but they certainly do not agree with all that you said (to comfort me). My arm forbids my chatting any longer. Think of me from time to time and send me a card occasionally. My faithful old heart will be with you. Your CLARA.

CLARA *to* BRAHMS.

BERLIN, *May* 7.

So the dear anniversary has come round again, but where, oh where, am I to send my greetings and good wishes ! I scatter them to the four winds, perhaps at this very moment they are hovering about you, and you become conscious of a feeling of vague contentment, while a thought wings its way back to me in dusty Berlin ! Where can you be ? Thank you for your note from Rome which made me very happy. I was very glad to hear that you had seen Felix. But you don't tell me what Billroth thinks of his condition or what he recommends for the future.[1] Felix also writes nothing about it, and

---

[1] Billroth's report was hopeful. He said there were one or two points in the lungs that were not quite right, but in view of the boy's youth it was possible they might heal even if it took a long time.

so it looks as if I must fear the worst. Please, dear Johannes, tell me frankly what Billroth says. I have long ago given up all hope and only do what I can for him. Anything else is beyond me !

As you may imagine we are very busy. Our goods and chattels go to Frankfort at the end of May. We were there at Easter and found a nice house in an open situation.[1] In June we shall so far settle things as to be able to find everything comfortable there by the beginning of October. But what a move it is ! ! !

Carnaval and *Phantasiestücke* have at last gone off to Härtels, after I had worried myself for days with the metronome on their account. I had bought myself a watch with a minute hand and the long and short of it is that I have given it up. You were quite right, the work is pure torture. It makes one quite desperate. Anybody who understands the pieces will play them all right, and those who do not understand them we need not bother about. . . . I am very anxious to hear where you are and where you propose to pitch your summer tent. I shall shortly be going to Kiel and shall finish there at Whitsuntide, so that I shall most probably be in Düsseldorf for the festival. Your D major Symphony and Faust are being played there, and I feel frightfully tempted to go. Farewell for the time being. Where shall I send this ? To Vienna, I suppose. With affectionate greetings, Your CLARA.

BRAHMS *to* CLARA.

PÖRTSCHACH, *June.*

Even to-day I shall not be able to write much, but I want to thank you again for your charming and affectionate letter. You will have no difficulty in believing that I know how to read and understand all you have written and felt. If on an occasion of this sort I wish that both my father and your husband might be back on earth again, I also feel that nothing will now be harder for me than parting from you.[2] Thus I beg you to believe that in spirit I was in very truth by your side and will

---

[1] 32 Mylius Strasse.

[2] This refers to the success of the Second Symphony at the musical festival at Düsseldorf at Whitsuntide, 1878. The letter in which Clara tells her friend about this seems to have been lost.

confess that on that beautiful spring morning here I allowed
my imagination to rehearse certain passages from the Symphony, and that it did not seem out of keeping with the surroundings.   Thank Eugenie again for having copied out Felix's
poems for me.   I have selected one of them.   The others do
not lend themselves to music.   As I believe that a song by
Felix will interest you I send it herewith, and as I do not like to
send it alone I am sending some other songs with it.   I also
send you some duets which I intend to publish with *Edward*.[1]
Please write and say what you think of them, and also whether
they and the songs please you (you might let me have a word
to say whether the music has arrived).   If you like, and provided your criticism is favourable, I will send you more.   I
read quite enough papers (particularly at such times), but I
do not get the Rhineland papers, so knew nothing about the
festival.   The A minor Concerto by Viotti is a particular
favourite of mine and I believe that Joachim chose it on that
account.   It is a remarkable work showing great facility of
invention.   It sounds as if he were improvising and the whole
thing is conceived and carried out in such a masterly
fashion.

About Hamburg, I wrote to you that I was in favour of the
Mozart (or the Mendelssohn) Concerto.   The public always
listen to the D minor in particular with reverence.   The fact
that people in general do not understand or respect the best
things, such as the Mozart Concerto and the above by Viotti,
is well known, and it is owing to this that people like ourselves
thrive and come to fame.   If only people knew that they get
from us in drops what they might drink by the gallon from
these sources ! . . .   If you are in Baden in the autumn, we
shall be able to do some wonderful work together [2] and also
take wonderful drives in the wonderful woods.   With this
pleasant prospect in view, I am, Your JOHANNES.

CLARA *to* BRAHMS.

FRANKFORT, *Sept.* 17.

It is a long time since I wrote to you, but oh, what have I not
gone through meanwhile and how utterly sad I am even now !

[1] Op. 75, 1.
[2] This refers to the Complete Edition of Robt. Schumann's works.

I am almost paralysed and can hardly do what is most necessary, and yet the work that lies before me is incredible. Just fancy, I had only been a few days in Munich when I got such acute neuralgia in my arm that I could not move a finger and had the most maddening pain day and night! This lasted fully three weeks and in the end morphia alone gave me relief. In addition to these bodily pains I underwent the greatest spiritual tortures that a mother can suffer. On our second day in Munich we received news from Marmorito that Felix was so ill that he could no longer be left alone. I telegraphed at once for him to come to Munich, but I was so shaken that I went about as if I were besotted. Of course this increased the pains in my arm. After much correspondence to and fro, Felix at last arrived, and his appearance when I saw him again —oh, it was heartbreaking! He staggered along like an old man and could not get his breath, besides which he coughed from morning till night and was only able to snatch a few hours' rest by means of chloral. In this state we brought him to Baden. There he revived a little, and after a week's stay my arm also improved so much that I dared to sit down at the piano again for a bit. We stopped at the *Bär*, but it was an awful time, and I was so ill with anxiety that the children urged me to go to Büdesheim for a day or two, which I eventually agreed to do, as I felt so terribly ill. Marie went to Frankfort, where there was a great deal to be done, but she came back to me on the 13th, so that I had the comfort of having her with me, though my birthday was indeed a sad one, for Eugenie had gone with Felix to Falkenstein—a consumptive hospital an hour's distance from here, which is said to be very good. He wanted very much to come and stay with us, and we wanted it too. But it was impossible to take him to a house which was not yet straight, without servants, etc. And so I begged him to go to Falkenstein for the time being. It was getting too cold in Baden, but in many respects he seems to be quite comfortable where he is. We can do nothing for him except alleviate his sufferings, for I have no longer any hope ; one lung is completely gone and the other is badly touched. But what a beginning in a new house and a new sphere of activity—it is very hard ! But it was a great joy to find that among the letters which Marie brought me at Büdesheim there was a greeting from you. I also received a happy message from New York,[1] where a boy has been born, and according to the telegram, all are doing well. I suppose we cannot expect to hear anything more for another ten or twelve days. It is dreadful! I have been here for a few days, but in an hotel. We cannot live in the house until the end of the month—at least not to sleep there. But during the last few days I have been practising in my charming room there in preparation for Hamburg, and had to get the cadenzas right, which I found extremely hard, as I could only catch the feeling with great difficulty. I have borrowed a few passages from you—you don't mind, do you ? Your news about Hanslick surprises me. Fancy their having invited him and not you ! [2] It is quite incredible ! I have a great deal of pain in both arms and don't know how I shall be able to play at Hamburg. But for this particular occasion I should hate to cry off ; I would only do so if I were absolutely obliged. But you will readily understand that I am in no mood for it, for my heart has never been heavier even in the bitterest moments of my life. To be old and healthy oneself and yet to see the life of a child, of a boy in the prime of youth, fading away—surely this is the cruellest trial a mother's heart can endure, and it is a trial to which I have been subjected for the third time. Nor could I bear it were it not that the love of my other children sustains me. God grant me further strength by safeguarding them !

I have been writing a great deal about our affairs, but I hardly have a thought apart from these troubles which drive everything else into the background. Joachim has written to me about your beautiful Concerto.[3] He says he is delighted with it but that it is very difficult. How I long to hear it ! But it is not so easy for me to get to Leipsic now as it used to be. Farewell. Write a word of comfort soon to Your old friend
CLARA.

CLARA *to* BRAHMS.

FRANKFORT, *Oct.* 8.
Neither your memory nor your pen happens to be right—the

---

[1] From Elise and her husband.
[2] To the jubilee celebrations of the Philharmonic Society.
[3] Violin Concerto, Op. 77.

concert in Leipsic is on the 24th of October.[1] This will surely be too early for you, as you will hardly have got back. If you cannot combine the journey with some useful object I would rather you did not come, for it is really such a long way, and I should feel uncomfortable if you undertook it on my account. I do not need to say more ; it is obvious. We are now in the deepest distress ; the doctor at Falkenstein refuses to keep Felix any longer because he cannot do him any good. Felix himself wishes to leave for the simple reason that he always wants to leave any place where he has been two or three days, and feels just the same when he is with us. But we cannot give him anything like the attention that he gets there, nor many of the comforts. Besides which there is incessant noise and music here—in short, we are at our wits' end to know what to do. You can imagine how all this depresses me. At the best of times my wings refuse to soar, but now they threaten to bear me down into the abyss. Farewell for to-day. With most affectionate greetings, my dear Johannes, and begging you to remember me, Your old friend CLARA.

CLARA *to* BRAHMS.

FRANKFORT AM M., *Nov.* 4.

A day or two ago I came back from Leipsic. It was a wonderfully beautiful festival, finer than I ever dreamt it would be, for I had always felt rather frightened of it, and lo ! it turned out to be a really magnificent and undiluted pleasure for me. What affection everybody showed me ! It could not fail to raise me above all earthly considerations. I felt wholly uplifted and blissful. The fact that, although you were on your travels, and the principal concert in Dresden was over, you did not see your way to come—and secretly I did not give up hope till Thursday—was quite incomprehensible to me. Neither could I understand that amid so many hearty congratulations, which came to me from friends and strangers alike, I had to go without yours and it pained me very much. Nevertheless I have the comfort of knowing that nothing I have done was responsible for this, and can only suppose that the world is made up of different sorts of people.

[1] This refers to the concert to be given in Leipsic to celebrate her jubilee as an artist. See p. 26, *ante.*

Felix is now with us, which in many respects is a great trial, but also in some ways a comfort. His condition fluctuates, but on the whole he is very weak. It is very hard to have to work in the midst of it all, and yet I suppose I ought to consider myself lucky to be able to do so. Let me hear from you soon and tell me how you fared in Breslau. A day or two ago, while I was at Leipsic, they performed your Symphony here, and it had a great success. I understand that Müller is going to perform it again. I am frantically busy, so must close for to-day. With affectionate greetings, ever your faithful old friend CLARA.

CLARA *to* BRAHMS.

FRANKFORT AM M., *Nov.* 7.

I was just about to revel in the piano pieces [1]—I can play some of them quite well now, but most of them are terribly difficult—when your letter arrived, and so I am writing to you at once to tell you how much I am enjoying them. A great favourite of mine is the C major, and yet you want to leave it out ? Why this one particularly ? If you leave out any at all I should prefer it to be the A major, for although its middle movement is charming, it is too reminiscent of Chopin, and the beginning is too insignificant for Brahms—if you will excuse my saying so ! In the C major piece I wish you would use the charming opening phrase again at the repeat, it would not be difficult, would it ? I don't much care for the four first bars after the repeat, they sound dry up to the bar

where it becomes more pleasing again. Then at the end the second bar

would sound better with another harmony. You use such a liquid one in the following bar, and this one is so dry. I am

[1] Op. 76.

practising the last part of the Finale hard in order to be able to
play it so that it does not sound so harsh.   It is rich in ideas
but a little harsh after the exquisite sound of the whole.   Please
do not leave the piece out.   It would be a pity !   I like the
first one in parts very much, but I cannot grow accustomed to
the sudden changes of time, so that I do not enjoy it as a
whole.   Number two is enchanting.   I also like number four,
the A minor, very much.   I am much in favour of the change
to 3/2 time at the transition, which lengthens it a little and
makes it more reposeful.   I also thought of some of the alterations you have made in the F Sharp minor piece, for instance,
what was

now goes in octaves, which sounds harsher, and it is the same
the second time.   Then I prefer the earlier version of the
return, in which it repeats the first theme and the bass takes it
up, because at the outset it does not keep on F Sharp in the
bass, and that is why I was always so delighted with this earlier
version.   Why did you alter it ?   I am also very pleased with
the augmentation at the return to the theme.   The two short
pieces in A Flat major and B Flat major are little pearls.   I
am in favour of repeating the first part of the A major.   I
think it would make the whole thing clearer.   I have written
more than any correspondence card would have held ; but all
these comments were in my mind, and possibly you may find
some of them at least justified.

   You must have received my parcel of proofs by now and have
seen that I have set aside all scruple, and yet you will have to
give my conscience credit for the fact that at least I always
look through the things before sending them to you, and then
leave the final decision to your judgment.   As to the *Impromp-
tus* and the *Papillons*, I have begged Härtels to look for the

manuscript at Hoffmeisters. Soon I will send you the *Phantasie.*

I cannot tell you how busy I am, and in addition I have undertaken one or two private lessons (at 30 marks a time ! ! !) which, however, I shall have to give up, because I cannot stand working three hours in the morning ; and the afternoons are impossible because there are other things to do. You see I have in any case to practise from one to two hours every day. But I have a number of charming pupils. I have just received an invitation from Vienna, from Frau Wagner, the widow of the actor at the Imperial and Royal Theatre, asking me to attend a charity concert. But one cannot go to Vienna for *one* concert ! This year I have again been obliged (with a heavy heart, I admit) to give up going to England, chiefly owing to Felix, whom I did not wish to leave for so long to the care of one of his sisters.

You haven't written to tell me how the Symphony went off at Breslau or whether you were pleased about it. If only people (like Sch. . . .) would refrain from composing ! It really is a pity ! In this place every Tom, Dick and Harry fancies he must compose before he has even mastered harmony (but this is quite between ourselves). So farewell for to-day. Please answer me concerning my own criticisms. I should be glad to hear what you have to say and would be interested to know your grounds for disagreeing with them. Yours affectionately, CLARA.

BRAHMS *to* CLARA.

VIENNA, *Dec.*[1]

. . . I do not know yet whether I shall be in Leipsic for the concert on New Year's Day, or whether I shall come to Frankfort for Christmas or after the 1st of January. You might write to me some time and say whether you can have me at your house (owing to Felix, surely not). Frank has also invited me but seems to be coming to Vienna for Christmas ? Will you ask him ? After all it doesn't matter whether

[1] A previous letter written by Brahms this month, which was full of technical details regarding Clara's editorial work, did not seem to be interesting enough for translation. This also applies to the first half-dozen paragraphs of the present letter.—TR.

I sleep in an hotel or not, I sleep well anywhere. We might arrange to be invited to Wiesbaden for the violin Concerto. A motet by me [1] ("Why ? "—it begins like this) was sung here last Sunday. I believe the audience was very pleased with it. . . .

If I come at Christmas I must implore you not to make any presents. I would do so willingly but I really haven't time to look about and choose. I do not include Czerny in this remark. I would have sent him long ago but I thought that, acting on my advice, you would naturally have bought him for the Conservatoire. With the most affectionate greetings to all from Your JOHANNES.

I really am curious to know whether you let me have the Schumann pieces before they are engraved afresh, for I don't mind telling you that seeing them afterwards does not amuse me very much.

[1] Op. 74.

1879

Clara *to* Brahms.

FRANKFORT AM M., *Feb.* 2.

DEAR JOHANNES,

. . . Things are far from well with us. Felix is visibly fading away and, although he keeps out of bed, the poor fellow endures unspeakable suffering which we share with him. I cannot tell you how miserable I am! I see him only for a few minutes at a time, because it always excites him too much. But my heart bleeds for him when I see him and, no matter what I may be doing, I can think only of him, the poor sufferer, and have to summon all my strength not to sink beneath the load. Surely this illness is the cruellest one can possibly imagine, for one can do nothing to give relief and can only stand silently by. The suffering is so incessant that the poor invalid cannot be distracted from it even for a minute. Alas, I am writing you a great deal about all this, but you can well imagine how full to overflowing is my cup of sorrow. It seems to me extraordinary that at my concerts [1] I can play with so much freedom and power, when all the time I am so miserable that I never forget my grief for one moment. But enough of all this. May I send you some proofs soon? Let me send you one more affectionate greeting, I don't suppose I shall accomplish much more than that to-day. Your faithful old friend CLARA.

Brahms *to* Clara.

VIENNA, *Second half of February.*

MY BELOVED CLARA,

Every letter I have received from you lately has prepared

---

[1] Between the 17th and 30th of January Clara gave concerts at Bâle, Zürich and Freiburg.

me for the sad news which has come to-day.[1] But when I held this one in my hand I felt sure of what it contained and as I opened it all my thoughts were with you. One would imagine that at such a moment one ought to feel relieved and uplifted. But I have never found it so. All the memories of the good things I have had in the past and the thoughts of all the good things I may yet hope for and expect, crowded in upon my mind. At the moment I only feel with double force what I felt before.

It is a good thing that Fate cannot assail me many more times. I very much fear that I should not bear it very well. But what I wish with all my heart is that everything that is given to mankind and which reaches them from outside, in order to comfort them in their trouble and to help them to bear it, may be vouchsafed to you in abundance, so that you may be able to endure this blow as you have endured many another hard one. I feel particularly sorry for Eugenie who was so devoted to him, but I am comforted to think that you two are together, that you help each other to bear your load, and take care of each other. I wish I could be with you, for no matter how long I may sit with paper and pen before me, I should find things so much easier if I could sit in silence beside you. Yours affectionately JOHANNES.

CLARA *to* BRAHMS.

FRANKFORT, *Feb.* 21.

Thank you, my dear Johannes, for your note which has comforted me so much. If I were to try to tell you of the days we have been through I could not describe all that I have endured. The worst to me was when they bore him away. What agony that was! But I am quite calm, though terribly sad. It really was a release which we ought to have desired. It was too awful, to witness such suffering, and we cannot help feeling relieved that he should have been freed from it. Even Eugenie is bearing up wonderfully, and she was, of course, the one I was most anxious about at this moment. Thank God spring is near at hand! I cannot help thinking sorrow can be borne more easily when one sees the

---

[1] Felix Schumann was released from his suffering during the night of February 15/16.

trees all budding—there is something comforting about it. Ferdinand was here for a day or two, but has gone away again, and everything is now quite desolate, and we are alone in this great house with nothing more to do for our loved one.

I cannot conclude these lines without asking you a business question which I should be glad if you would answer immediately. You know that Franck's resignation has been accepted, and as for the moment he has not got another post, he intends to give lessons, etc.[1] I was wondering whether we could not give him a few of Robert's orchestral and choral pieces to revise ? He has the time and would thus earn a little money, because I would, of course, discuss the business side with him first, or better still, in order to spare us both any embarrassment, I might ask Härtels to settle the matter, and to deduct his fee from mine. In this way Franck would earn a little, a good deal would be taken off my shoulders, and we should reach our goal more quickly. Did you not once tell me that you thought very highly of Franck as a musician ? In any case we could judge, or rather you could judge, whether he has any skill in revision, as soon as he has revised one piece. Of course I shall do nothing in the matter until I know what you think about it. I shan't even write to Härtels, unless you are in favour of it.

Please answer me quickly about this matter, for no one can tell how long Franck will remain here. I shall be very sorry if he goes, for in my opinion he is the only musician here and is, into the bargain, such a good fellow, so honest and straightforward. Farewell, my dear Johannes. Think of your old friend CLARA.

Your sister wrote to me several times and showed so much sympathy. I sent her a few lines the other day.

BRAHMS to CLARA.

VIENNA, April.[2]

. . . Many thanks for the Roman History. But I cannot help thinking of the sack in which it was so carefully packed,

---

[1] Ernst Franck, Musical Conductor.

[2] The letter begins with a page and a half of technical and other details about the Schumann edition which it was thought were not sufficiently interesting to be translated.—TR.

particularly when I bear in mind that I shall soon have to be
sending the Concerto parts to Amsterdam.   I am very anxious
to know whether Sarasate played the Concerto to you, and
how he interpreted it.   I should love to practise it with him.
I have been interrupted and cannot therefore tell you as fully
as I had intended with what joy I sauntered about the Prater
on Sunday.   It has an atmosphere all its own, and I could
not help being amused yesterday when I thought of the new
Vienna (Café) in Hamburg and Berlin.   What is the good of
all these fine Vienna Cafés and what is the good of all the
palms and everything, if the Viennese public is not there too ?
Nowhere can the amiable and cheerful character of the Viennese be so fully enjoyed as on a stroll through the Prater.   For
you it would be somewhat of a trial, for the beautiful spring
weather has lured thousands from their homes.   If you happen
to be sending me anything in the next day or two I should be
particularly glad if you would add Felix's poems to the parcel.

With hearty greetings to the Francks, etc. etc., Your
JOHANNES.

CLARA *to* BRAHMS.

FRANKFORT AM M., *May* 5.

I am sending you only a birthday greeting to-day but it
is a most affectionate one.   Once more has it come round,
the day which gave you to the world, and how splendidly
have not all my good wishes been fulfilled hitherto !   Every
year has been better than the last for you, fruitful in creations
and lavish in recognition, honours, gold and how many other
things !   If only spring would not show such undue hesitation
this year !   On the 7th of May it ought to stand before us in
its fullest splendour.   What a good thing you are not in Italy.
That would be hateful.   Complaints about it are coming in
from all quarters.   How it would have spoilt the impression
you had of it last year. . . .

I was very much surprised to see that you had been offered
the post of *Cantor* [1] at Leipsic.   But you do not write as if

─────────

[1] The full meaning of this word is not clear.   It was probably connected with the work of training and conducting the choir.   The post
was vacant at the time at the *Thomasschule* where Brahms was to
succeed Ernst Friedrich Richter.—TR.

you wished to accept. When you answer, do make yourself
clear. Don't keep the people in suspense. . . . In any case
I should not advise you to accept. Leipsic is no longer what
it was. Farewell for to-day. Celebrate the great anniversary
as cheerfully as you can. At all events the Fabers won't be
slow to help you in this. Unfortunately all I can do is to
send my most affectionate thoughts speeding to you. Your
faithful old friend CLARA.

The children send their heartiest wishes. They are all well
and even I continue to be in better spirits. I often feel the
clouds gathering about me, but they do not burst; I have
set my face against that. . . . I cannot help thinking about
Leipsic. The attractions of the post are only illusory, it has
no other. You would want more than that to make you leave
Vienna, don't you think so ? You ought to have charge of
the concerts as well. But there are such a number of them
that you would soon get sick of it. Let me know what you
do about the matter, and now quite seriously, adieu !—

CLARA *to* BRAHMS.

KIEL, *June* 21.

. . . What a pity it is that you have found nothing suitable
among Felix's poems. How fine it would have been to have
had a bunch of them bound together by your music ! I cannot help thinking that he never polished them up sufficiently,
he just jotted them down as they entered his head. They are
not devoid of talent but there is nothing great about them.
For Felix showed talent in a number of things but exceptional
gifts in nothing. It is possible that these might have developed later, for his illness prevented him for years from engag-
ing in any serious study.

After a long interval I received news of Ludwig the other
day, but it was so terrible that my heart gave way. . . . To
think that a poor unfortunate fellow like that goes on living
and that the other, who was intellectually so gifted, and to
whom life with all its joys held out its arms, had to die. Why
should this be ? . . . Yesterday I received the good news
that the monument in Bonn is to be unveiled in the spring.
I seriously hope that this time you will not fail to be there,
I mean playing an active part.

To-day I am sending you a product of my brain.[1] If you must smile compassionately, keep it to yourself. But if you want to scold me about it, don't hesitate. I can stand that all right. But, as a matter of fact, it deserves neither the one nor the other. I am leaving here on the 27th. The massage has done me good and my stay with these charming and really magnanimous people has had an even more beneficent effect upon my spirit.[2] If only I had a couple of friends like them in Frankfort! They are so quick to sympathize with every thought and mood. Such intercourse is a real joy! Take care of yourself, enjoy the pleasures of land and water and remember Your old friend CLARA.

BRAHMS *to* CLARA.

End of June.

. . . Wretched Ludwig and still more wretched Felix! I shall let the poems lie for a bit, for it would be a great joy to me if I could produce some small souvenir to his memory. I am very anxious to hear more about the festival in Bonn. I know nothing more than your casual mention of it. Is there to be a musical festival in connection with the unveiling? And how can I take an active part in it? Proud and pleased as I should be, I don't see what I could do. As for appropriate verses and music, I don't like to think of such things, and for this festival a piece by me would not be so fitting as for the last festival. Except for the violin Concerto I prefer not to share the honours with Joachim as conductor, nor push myself in front of Wasielewski. It would be better if I could think of something good for the unveiling, although perhaps for such an object it would be preferable to have somebody with more skill and a lighter touch than I have even if the standard of his work were lower. It seems so strange to me that a minor musician should be called upon to sing the praises of a greater. But in any case I should like to know sometime what the plans are.

With all this I have not written to you about the most

---

[1] A March composed by Clara to celebrate the Hübners' golden wedding.

[2] Ever since the 31st of May Clara had been undergoing a massage treatment in Kiel, and had lived with the Litzmanns.

important thing of all—the new opus. But in order to do so
I should have to cut my pen afresh and take more paper.
Let it suffice for me to thank you for having sent it to me.
I played it to myself with all due solemnity, and thought how
great must have been the Hübners' delight with it.

With love, Your JOHANNES.

In your next letter don't leave my opus to the end, I don't
want it to receive short commons.[1]

BRAHMS *to* CLARA.

End of June.

. . . N.B. Surely my *Requiem* will not do for this occasion
at Bonn ! It would also be rather risky after the summer
holidays. In any case I am very glad about the Bonn festival,
as I am about everything that brings you and me together—
and for other reasons too. But one day before, and one day
after the festival, I must really be allowed to stay in Fr !—
Heartiest greetings to your two daughters. Your JOHANNES.

BRAHMS *to* CLARA.

(July ? .)

Herewith I am sending two pianoforte pieces on to which
you can fling yourself heart and soul if they please you at all.
Incidentally you can also find out whether the cure has worked.
Please let me remind you on no account to let the pieces go
out of your own hands, unless one of your daughters would
like to practise them ! I hope to hear from you very soon
about them and to know whether number two has given you
any pleasure. Heartiest greetings to everybody in Düsseldorf
and Frankfort, Your J. B.

CLARA *to* BRAHMS.

DÜSSELDORF, *July* 10.

I must send you a line to tell you how deeply moved I am
by your Sonata.[2] I received it to-day and of course played
it through at once, and had to cry my heart out afterwards
for joy over it. You can imagine how delighted I was when
after the first enchanting movement, and the second, I again

[1] This refers to the Sonata Op. 77 sent with the previous letter.
[2] Op. 78.

came across in the third my own beloved melody, with its exquisite quaver movement. I say *my own*, because I don't believe anyone can enjoy this melody as deeply and as thoroughly as I do. Fancy finding this last movement after all the beauties that had preceded it ! My pen is feeble but my heart is full and yearns towards you in gratitude. In spirit I press your hand. I expect to be in Frankfort on Sunday, and then I shall play your Sonata at once with H. I must practise the other two pieces first, and I think they will go all right then, as most of the other pianoforte pieces have ; for, apart from the F Sharp minor, I have gradually learnt to love them all. I shall stop in Frankfort until the 19th or 20th. Write to me there again. Farewell, dear Johannes. Ever your faithful friend, CLARA.

CLARA *to* BRAHMS.

WILDBAD GASTEIN, AT GRÜBER'S, *July* 26.

To return to the subject of my short note the other day, I am now writing to say that I have tried the Sonata with Heermann. We were so glad of the opportunity that we went into the work quite thoroughly. The way you have blended all the motifs together strikes me as wonderful. How charming the dreamy accompaniment of the last motif ♩ ♪ | ♩. sounds at the beginning of the first motif. It is as if the spirit of the whole piece were wafted to one's ears at the very opening. I find the general character of the Sonata most enlivening. The grace and warmth of the melodies, and the masterly way you treat all the motifs, captivate one's heart and soul from the first to the last note. What heavenly passages there are in it, not to mention the beauty of some of the organ points ! And then the ascent in the last movement of the first melody where it finally returns and rises and falls full of sadness and yearning ! For such feelings sound alone, and not words, are adequate. A few small points which occurred to me I will tell you about later if you like. This will do for to-day, together with my thanks for all the joys you have given me. Many people may be better able to speak about these things than I am, but no one can feel them more deeply than I do. The deepest and most tender chords of my heart vibrate at the sound of such music.

It is a real privation to me to have no piano, but it is impossible here, so I must put up with it. We have been here for two days, and, after having had the most appalling weather on our journey, it is now magnificent. Although she can only take a few steps at a time, Marie has stood the journey well, and feels better every day. The doctor thinks she will soon be quite well.[1] Throughout the whole of the time (and it would have tried the patience of Job) she was an angel of resignation and cheerfulness, and I was forced to admire her in silence. It was no joke to have to lie in bed for eight weeks when she was not ill or requiring rest, and she always cheered Eugenie and myself when we were both feeling sad. . . .

I enclose a letter from Härtel. What do you think of it? Unfortunately Härtel is not here as I thought he was. It would have been so much better to have discussed many things with him. I should like to have asked him about several matters connected with the publication of a book of letters linked together by means of biographical explanations, and particularly about what arrangement one makes with the compiler—Jansen, for instance. I made the acquaintance of the latter a little while ago in Hamburg. . . . He told me a good deal that I did not know, and interested me very much. I have made a start with the copying and have secured a little help with it. But the more conscientiously one approaches such an undertaking, the more difficult does it become.

Nothing is yet settled about Bonn. Joachim has suggested a concert where he would play your Concerto. I should also play, and Schumann's *Requiem für Mignon* would be given ! ! ! I must confess that the choice of this piece is quite incomprehensible to me—not to use a more drastic term ! I spoke to the gentlemen about it and told them that, in my opinion, there is only one Requiem suitable for the occasion and that is yours conducted by yourself. From the first they had agreed about a *Requiem*, and as the unveiling is not to take place, according to Joachim's proposal, until the end of October there would be time enough to practise it. They were also in favour of giving a memorial concert in the winter, at which Joachim and I promised to play (for Donndorf's benefit). So it is quite possible that the unveiling may be fixed for the

[1] She had broken her knee in the winter.

beginning of October after all, and that singing will only take place at the grave. As soon as I hear anything for certain I will let you know. Joachim was not asked to conduct but only to play. Donndorf charged so little for the monument that they would like to give him something extra. . . . I must close for to-day, we want to try and catch the fine weather. Farewell, dear friend. Your loving old friend CLARA.

BRAHMS *to* CLARA.

[VIENNA], *Sept.*

Ever since I returned the day before yesterday I have been wanting to write to you. Now here is the letter at last ! I will deal with your business questions first. If only you were not up to your old game, worrying about things that don't matter ! . . . Do not allow yourself to be harried by Härtels. This for the hundredth time ! They are always pressing other people but are never in a hurry themselves, or even prompt.

I am so glad to hear that your house at Baden is sold. It would have been a difficult and expensive matter to keep it as a souvenir. I am happier still to hear that you are both better. I hope you will both live comfortably and quietly and that things will continue to improve. What is happening about Bonn ? Are you going there in October ? We had a beautiful and most enjoyable journey. We travelled through strange, interesting and frequently beautiful country in the most magnificent weather, and incidentally treated ourselves to a little music and also to an occasional drink. A couple of weeks fly quickly by in this way and are not hard to bear ! Unfortunately I have a heap of letters here, chiefly long-winded communications about concerts, or I would write in greater detail. I should often feel inclined to undertake these concert tours if one could give a concert every other day and have time to get to know the country and the people. But the modern virtuoso is too grasping for this. There has to be a concert every day, and all one can do is to arrive an hour before the concert and be off again an hour after it. I can think of nothing more detestable or more contemptible than this kind of occupation. And yet people like us are so well treated. We are received by the mayor and the Directors at the station, introduced immediately into the best circles, and they all vie with each other in being as kind and as friendly to us as possible.

On the other hand, though a man like Billroth may go to Hungary or other parts of the world much more often, he sees no one except the Jews he has to operate upon. But we can see everything and hear everything that is worth while, provided we are not hustled. We gave concerts in Arad, Temesvar, Kronstadt, Pressburg, Hermannstadt and Klausenburg. It was interesting everywhere. But I will describe it to you more fully when I see you some time. . . . Meanwhile I send you hearty greetings and hope to send you more soon. With best wishes to you all and the Francks, from Your JOHANNES.

CLARA *to* BRAHMS.

FRANKFORT AM M., *Oct.* 12.

I have long hesitated about writing this letter, but it must be written at the risk of making you angry. . . . From the enclosed letter you will see how anxious Härtels are that the work of revision should proceed as quickly as possible, and that they are not only concerned about those works they have published themselves, but with them all. I must repeat that this business is weighing heavily on me and that I have but one wish at present and that is to dispose of it at the earliest possible moment. To make a person of my age treat such a matter lightly is impossible. You wrote to me the other day that the works you were sending (to Härtels) had already gone, but you still have Op. five and six.

I cannot help thinking that in any case this business is taking up a lot of your time, and it would be far better if you were only appealed to in the last instance, and were to allow a few others to co-operate in the earlier stages. I should very much like to employ Franck in this capacity. . . . Woldemar has also repeatedly said that he would gladly collaborate with us, and in this way I should be able to distribute the work, and more particularly the orchestral pieces, between these two. Please let me know as soon as possible, but not in your first transport of indignation, what you think about this.—If you bear in mind that I have not very much longer to live you must sympathize with my wish to get the work done as soon as possible. For you know only too well how many other calls I have upon my time, and must realize that at my age I no longer possess the elasticity necessary for continuous work of this kind. So weigh everything carefully. Perhaps you will then take a different view of the matter. Incidentally I should like Härtels' letters back some time. . . . I will end with heartiest greetings from us all, as ever, Your CLARA.

BRAHMS *to* CLARA.

> VIENNA, *Oct.* 14 (?).

In the first place let me tell you that it is impossible for the greatest difficulties or for anything at all to make me the least bit angry with you (I don't even like to use the word), or to have anything whatever against you. I am only joking when I scold you because you will give yourself so much unnecessary trouble. Thus I am against you for your own good. . . . I am in entire agreement with everything you do even in regard to Franck and Bargiel. As far as I am concerned, I have no objections to anything, and shall always be ready, whether at the beginning or the end, to do everything you want, or what I myself believe to be in your interests. If occasionally I advise you not to draw many, or too many, assistants into the business, again I speak only in your interests. For if you do, you have to weigh and to consider the opinions of three people, and thus merely treble your work and your difficulties.

Secondly, I really cannot see why you should spend your money in this way, because I see you intend to pay Franck, for instance. This goes very much against the grain with me, but once again only because I am for you against yourself. However, so that we may see the end of the matter, just try giving the Symphonies to both of them—say the B Flat major and the C major to W. and the B Flat, the E Flat and the D to Franck. But don't forget to remind them to write their ? as lightly as possible in pencil on the score, so that the whole thing does not get scrawled over from the start.

And now let me further beg of you to feel quite safe about the things you send to me, and about my orderliness in such matters. What about giving some songs as well as the Symphonies to your two friends and co-revisers, so that the business may be attacked from all sides at once ? I can think of no work of Schumann's that is likely to hold us up for long. I should only like to put aside the symphonic studies and the F minor Sonata for the present, so that I may gradually come to some conclusion as to the best way to deal with them. Otherwise everything can simply be prepared for engraving straight away.

Now I should very much like to indulge my curiosity and ask you a question about Stockhausen.[1] But both you and your two dear secretaries [2] have too much to do and can ill afford the time for gossip. So my curiosity must be stifled until I see you in January.

So now send off a parcel of music at once to W. and Fr. and then, either direct to me, or after you have looked at it yourself, for me to see. I shall put my papers here in order, and send you and Härtels your allotted portion. With heartiest greetings to you all, Your JOHANNES.

CLARA *to* BRAHMS.

FRANKFORT, *Oct.* 22.

. . . Now here is another matter, and once more it concerns Robert's correspondence. There is a young man in Breslau called Max Kalbeck—you must surely know him too. My friends in Breslau have strongly recommended him for this work, and as he is intimate with Heyse, I asked the latter about him and received the enclosed reply, in which Heyse says that he is a very suitable man for the work and that I can trust him entirely. Perhaps you know him better than I am aware and can tell me something about him.

As you see from the letter he would be able to come to Frankfort from time to time in order to examine all the papers concerned under my roof. Please return the letter and answer me some time, but not later than a fortnight hence, as I shall then be going to Breslau and could discuss any further questions with him. The other day Härtels sent me a popular edition of my compositions published by them, and in it I found "*pièces fugitives*" translated by "*fugierte Stücke*."[3]

---

[1] Owing to differences with Raff, Stockhausen had resigned his post at the Conservatoire.   [2] Marie and Eugenie.

[3] "*Fugierte Stücke*" means pieces composed in the style of a fugue.—TR.

What do you think of that? And now farewell. With heartiest greetings from us all, Your old friend CLARA.

CLARA *to* BRAHMS.

(*Dictated.*)

LEIPSIC, *Nov.* 11.

To-day I must tell you about something which for the last week has kept us in a state of almost feverish excitement. I have, as a matter of fact, made up my own mind about it, but I should like to know your opinion. I must give you some sort of introduction, and then I will enclose the documents herewith so that you may gather all you want to know from them.[1] . . . Please let me know at once what you think about it. Also please let me have the letter back. But above all do not mention the matter to a soul until I have taken a definite step. Write to me here as I shall stay here until Saturday. I really do not feel in the mood, nor have I time for any more. You can imagine how hard this journey was for us, but it is a good thing that I still have a week left. Nobody knows about it in Frankfort. With heartiest greetings from Your old friend CLARA.

BRAHMS *to* CLARA.

Nov.

Men are not all made of pure gold. In fact they very seldom are; but every time you find this out, or imagine you have found it out, you are horrified and filled with astonishment. Perhaps this time your astonishment alone will suffice and Raff's gilding will survive the test. Of course I see the thing just as you do, and in your place would leave no stone unturned to straighten it out without delay, for it may mean a good deal to the poor young woman. For the moment, however, do not think the worst of Raff. . . . My own idea

---

[1] During her stay in Schwerin two years before, Clara had promised the mother of a young pianist that she would take her daughter as a pupil. The girl arrived in Frankfort in October, 1879; but Raff, although he knew of Clara's intentions about her, handed her over to another teacher (Fälten) without consulting Clara. Clara regarded this as a great grievance and, as will be seen from this and the following letters, could not be pacified for a long time. Thanks to Brahms's advice, however, a quarrel with Raff was fortunately avoided.

as to what has happened may seem plausible to you and I will describe it briefly. R. has a very difficult position. He has to consider a hundred points of view ; he is bombarded by all sorts of requests and claims, and he has to conciliate and distinguish between all manner of conflicting interests. Now it seems not improbable to me that in this case, as well as in many other similar cases, he is very often tempted where you are concerned to try (always in secret) to patronize you a little. In spite of all his respect for you—aye, and his sympathy for your beautiful nature, he imagines that as director he has a right to keep certain things to himself and to take care behind your back that matters do not go too far.

In the interests of his institution he is probably only too willing to hand over the more distinguished pupils to you. Also he does not feel inclined to spoil bursars too much at first, etc. I could write many other such etcs. But perhaps you will agree for the moment that his behaviour may possibly be excusable after all. If I were you, therefore, I should write to R. a polite and serious note to the following effect . . . that you are quite ready to believe he had his own very special and valid reasons for acting as he has done, but that in view of the friendly promise he had made you, you had encouraged the girl to undertake the journey, and, anxious though you are to recognize whatever grounds he may have had for his action, these could not affect your decision, which could only be to have the girl placed at once under your tuition. . . . In my opinion you will then get a very polite letter from him saying that he had not thought the matter as important as all that, and that he wished to avoid giving the girl *omelettes aux confiture's* [*sic !*] too soon, etc. . . . Greet all our friends in Leipsic, your hosts,[1] my hosts [2] with whom unfortunately I, as I feared—well, etc. etc.

Let me have a line announcing the result. Yours most affectionately, JOHANNES.

CLARA *to* BRAHMS.

LEIPSIC, *Nov.* 15.

I think your advice is very good. And yet I don't like the idea of scrambling for a pupil, who by now has got used to

[1] The Fregers.   [2] The Herzogenbergs.

her own teacher, and whom I should therefore have to snatch away again. . . . Your idea that I should appeal direct to Raff was also the first that occurred to me ; it seemed to me the most human course of action. . . . My main consideration must naturally be the good of the girl herself. Please let me have a word in Breslau where I am just going, to tell me what I should do, particularly if Raff does not agree to my demand. With hearty greetings and thanks, Your CLARA.

BRAHMS *to* CLARA.

November.

If my advice was good at first, it is so still, and is not the least bit modified by any fresh communications. As a matter of fact all the questions are already answered in the first letter or else provided for. . . . Moreover, there is no reason whatsoever to go over Raff's head and to appeal direct to those above him (the governing body). If you write to him on the lines I have suggested, everything will be all right. In two days you will ask him for an answer. If he sends you an unsatisfactory or obstructive reply, decline to consider it, and settle the thing quickly by reiterating your demands. . . . Until you have done something in the matter, or heard something about it, I really don't know what more to say. But I know what will happen. You will all go on discussing it from every point of view for so long that the girl will have learnt all she has to learn from Fälten, and will leave your establishment fully qualified. . . . So see whether you can't manage to write a firm but friendly letter to Raff. . . . And now give my best greetings to everybody in Breslau, particularly your hosts. In this connection I cannot help thinking of my dear Leipsic hosts whom I seem to have offended in some way. I should be particularly sorry to have done so, more especially in their case. But I leave the world to go on as it likes. I am only too often reminded that I am a difficult person to get on with. I am growing accustomed to bearing the consequences of this. Yours affectionately, JOHANNES.

CLARA *to* BRAHMS.

FRANKFORT A/M., *Nov.* 29.

I received your letter in Breslau just as I had sent mine off to Raff.   So you see, I overcame my " womanly fears " before receiving your admonition. . . .   It really is a tiresome business, and I shall be very glad to see it satisfactorily settled. I should hate to have a scandal.

The time is drawing near when I am to hear your Violin concerto played by Joachim.   This will take place here on the 5th.   I am very much hoping that I shall then be able to play the Sonata with him.   In Breslau they are waiting for you and your third Symphony in connection with your Doctor's degree.[1]   I wonder what the truth of the matter is.   I have now got to know Kalbeck and I find that he has many qualities which are very desirable for the work in question. But it is not an easy thing to hand over such confidential matters to a complete stranger.   Farewell for to-day, and let me hear from you soon.   Your old friend CLARA.

P.S.   Please send the copies back.   It is amusing to see that Raff has answered me just as politely as you said he would, though without settling the matter.   Have you accepted any engagements in Germany ?   I should like to know about them.

CLARA *to* BRAHMS.

FRANKFORT AM M., *Dec.* 8.

Through Fräulein Fromm I have just received a letter from Raff in which he officially hands her over to me ! . . .   So now I have her, and after she had played me over a short piece, I recognized that she had more talent than all the others. . . .

And now to something more cheerful—Joachim's stay here, which has afforded us an enormous amount of pleasure.   He played your Concerto wonderfully, and I revelled in it.   We also played your Sonata at various times, and I believe it went beautifully, whilst some variations of his own, which he played as well, were very interesting.   I could not help thinking that here and there they were reminiscent of Brahms. He was very charming, and so jolly, as he always is when his wife is not with him.   I suppose you know that Franck is going to Hanover ?   It is a good thing for him, but we are very sorry about it.

[1] In March, 1879, Brahms was given the degree of Doctor by the Philosophical Faculty of Breslau.

I should like to talk to you about a good many other things, but I am so frantically busy that I have scarcely time for the most pressing duties. I hope I shall see you in January. You know that you are always welcome here at any time, festival or no festival. So farewell for to-day. Your affectionate CLARA.

This week I am going to Carlsruhe, but shall be back on the 14th.

1880

CLARA *to* BRAHMS.

BÂLE, *Feb.* 22.

DEAR JOHANNES,

. . . I am sorry to have annoyed you once more, but you might have ascribed my action to my conscientiousness and shown a little more patience. I shall often have to worry you again with my questions and doubts. I can hardly help doing so, for without your assistance I should never have undertaken the work. Besides, I must tell you that in regard to the trios, the quartets and the quintet, you have done me an injustice. I wrote to Härtels exactly what you told me to, whereupon they replied that they were very much astonished to hear from me that the pieces were so correct that they could be engraved afresh without revision. This frightened me, and I informed them that they had misunderstood me ; all I had meant was that they could proceed confidently with the first proofs. They then, for some unaccountable reason, sent me everything, including all the things that had long ago been forwarded to them without revision on my part.

Unfortunately, Rudorff cannot collaborate with us, for he has still too much to do on the Mozart edition. So we shall have to be content with Bargiel, Franck and Volkland.

With regard to the Bonn affair, Wasielewski has taken the liberty of inviting you " on my behalf " to play. I know nothing about this, and would never have dared to send you such a request, without at the same time begging you to conduct some more important work. I told the Committee of this. Of course it goes without saying that I should be very glad if you did play, and that there is no one whom I should be better pleased to see at the piano on this occasion than yourself. Incidentally, the gentlemen of the Committee begged me to play also. But my feelings are against contributing to the programme on this occasion. I agree that the question can be looked at from various points of view. Please write and let me know whether you think my scruples are justified. I am not quite clear about it. I approve of the *Phantasie* but do not care so much for the Duet, as it was played at the Schumann festival. Farewell, and heartiest greetings from Your CLARA.

BRAHMS *to* CLARA.

VIENNA, *March* 2.

DEAREST CLARA,

I think I have often begun my letters by telling you that if you fancy you see impatience or ill-will in them, this has nothing to do with me, but concerns either you or both of us. For you, no trouble I can take is too great, nor can my patience be too sorely tried, provided my efforts are not in vain.[1] But unfortunately that is precisely what they generally are. Your Cabinet meetings over breakfast always revive all the old doubts ! ! ! !

I can't help what Härtels say, but apart from about twenty-five pieces, there would be absolutely nothing to do on Schumann's works, if only they would provide themselves with a good reader. We shall have to keep a sharp look-out on the first pianoforte pieces and later on upon those coming from the Schubert publishers. It is not our job to see that the engraving is correctly done. That should not concern us. And for Heaven's sake don't mind telling them this. Now let me thank you for the magnificent candlestick which Betty has brought me.[2] It decorates my room wonderfully. . . .

I have certainly been invited to Bonn also in order to conduct my Violin Concerto. But I don't like the idea at all. J. ought to play Schumann's *Phantasie*. For the time being I have consented both to play and to conduct, provided that

---

[1] A passage from Clara's Diary for Sunday, December 29, 1879, throws some light on this sentence and on her reference in the previous letter to her misunderstanding with Härtels. The passage reads: " I was at home alone in the evening and talked much to Brahms about Härtels' edition of Schumann's works. He is not at all the person to banish my scruples. On the contrary he always says that proof-correcting is unnecessary as the engravers always make fresh mistakes." *Life*, Vol. II, p. 352.

[2] This refers to their common friend Betty Oser.

you do not intend to play and that the programme does not consist exclusively of Schumann, which I do not think would be suitable. Heartiest greetings to the whole breakfast-table. Your JOHANNES.

CLARA *to* BRAHMS.
FRANKFORT AM M., *April* 3.

On receipt of your letter I wrote immediately to Schaaffhausen [1] about the chorus from the *Peri*, and I have just received the enclosed reply. It would really be delightful if you would arrange the chorus for wind instruments. As you will see from the letter, however, this would have to be done very quickly and I don't know whether it is not presumptuous to expect this from you just now. Please send me a card so that I may know what to answer Schaaffhausen, or better still send a card to Schaaffhausen direct. But let me hear too, so that I may rejoice over it. What do you think about the words for the chorus ? Shall I ask Kalbeck to do them ? Or can you think of anybody else ? . . .

Farewell, and let me hear from you soon. Your CLARA.

CLARA *to* BRAHMS.
FRANKFORT A/M., *June* 6.

. . . Rudorff has now definitely been appointed to Bruch's post. My poor brother Woldemar is very much upset about having been overlooked. It is doubly hard on him, for he was Rudorff's teacher and is much older than he is. Poor fellow, he evidently has no luck !

If you want to know more about us, you will find Franck the best reporter on the subject. I thoroughly enjoyed seeing him again. Unfortunately we are threatened with fresh losses here. I understand that Koning has applied for the post of Conductor at Mannheim. If he gets it we shall have lost another good musician. I should like to have seen a serious musician and one more sympathetic to me in Heymann's post here, and had thought of Grabau in this connection. But I can do nothing. The Board of Governors are thinking of Sahr and Raff. But nobody really knows, except that he [Raff ?] is in favour of some one who represents Liszt and Rubenstein—in short the

[1] Professor Schaaffhausen of Bonn.

modern tendency ! ! ! He came to me the other day and seriously asked me whether Marie and Eugenie would not be willing to take charge of a preparatory class for me, in which case
he was prepared to give them definite appointments as teachers
(that is, assistant teachers for me only). Marie was very much
against our being bound to the school any further, and wrote
refusing. But then Dr. Hartmann came on behalf of the
Governors and made the same request. So that now the matter
has a different complexion and we are thinking it over. Have
you any ideas on the subject ? If so please let me know them.
Of course, the children would not bind themselves for a longer
period than I have done. And now adieu. Let me hear how
you like Ischl. I suppose one may not inquire about Symphonies, Operas, etc. ? Your old friend CLARA.

CLARA *to* BRAHMS.

FRANKFORT A/M., *June* 29.

I should have liked to answer your kind letter at once, but I
am really so busy now that I don't know what to do. This
month I have to make up several lessons I have missed, and,
in addition to that, almost every day has brought a desperate
mother or father who wished to have their daughter tested.
I find that this sort of thing not only takes up my time, but also
upsets me, because I have to reject the majority of them, and
that always means tears. They have now come to a definite
arrangement with Marie. The whole Board of Governors
interested themselves in the matter, and so she was well able
to accept. But they did not both want to be bound, and I
think they are right. It does not look well for the whole
Schumann family to be at the school. Eugenie is now helping
Marie (as the latter was anxious for her to do), but she is not
regarded as an official teacher. We have made our position
secure in every way, and I have had my agreement altered so
that I can give six months' notice instead of eighteen. . . .
With heartiest greetings, Your old friend CLARA.

CLARA *to* BRAHMS.

FRANKFORT A/M., *July* 5.

I am very anxious about the pains in your ears. Do they
affect your hearing ? Or are they external ? I have just

heard that you have been sitting out in a field and so caught cold. I wish you would be a little more careful. We do not remain for ever young, and are constantly reminded of it. Let me know how you are, nothing more. I am anxious, more anxious than you probably are yourself! As we grow old we lose our elasticity, I feel this very strongly. I dread going away as if it were something terrible, and yet in the most secret corner of my heart, I am looking forward to it, for it is high time I had a rest from this tiresome work. . . . So please, my dear friend, let me hear soon that you are better. . . . Elise had a second boy yesterday. The telegram says that she is doing well. Most affectionate greetings, Yours, CLARA.

CLARA *to* BRAHMS.

HOTEL MARIENBAD, MUNICH,[1] *July* 8.
Like the torment that I am, I am coming to you to-day with another request. Although you always say that we never follow your advice, as a matter of fact we do so almost every time. And to-day I propose once more to rely on it. Following your advice, I carefully studied Czerny's course and find it excellent. We have already copied quite a number of exercises out of it, and when I was in Leipsic last year I asked Abraham [2] whether he would not be prepared to publish a small selection of those studies (finger exercises) which seemed particularly useful. Naturally I had not the remotest intention of doing it myself, but a little while ago Kranz, who is the head of Spinnas, the Hamburg publishers, called upon me, and said that Peters had spoken to him about the matter, and that he would be very glad to publish such a volume if he could be allowed to put my name on it.

I told him that I would try to do it (as a matter of fact, I think it is very important for teaching purposes that such an edition should be prepared), and get Marie to help me, for as she is more concerned than I am with the technical side of the

[1] On the 7th of July Clara had left Frankfort to visit an exhibition at Munich. Then she went to Oberammergau, where she saw the Passion Play, whence she proceeded to Schluderbach and stayed there with friends until the end of August.—TR.

[2] Head of the publishing firm of Peters.

pupils' work, she is very much interested in it, and has already made a selection of those exercises which she considers particularly useful.   But I should not like to undertake anything of this sort without your advice, particularly as I have to put my name to it.   Kranz says he must have it by the end of July, and I want to ask you whether you would mind my sending you the course to look at.

If you should agree with my idea, let me know at once what you think about the financial side.   Shall I do it for nothing, or shall I ask for a fee ?   The work will take up a fair amount of my time, and it is not improbable that Kranz will make a good thing out of it.   You are so practical in all these matters that you will surely be able to advise me.   If we are to undertake the task at all, we should like it to appear in the autumn. There is therefore very little time to lose, and I should be grateful if you would let me know as soon as possible.   Let me have a card here at the above address to say whether you have time to look through the course.   Do not forget to add news of your health.   With greetings from us both (at the present moment Eugenie and Fillu are floating down the Danube in the direction of Vienna), Your CLARA.

CLARA *to* BRAHMS.

SCHLUDERBACH, *July* 26.

Just a line to tell you that we came here three days ago, and that the air is so perfect that, although the neighbourhood is not what I should choose for my depressed spirits, we have decided to stay here. . . .   Will you be so kind as to send us back Czerny's Course with the advice I asked you for ?   The packing need not trouble you, as it is not for foreign parts. . . . .   How are you, my dear Johannes ?   Have you got rid of your ear trouble ?   I should be so glad to hear that you had. With hearty greetings from Marie and myself, Yours ever, CLARA.

CLARA *to* BRAHMS.

SCHLUDERBACH, *Aug.* 7.

In the first place, a thousand thanks for the Course.[1]   I had

[1] Stimulated by his examination of these exercises, Brahms wrote his *Fifty-one Exercises for the Pianoforte* about this time.

no idea that I was giving you so much trouble, and only realize it now that I have seen how carefully you must have gone through it in order to do what we wanted. I only wish I could do something for you in return.

I should like to ask you a number of questions, but as we intend coming over to Ischl for two days, I won't waste your time or mine, but will wait till I can speak to you. You will be in Ischl until the end of August, won't you ? . . . I am very much worried by my state of nervous irritability and often feel quite desperate about it. For the last three or four weeks, for instance, I have had melodies continually running in my head, particularly at night, and cannot get rid of them. It is a little better now, but occasionally I have a night when I do not sleep a wink. Of course I don't play any music, although we have an upright piano here. Neither do I hear any, and I am tormented by the dreadful thought of how I shall get on when I have to start my teaching in the autumn. But I must hope that my nerves will grow stronger in time. I really did too much during the last months in Frankfort. . . . Farewell for to-day. Write soon and tell us whether we shall find you. And once more, with many thanks and most affectionate greetings from us both, Your old friend CLARA.

CLARA *to* BRAHMS.

SCHLUDERBACH, *Aug.* 13.

. . . My principal object in writing to you to-day is to discuss the Course. Something you say in your letter seems to show that you are in some doubt about it, and as this has revived misgivings that have long been latent in my own mind, I wish to implore you to give me your opinion quite frankly. Up to the present Marie has been working at it almost alone. I did not encourage her to do so, because, after all, we are mere laymen in these matters, and have not spent our life in dealing with them. And that is why I felt doubtful as to whether we could carry out the work sufficiently correctly and logically. Marie, however, threw herself heart and soul into it, not with any eye to the fee but because of the interest of the subject, and because she believed that a selection of the kind would be of the greatest use to pupils. But if you are doubtful whether we can turn out the work satisfactorily, please do not have any hesitation in saying so, for if we were guilty of any blunder, no fee would make up for it. I told Marie from the very beginning that I could not devote much time to the work. I should not have worried you with this matter again, and would have waited until we met, but Kranz is pressing for an answer, and I am therefore obliged to fly to you. So please be quite frank. The excellence of our work is all we are thinking about. Thank God we don't depend upon the money it will bring in ! . . . I shall probably remain here until the 20th. I feel very much better. Your old friend, CLARA.

CLARA *to* BRAHMS.

BERCHTESGADEN, *Sept.* 18.

I have been wanting to write to you all this time to ask you whether you had not perhaps caught cold on that bitter night (after leaving here).[1] But a letter has just come from Fillu who saw you in Salzburg with Nottebohm, and I was relieved. I must thank you once more for your visit and for the artistic joys you gave me while you were here. Unfortunately I am compelled to plague you again with the Härtel business, as I have more time to deal with everything here than in Frankfort. So I beg you to answer me here by return, please dear Johannes, for my sake ! It relates to the various signs of expression, such as " solemnly," " lively." I cannot agree that these should be Italianized, particularly in the case of such a thoroughly German composer as Schumann. On the other hand, I think that the Italianization of the names of the instruments is very good. Surely it does not matter if the latter are Italian and the former German ? It doesn't seem to me at all important, but I do think the signs ought to remain as Schumann wrote them. So please let me know your definite opinion at once. It must be settled now because the *Requiem für Mignon* is to be printed in the winter. Of the eighty letters which I received for my birthday, I have answered half. In addition to this, there were heaps of other things to do, so I am very busy. Farewell, your old friend CLARA.

---

[1] Brahms and Joachim had visited her at Berchtesgaden on the occasion of her birthday. For an account of this see *Life*, Vol. II, p. 355.—TR.

BRAHMS *to* CLARA.

VIENNA, *Nov.*

One no longer knows what to say when God sends you further trials. I am sorry for Ferdinand.[1] But I am much more sorry for you, and that you should have to experience such a thing in your own house is beyond a joke and most unfair. I hope that by now you have had the pleasure of seeing him leave you quite recovered. . . . I don't suppose you will have enjoyed Raff's No. 29 very much. But what are we poor low-class composers to do ? People chide the majority of us for writing too much and in the same breath scold the others for writing too little ! I am at a loss to discover where we are to find time to do any writing at all. . . . Heaps of concerts are being given here, and my music, particularly the chamber music, is having a terrific vogue. On Sunday they are singing the *Schicksalslied*. As to the Overtures, the violin parts are already printed, and, quite between ourselves, I am having the one for four hands printed so that you may have it on your table at Christmas. I shall have to come later, as I shall be in Germany at least until the end of January. On January the 13th I shall give the Overtures in Leipsic, but—and this sounds really tempting to us—they are doing my *Deutsches Requiem* at the Hochschule in Berlin, and it is just possible that on the following morning the Overtures will be played in order to amuse the young people. I shall probably go there, as I have never heard them do anything yet, and it would be kind and grateful to go. . . . Billroth is trying to tempt me to go to Italy in April to see Naples and Sicily—and he will probably succeed. You ought also seriously to think about going there some time. If only I were more practical I would offer myself as a guide. But would not Marmorito go with you to Venice, Florence and Rome ? With affectionate greetings to you and yours, Your JOHANNES.

[1] Ferdinand Schumann had fallen seriously ill with rheumatism and had gone to Wiesbaden for the cure. But at the end of September he went to his mother's house in Frankfort for a few weeks to convalesce.

1881

CLARA *to* BRAHMS.

14 HYDE PARK GATE, LONDON, March 23.

DEAR JOHANNES,

Not a day has passed without my wishing to write to you, but how seldom have I been able to find time, and how frightfully busy one is here ! The days fly by like anything. You have probably seen from the newspapers that I am quite well. Never have they received me more enthusiastically,[1] and up to the present everything has gone very well with me. I have now played six times, and have five more concerts ahead. The greater part of my visit is already over. On the 11th of April I shall play for the last time. Then we return home, where we expect Elise after Easter. You must be getting ready for the Utrecht music festival. When does it take place ? I should think you would have to come *via* Frankfort. I often think about your coming here. What a reception you would have ! But you would also feel most uncomfortable, although in many respects England has changed a good deal. Everything, however, is still very formal. You must be satisfied with these few lines. I only wanted to let you know that I was thinking of you. Do the same soon by me. Your old friend CLARA.

P.S. Just one request ! I think we are sufficiently friendly for me to dare to make it. The point is this—I should like to make you a present of a fine trunk (they don't make them so well in Germany as they do here). But I should like to know how large you would like it to be. It would be a pity if I bought one either too large or too small. Take a piece of string or ribbon and cut one piece for the length and another for the

---

[1] On the 20th of February Clara, accompanied by her daughter Marie and Fräulein Betty Oser, had set out for a concert tour in England.

breadth and send me both in an envelope. I should like to give you this little pleasure, and even if it is prosaic, surely prose is part of our life ! But send me the measurements soon. Once more, adieu.

BRAHMS *to* CLARA.

ROME, *Wednesday, April.*

DEAR CLARA,

I was very glad to receive your letters from the post office. I got the first in Siena and the second here ; for I had a cart-load of letters sent to this place. But here I neither care to write nor can write, no matter how small I begin my scribble on the small note-paper.

How often do I not think of you and wish that your eyes and your heart could have the pleasure which eye and heart enjoy here. If you stood for only one hour in front of the façade of the cathedral at Siena you would be beside yourself with joy and agree that this alone made the journey worth while. And, on entering, you would find at your feet and throughout the church no single corner that did not give you the same joy. On the following day in Orvieto you would be forced to acknowledge that the cathedral was even more beautiful, and after all this to plunge into Rome is an indescribable joy ! I would never stop urging you to come here if I were a more competent guide, and also if I had the courage to help you bear the hundred and one small worries which increase the difficulties of a journey for you women, and which at your age are entirely comprehensible. I think you ought to try travelling with Marmorito one of these days, or next autumn with Elise and her husband, and Marie and Eugenie. Every little detail rewards one for the journey, and the more slowly and the more comfortably it is taken, the more enjoyable it is. Venice, Florence, Rome, Naples, and as many other places as possible, and what you will between !

Up to this point I have travelled with Billroth and Nottebohm. In all probability I shall go with the former next Monday to Sicily. On the return journey I shall stop here again and perhaps at some other places.

Now let me hasten to thank you for your kind offer to buy me a trunk. As a matter of fact, I am well supplied with such things. I am really so little used to luxury and refinement that to spend money on me in this way would be a pity. Besides, think of the trouble the thing would give you. But if you insist on buying it, let me beg you not to make it bigger than the one I am used to. Of course I must be able to carry music in it. But the principal thing in a receptacle of this sort seems to me to be that one can reduce it to half its size if necessary. My present one, for instance, is only half full, and I can take it in the carriage with me (in spite of the fact that it is now packed and heavy only with thick guide-books). Buy only Baedekers for Italy ! For my taste and need, two portfolios of music should give you the measurements. But, as I say, in my case the trouble is not worth while.

I shall certainly not go to Utrecht. My address here is Hotel Orient, Via del Tritone. I shall in any case pass through here on my way back, and propose to stay here a little while again. You and Elise ought really to decide to come to Italy in the autumn, and it is to be hoped again in the spring. I think the spring is the best time, because there are not so many tourists as in the autumn. We still have the best time of the year before us. It is quite early yet and everything is gradually coming out. You can have no conception of how beautiful it is, and you have only to take the trouble to enjoy it in comfort. Next year you must see that you are free at the end of March when I shall be able to be with you the whole of the journey,— by that time I shall have become a thorough Italian, and shall be able to be of use to you. That things should have gone well with you in England was only to be expected. But I am glad, for your sake, of the rest in Frankfort. With affectionate greetings to you and Marie, Your JOHANNES.

BRAHMS *to* CLARA.

ROME, *Monday, April* 25.

Here I am again with a short though hearty greeting. I only want to say that I am travelling slowly homewards. On Thursday I propose to go to Siena where on Friday I hope I may have the pleasure of gathering a *poste restante* greeting from you. I was very glad to hear that you reached home happy and well and not over-tired. My whole journey has been full of the most glorious experiences. Unfortunately I

have not the time—nor the gift—to write about them. In
Sicily too, particularly at Taormina and Girgenti, it was in-
describably beautiful. I also went to Catania and Palermo.
At the latter place I made the acquaintance of the Director of
the Museum whom Felix frequented, and with whose wife he
used to play music very often.

Billroth left for home a few days ago, so that for the third
time this year he will witness the coming of spring—though
this time it will be slow. In Sicily strawberries were almost
over. Here they are just beginning, and where you are they
are a delicacy yet to come. At night on the steamer when we
were returning from S., Billroth helped a little stranger into
the world! It made him forget his sea-sickness and everything, but he was successful although the operation is not his
speciality. . . . I expect to be home in the early days of May
—as a matter of fact this is wrong, and next time I shall not
allow anybody, not even myself, to mention going home. Let
me implore you to make your plans now for a trip to Italy in
the autumn! Go to Venice, Florence, Perugia, Assisi—Rome,
and then back through Orvieto, Siena and Florence, or better
still take Naples on your way, where, in Dorn, the Director of
the Aquarium (a brother of Frau Wendt of Carlsruhe) you will
find a most agreeable cicerone. Affectionate greetings, Your
JOHANNES.

CLARA *to* BRAHMS.

MYLIUSSTRASSE 32, *May.*

I suppose I may take it for granted that you are back in
Vienna, so will send my birthday greeting there. I thought
that on your way back from Holland you would celebrate it
with us here. I should have loved you to pick up your little
trunk here yourself. I shall now take it with me to Austria
(Gastein) and send it to you from there, so that you will have
no difficulties with the customs.

How do you find Vienna now? It must be cold after the
magnificent spring in Italy. Why did you come back so
soon? You could have enjoyed a longer time in Italy.

My arm is not well. Writing gives me trouble and pain.
That is why I shall polish off some of my business letters by
dictation. As regards the life we have been leading, let me tell

you that Elise and her husband are very happy.[1]   The children
are charming, the youngest one particularly so.   But unfortunately they cannot remain in Europe later than the middle
of September, so that it is impossible to make any plans for a
trip to Italy with them.   They leave us in a fortnight in order
to join us again in August, when Marmorito will perhaps also
come with his little Robert.   We are hesitating between a
place in Switzerland and Vordereck near Berchtesgaden.   I
hope you will celebrate your birthday wisely but not too well
and that the thought of the warm hearts that beat for you in
cold Germany will bring a glow to your own.   Your old friend,
CLARA.

BRAHMS *to* CLARA.

VIENNA, *May.*

In the first place heartiest thanks for the letters received in
Italy and here.   But Elise really must postpone her return
journey for a month and go with you to Italy.   You ought to
go from the middle of September to the end of October, and
travel with the firm resolve of returning thither next spring,
even if everything does not come up to your expectations, or
precisely on that account.   Moreover, I hope that you will
have fine weather for the trip, I mean, practical weather—
weather which is more pleasant for human beings than for
insects.   There is only one thing I am troubled about and
that is how you will arrange your journey.   You ought to
make it a hard and fast rule to see only a little at a time and as
slowly as possible.   Set aside a few hours in the morning for
sight seeing, and every afternoon go for a drive.   Everybody
will be recommending you a different town, and in each town a
different church or a different gallery as the most important
thing to visit.   But in Italy it is a mistake to make inquiries
about what one has not seen.   One can easily see too much,
and it is really fortunate that music is not also one of the attractions there.   On the contrary, it is atrocious, otherwise one's
brain would reel. . . .   One sense has a long rest.   It is true
that I diligently listened to everything that interested me.   But

[1] They had met Clara in London and had made the return journey
to the Continent with her.

you would have derived but little pleasure from it. You must keep our musical friends (who are very kind and polite) severely at arm's length. As for Conservatoires—I am not at home, not even in the country ! To give you the items of one programme taken at random would be to give you the lot. I only hope yours will not be any longer.

A few days in Venice make the most glorious prelude and would be most comfortable and enjoyable for you. All you need to do is to saunter round the Piazza San Marco, and to sit in a gondola and be taken about. Here and in every other town you must not miss the fruit, vegetable and fish markets, and cheerfully give up a gallery or a church for the purpose. Then go direct to Florence. Once there, the question is whether it would not be best for you to take comfortable rooms for the whole of your stay. There are some very good and cheap ones to be had. And then be careful not to see too much. One room in a gallery, and perhaps merely the gates of the Baptistery—this would be quite enough for you. And in the afternoon, go for a drive. Above all avoid tearing through all the galleries and churches. If you have nice rooms there I would perhaps take an occasional trip either to Siena or Orvieto, or to Perugia and Assisi. Or else take these places on your way to Rome and back. But once more let me implore you, don't do more, and do this slowly and in comfort. If you can allow yourself breathing space in a town like Siena you will get something out of it. You will never get tired of contemplating the cathedral, and you can take wonderful drives round about there (my way of running about).

And now comes Rome ! This is a whole world, and you will require an enormous amount of caution in order to derive enjoyment and not merely fatigue and bewilderment from it. The longer you remain there and the less you exert yourself, the more you will enjoy it. You would then find a journey to Naples and a quiet tour of the place very refreshing ; but perhaps you will leave that till the spring when, if you travel in April and reach Naples towards the end of May, you would find things at their best. If you limit your programme to this and take it moderately and slowly, I shall be satisfied. And now give my heartiest greetings to all your family and keep Elise to her word about Italy. I may also perhaps go and act

as your guide for a bit.   But what is more I should restrain you,
which is certainly no easy task, when enchanting things chal-
lenge you from all sides.

Most affectionately yours, J. B.

CLARA *to* BRAHMS.

WILDBAD GASTEIN, *July* 15.

Enclosed I at last send you the key of your little trunk, which
you will have received from Zell.   The score of *Genoveva*
Vol. I) is packed in it.   But Franck will only join you in two
or three weeks, I suppose.   There is another key to the trunk
which I have kept in case you should lose yours.   I did not
want to bother you with it.   And now let me thank you for
your kind letter which I have been unable to answer because
we were travelling about.   We had a magnificent time at Zell
am See, where this time we were favoured with the most beautiful weather.   It is also very fine here, where we arrived the
day before yesterday.   Thanks to the doctor's help we found
some nice rooms, and we shall probably stay for a month.   But
we shall find it difficult, because Elise is awaiting us in Flims.
That is why we had to give up all idea of Berchtesgaden.
This time I have Marie and Eugenie with me.   Fillu is with
her mother, and Fräulein Houfer in Vordereck.   I surely must
have told you about my little gathering for the benefit of the
poorer pupils.   It has enabled me to send Fräulein H. to Vordereck to restore her nerves, and this was a great joy to me.
The girl deserved to be singled out in this way, for she is one of
the most talented of my pupils, after Fräulein Fromm, whom I
have also been able to help very considerably.

A few days ago I had a letter from the Herzogenbergs from
Jena, where they are taking a cure.   They are going to Globen-
stein in the Tyrol.   We shall scarcely be able to see each other
this summer, which I am very sorry about.   They were always
such excellent travelling companions.

I have got a small but very good piano here from Streicher,
which he sent to me immediately with the utmost willingness.
I am particularly glad to have it for the children's sake, but I
also use it to correct the songs (now).   I ought really to write
another long letter full of complaints, and it almost drives one
mad, and makes one a little unjust into the bargain.   I am

delighted about the *Concerto*,[1] but am suspicious of the word
" small " in front of it.   I shall be quite satisfied if, after all,
I can manage to play it !   You could quite well send it to me,
for, as I say, I have an instrument here, and it would be a real
joy to me ! ! !   But now I must close.   Let me have a card to
say whether the little trunk has arrived, and if you will let the
card grow into a letter you will double the pleasure that you
will give to Your affectionate CLARA.

P.S.   I have just received 710 francs on account of author's
royalties from Durand, and I am once more annoyed to think
that you have taken no steps to do the same.   Even if you did
not want it yourself you could find some use for this extra income which would give you pleasure.   I thought I had drafted
out a formal letter for you about it ?

CLARA *to* BRAHMS.

GASTEIN, *July* 20.

I have just received your card with the surprising news that
you intend to pay us a visit.   But this raises the old familiar
doubts in my mind as to whether you are likely to be happy
here at the present moment.   You will get no variety, no interesting friends, and on Saturday my brother Alwin is coming
for the cure, and will of course be with us the whole time.
Won't that bore you ?   I am also expecting a niece and her
husband from Schneeberg, but the latter will probably only
arrive on Friday.   I was wondering whether we could not
have a more pleasant meeting somewhere else—in Baden-
Baden, for instance, where we shall probably go towards the
middle of September with Elise for about a week or a fortnight, going on there from Flims.   What do you say to a meeting there ?   In any case wire me the day of your arrival here
if you decide to come, so that we can find a room for you.   And
also please do not come before Sunday, when my niece will
have gone.   Let me have a word of news. . . .   So now adieu !
I want to get my letter off at once.   With affectionate greetings
and awaiting your reply, Your old friend CLARA.

[1] This refers to the *Concerto* in B Flat major, Op. 83, about which
Brahms had also written to Frau von Herzogenberg, describing it as a
" quite small " pianoforte Concerto, with a " quite small sweet "
Scherzo.

CLARA *to* BRAHMS.

WILDBAD GASTEIN, BEI MÜHLBERGER, *Aug.* 1.

I received your card saying you could not come. It upset me although I was responsible for it. You see, my dear Johannes, I knew that if you came here it would be for my sake. But if you put yourself in my place you will understand how very much it agitates me, when you are dependent on me alone for entertainment, to have somebody else constantly with me who must bore you, as would have been the case now. So do not be cross with me. You know me too well to misunderstand my motives. I hope we shall see you again in the autumn, and then Elise will share the pleasure. . . .

On the 6th we shall leave here, and shall go *via* Munich, Lindau and Chur, to Waldhaus Flims, Graubünden, Switzerland. Let me hear from you there soon. I do hope you are not cross. Your old friend CLARA.

CLARA *to* BRAHMS.

FRANKFORT A/M., *Nov.* 15.

So here I am again at last safe and sound.[1] In the first place let me thank you for your dear letter to Hamburg which reached me at Friedchen's. I saw Elise [2] several times, and was once more delighted to find her so happy with her husband. If only she did not have those dreadful headaches all the time ! And then there is the poor invalid daughter ! How sad it is ! I was heartily glad to have your reports about Meiningen. I hope you will soon be able to tell us more about it yourself here. Your room will always be ready for you whenever you pass through, but if you should play here I hope you will be able to stay a bit longer. . . . Now adieu.

With affectionate greetings, Your old friend CLARA.

[1] After concerts in Hamburg and Hanover, Clara had paid visits in Düsseldorf and Kiel.

[2] Brahms' sister.

1882

Clara *to* Brahms.

FRANKFORT a/M., *April* 17.

Dear Johannes,

I received your letter in England,[1] and it had not been opened, as you seemed to take for granted it had. I never allow letters from intimate friends or relations to be opened by other people. Well, first let me thank you for your letter, and tell you that I arrived here safely a few days ago. The reception I was given in England was heartier and more enthusiastic than ever, and everything else was all that could be wished. I am now getting into my old groove again here. Friedchen wrote to me from Hamburg about the concert and your visit which she thoroughly enjoyed. But she regrets that the Sicilian Society did not sing. I have not yet heard the *Nänie* and am longing to do so. A lot of Wagner is being given here—the *Rheingold* and the *Walküre*. One of these days I suppose I shall have to have it inflicted on me, if only on Dessoff's account.[2] I found Raff very much altered ; he looks very ill and I feel very sorry and anxious about him, for it seems to me that they are pressing him very hard just now. I hear a good deal, from which I draw my own conclusions. But naturally I keep it all to myself.

We have not yet made any plans for the summer. I shall have to stay here until July to make up the lessons I shall miss in June, when I shall have time to think things over. But I am seriously considering Italy for September and October.

[1] Clara had been on a concert tour in England from February the 26th to April the 8th.

[2] On April 26 she attended a performance of the *Rheingold*, on the 9th of May the *Walküre*, and on the 16th the *Rheingold* again " in order to see what the instrumentation was like." On the 18th she went to the *Walküre* again (" I wanted to study the music a little more "). See also *Life*, Vol. II, p. 362.

You will probably have gone into the country by now. I found many things awaiting me here and many letters to answer. I have also had all sorts of adventures with pupils, but not of an unpleasant nature. Farewell! Let me hear from you soon. Your old friend CLARA.

CLARA *to* BRAHMS.

FRANKFORT A/M., *July* 25.

DEAR JOHANNES,

Still very much shaken by the news, I am writing to tell you that after he had undergone the most incredible strain owing to the examinations, Raff passed away peacefully last night. His wife found him dead in bed this morning and has at least the comfort of knowing that he died painlessly in his sleep. For although she was lying at his side, she heard nothing. Everybody said that he ought to have spared himself and not have taken part in everything in the school in the oppressive heat. But he would listen to no advice. In spite of the fact that I was never very friendly with him I am deeply grieved for his wife and daughter, who were devoted to him. I wrote to you about him yesterday,[1] and now have this news for you to-day.

With most affectionate greetings from Your CLARA.

CLARA *to* BRAHMS.

GASTEIN, *Aug.* 1.

A trio [2] like yours was a real musical tonic. If only I had the instruments to hand! For there was much at which I could only guess, and all I have is a poor little upright piano. Here is indeed another magnificent work! So much in it delights me, and how I long to hear it properly played! I love every movement and how wonderfully it is developed! I am

---

[1] In this letter, which dealt chiefly with the business of the Schumann edition, Clara wrote : " We are very busy now at the School with the examinations. I think our pupils will do well, but in the intermediate classes the results of the first days of the examinations have been incredibly bad. The gentlemen of the Committee would very much like to make various alterations. But nothing can be done with Raff, and he is, moreover, so ill that the Committee dread the consequences if they oppose him with any vigour. This is a very bad state of affairs."—TR.

[2] Pianoforte Trio in C major, Op. 87, finished at Ischl in June.

so charmed with the way in which one motif grows out of the other, and phrase follows phrase. The scherzo is exquisite, as is also the andante, with its lively theme, which must sound quite original in the placing of the double octaves. How fresh the last movement is and, moreover, interesting in its thoroughly artistic combinations! I suppose you will allow me to mention a few small points that have struck me.

On page 3, system 2, I do not like the change to the minor, for which I can see no necessity. For what immediately follows is once more definitely major. On page 4, in bar 4, the triplets strike me as odd, as if they were only there to fill up the space. Page 15, system 3, and page 16, first bar, the turn does not please me. It seems to me somewhat trivial, if I may say so, which is quite unsuitable to this music. Without the turn the passage sounds much nobler. In the scherzo, which I find quite entrancing, the trio does not seem to me important enough, and coming after the scherzo, which is so delightfully varied, it is lacking in charm and sounds as though it had been thought out rather than felt. Forgive me! You must take into account that I have not heard it in its full effect, but only imperfectly. At the very first time of playing it struck me that in the last movement the bar which seems to be tacked on at the end looks as if you had tried to broaden the effect of the conclusion with it. It would please me much better if it ended briefly and briskly so

When is it going to appear and where? How you whet my curiosity when you say you have done something else that is better! But I do not wish to pry into your secrets. I rejoice over what is to hand and thank you for sending it to me. I return it with this letter and beg you to let me have a card, *poste restante* Lucerne, so that I may know you have received the trio safely. We shall leave here on Saturday the 5th, and reach Lucerne on the 8th. I am very much relieved by what you tell me about the gentlemen at the school.[1] So with most

In a previous letter Clara had expressed her anxiety regarding who was to take Raff's place. She says: " I think I would be in favour

affectionate greetings, dear Johannes, and renewed thanks for the great treat you have given me—Marie also sends you greetings. Your old friend CLARA.

P.S. I saw in the papers the other day that you were engaged. Of course I do not believe it, because you would never have allowed your old friend to hear of such a thing through the papers. Have you met any nice people in Ischl this year ? Is Brüll [1] there ? If so, give him my kind regards.

CLARA *to* BRAHMS.

DEGENBALM BEI BRUNNEN, KT. SCHWYZ, *Aug.* 10.

Before asking you to send the *Parzenchor*,[2] I was waiting to see where we would settle down, and as we are now staying here until the 25th of August I beg you most urgently to send it at the earliest possible moment. Many thanks for Billroth's interesting letter and for sending me the poems which had prepared me for what was to come. How wonderfully Billroth understands what to say to you about your things, and what penetration and subtlety he shows ! His comments always make me feel ashamed—not because I think he feels or understands your things better than I do, but because his way of expressing himself makes mine appear so amateurish. If I am conscious of my own inadequacy when I am writing to you, I become doubly so after I have read one of his letters. Nevertheless, you always give me great pleasure in sending them to me, because I always learn something from them. May I keep the letter a little while ? I should like to show it to Eugenie, and she will not be here for a week. The place we are in is magnificent, surrounded by the most luscious meadows and in the distance the Uri Rothstock Glacier. In front of us we have a strip of the Vierwaldstätter See, and right opposite Seelisberg. But we at the Degenbalm might be right in the country. It is enchanting, and we are always discussing whether some day we

of Wüllner, who would probably be glad to leave Dresden at this juncture. But naturally I shall keep quiet until I am consulted. In any case we may expect great changes. . . ." As a matter of fact Wüllner declined.—TR.

[1] Ignaz Brüll.

[2] *Gesang der Parzen*, Op. 89, finished in July. He had been inspired to the composition of this work by Charlotte Wolter's acting of *Iphigenie* at the *Burgtheater.*

shall not spend the whole summer in some such place. The fly in the ointment, as far as I am concerned, is the *table d'hôte* morning, noon and night, when the dirty tablecloths always annoy one and spoil one's appetite. But this is a mere detail compared with the glorious scenery and air, which is particularly fresh and pleasant, and not in the least sharp. . . .

May I show Billroth's letter to Grimm ? I am sure he would read it with the greatest interest. But tell me frankly if you would prefer me not to. Now I must close, but I am much looking forward to getting your parcel. We have a piano here with which, at a pinch, we might manage. Farewell, with most affectionate greetings, Your CLARA.

CLARA *to* BRAHMS.

DEGENBALM BEI BRUNNEN, KT. SCHWYZ, *Aug.* 23.

I am writing to you to-day with my heart full of joy after having spent a glorious hour with your *Parzenchor*. What a work it is ! How thoroughly genial ! What depths of beauty it contains ! And how it stirs one from beginning to end ! You have succeeded wonderfully in rendering the sombre mysterious power of the words in your music. How moving are the gentle but melancholy words in the one-crotchet movement. Words fail me to tell you the joy I have had from the piece—the gloomy beauty of its harmonies. The progression in the second bar, of which Billroth speaks, and in regard to which I don't quite grasp his meaning, is precisely what stirs me most. I admit that it is bold, but the A in the bass, and the F Sharp and G in the melody make it appear quite consistent with the rest of your conception, and the end, where the F Sharp minor progresses softly and sadly on its way till it merges into D minor is a fine example of your genius. How remarkable the end is ! For a long time one seems in the spirit to be nodding one's head with the old man until at last one slips into dreamland. It is not easy suddenly to find oneself in D minor at the end. But here the words help one, and one marvels at the way you have understood and translated them. A small point struck me the first time I looked through it and each time afterwards when I played it. On page 15, in the three-quarter time after the second passage *a capella*, and before the orchestra comes in on the dominant of D, you have the same harmony two bars before, and this, in my opinion, weakens the entrance of the orchestra ; besides which I would rather do without the double repetition in the tenor :—

it is the one passage in the whole work which strikes one as rather tame, and as a sort of sham transition which seems to me quite unnecessary. I would suggest doing away with the two bars altogether, or else having in them the same harmonies as in the fifth and sixth bars of this movement. Just look at it again, and perhaps you will think I am right. If not, then forgive me for having spoken so frankly. But we must hear the piece soon. I will speak to Müller [1] about it at once. Thank you so much for having already given me the pleasure of making its acquaintance. . . . And now farewell ! Let me hear from you soon how things went in Aussee [2] and whether your trio pleased you. I hope it did, for otherwise you would be ungrateful to yourself. Everybody here sends you most affectionate greetings but especially Your old friend CLARA.

[1] The Musical Director at Frankfort.

[2] At Professor Ladislaus Wagner's house here Brahms' new chamber-music piece was played for the first time at a matinée to guests who had been specially invited.

1883

FRANKFORT A/M., *Feb.* 22.

DEAR JOHANNES,

As I hope you will be returning here in March I prefer to tell
you by word of mouth what happened at the School.[1] Such
scandals are thoroughly distasteful to me, and I must confess
that I have hardly read anything about them. As the occasion demanded we all gave a helping hand, for I thought that,
since we belonged to the institution, it was our duty to do
what we could. But soon everything will be in order. If
only we could find a good pianoforte teacher ! How difficult
that seems to be !

The fall I had in Berlin is now a thing of the past, but it
might have been very much worse than it was.[2] I had a deep
cut on my forehead, a bruise on my left hand, and was black
and blue all over. The traces of it are still to be seen and my
hand is not yet right. Nevertheless, I risked giving the concert and played in great pain, although I forgot both anxiety
and inconvenience owing to the reception I was given. I don't
think I have ever experienced such wholehearted enthusiasm.
And thus, in spite of everything, I came away with pleasant
memories of the trip. When are you coming ?[3] I should like

[1] On January 21 Clara writes in her Diary : " Herr v. Mumm called
on me and told me of the revolution in the School (one can call it nothing
else). Three have given notice and three others have been given
notice. There is a complete transformation—but it was needed. The
lack of discipline was incredible."—*Life*, Vol. II, p. 369.

[2] She was about to give a concert in Berlin when she fell down the
stairs of a friend's house.

[3] Brahms had spent Christmas at Clara's house and in passing through
Frankfort in January he had also stayed there a day or two. Concerning the strained relations revealed in Clara's Diary at about this
time, and which Kalbeck comments upon in his Life of Brahms, we
must bear in mind that Kalbeck had reasons of his own for being

to know, as I want to be here. . . .   I suppose you know that Stockhausen is taking up his post at the School on the 1st of March ?   Adieu for to-day.   I have a mass of letters of condolence to answer, so shall spare myself more until I see you. With affectionate greetings from all three of us, Your old friend CLARA.

CLARA *to* BRAHMS.

FRANKFORT, *March* 26.

DEAR JOHANNES,

I expect you are now getting ready for your new triumphal tour, and so I am sending you one more greeting to Vienna. I only came back a day or two ago from Leipsic, where I had a very pleasant time.[1]   I spent some particularly delightful hours with the dear Herzogenbergs, from whom I heard to my joy that you had recently paid them a visit. . . .   What a pity it is that you cannot produce your *Parzenlied* in Cologne.   But it would be a bitter pill for Hiller who once wrote me a pathetic letter saying that since you had composed it his own piece on the same subject had been buried.   I did not write to you about it because it grieved me, although it was one of the best things he has ever composed.

This week Scholz has been introduced to the pupils as Director of the School, and has made a good impression upon everybody.   I hope things will go well now, provided no one plays either him or us any trick.   Well then, let us hope that we shall see each other soon.   Let me know in good time when you are coming, because our spare room is often occupied just now and I should like to keep it free for you.

Affectionate greetings from Your old friend CLARA.

CLARA *to* BRAHMS.

FRANKFORT, *Morning, Dec.* 5.

You have given yourself a nice job with that Schubert !

annoyed with Clara just then.   It was at this moment that she cancelled her agreement with him for the publication of Schumann's papers.   Her reasons for this were both business and personal, which made collaboration with him intolerable to her.

[1] She went to Leipsic on the 8th of March, and played there on the 10th in a quartet, and on the 15th at the Gewandhaus.

Why did you do it if you are so little in sympathy with it ? [1]
It is a gigantic undertaking. It is true that they could not
have addressed themselves to anyone more competent for the
task, for you know the works so well. On my journey home
the day before yesterday I visited Hiller and found him intellectually very fresh but spiritually depressed. I cannot understand why he has not resigned his post of Conductor, for it
does him more harm than anything else, it not only affects his
health but also his position as a musician. The last thing in
the world that I could endure would be to be pitied on appearing before the public. If he were to retire, there are so many
other things he could do. His family is very miserable about
it. I don't think I shall ever see him again, and I had great
difficulty in controlling my sorrow when taking leave of him.
To-morrow morning we are expecting Ethel Smythe [2] for a day
or two. I am surprised at the progress she has made and
even if she has no originality as a composer, I cannot help feeling respect for such ability in a girl. I close with affectionate
greetings from us all, and let us hear your plans soon, Your old
friend, CLARA.

BRAHMS *to* CLARA.

VIENNA, *Dec.*

The enclosed would really be the proper place for a few graceful verses. But they will not end properly and above all they
refuse to be beautiful, so I prefer to tell you in prose that I
wish you all the happiest of Christmases and New Years. I
shall be able to picture the merry pupils' evening in my mind's
eye and shall live it in my thoughts. I shall see the whole
company of girls marched on to the platform in the highest of
spirits, with every possible noisy instrument in hand and
mouth, and you sitting solemnly at the piano all the while, as
if the business in hand were a Bach Fugue in a minor key.
Then will follow the scuffle for the sweet things that have been
won !

What a pity it is that no description of the function will

---

[1] This refers to Brahms' revision of Schubert's big orchestral works
for the firm of Breitkopf and Härtel.

[2] Dame Ethel Smyth, the well-known composer and pianist, pupil
of Heinrich von Herzogenberg.

appear in the *Frankfürter Zeitung*.   I always look most carefully at this paper to obtain news of everything there, but on
the whole find much too little about the Hochschule and the
girl pianists and singers opposite the *Bockenheimer Tor*.   You
never mention the school, and that is a good sign, because it
shows that under Scholz things are getting better and more
comfortable every day.   There is sure to be a great change here
soon among the musical conductors and Directors.   It is at
such moments that one realizes how glad everybody is to come
to Vienna.   And yet on the whole I cannot help thinking that
we have very little to offer.   With the political situation as it
is, everything must go from bad to worse.   Now please greet
everybody for me and tell Fräulein Filu that she ought to send
a nice description of your pupils' Christmas evening to the
Frankfürter Zeitur g.   Most affectionately, Your JOHANNES.

1884

CLARA *to* BRAHMS.

FRANKFORT A/M., *Feb.* 11.

DEAR JOHANNES,

I don't know where this letter will find you, but I can't refrain from writing it because my heart is so full. I have spent such happy hours with your wonderful creation,[1] (I have played it over several times with Elise [2]) that I should like at least to tell you so. What a work! What a poem! What a harmonious mood pervades the whole! All the movements seem to be of one piece, one beat of the heart, each one a jewel! From start to finish one is wrapped about with the mysterious charm of the woods and forests. I could not tell you which movement I loved most. In the first I was charmed straight away by the gleams of dawning day, as if the rays of the sun were shining through the trees. Everything springs to life, everything breathes good cheer, it is really exquisite! The second is a pure idyll; I can see the worshippers kneeling about the little forest shrine, I hear the babbling brook and the buzz of the insects. There is such a fluttering and a humming all around that one feels oneself snatched up into the joyous web of Nature. The third movement is a pearl, but it is a grey one dipped in a tear of woe, and at the end the modulation is quite wonderful. How gloriously the last movement follows with its passionate upward surge! But one's beating heart is soon calmed down again for the final transfiguration which begins with such beauty in the development motif that words fail me! How sorry I am that I cannot hear the Symphony now that I know it so well and could enjoy it so much better. This is a real sorrow for me. A few days ago I sent it to the Herzogenbergs. I found it very difficult to take leave of them.

[1] The Third Symphony.
[2] See *Life*, Vol. II, p. 372.

It is a godsend to have people whom one is so fond of, and to whom one likes to give such pleasure. I shall leave here on the 24th and, if all goes well, shall return for Easter.[1] Farewell. That things may go well with you now as ever is the wish of Your CLARA.

CLARA *to* BRAHMS.

FRANKFORT A/M., *Feb.* 23.

DEAR JOHANNES,

It is unfortunately impossible to postpone a Museum concert. They would rather let Frankfort perish than let such a thing happen.[2] The last of the concerts is on the 29th of March and I shall not be there then either, provided I am not recalled before owing to illness, etc. I am at least comforted by the thought of Düsseldorf. I intended going there on my way back from London (for Easter) but now what I shall do is to go straight home and then proceed to Düsseldorf at Whitsun. I suppose you will give your Symphony there too ?

It was a strange coincidence that my letter should have reached the Herzogenbergs while you were there. I had no idea that you were going to Leipsic, and would have thought it out of the question had it not unfortunately been true. I say " unfortunately," for really the Leipsic public do not deserve to have your works produced there by you yourself. Here there is some talk of having a concert at the Conservatoire in your honour. But I have told them that they ought to spare you the ordeal of an evening when you would hear only your own works performed. I hope I was right. My English address is the same as before—14 Hyde Park Gate, Kensington, London. . . . I am travelling with Marie ; Eugenie is remaining here. I need hardly say how pleased she would have been to ask you to put up at our house as usual, but it is precisely here that this would not do, it would be sure to lead to talk, which is better avoided. I have my head full of a thousand and one things, as you may guess, so will close. That you may have every happiness is the hearty wish of Your CLARA.

---

[1] This was to be her sixteenth concert tour in England.

[2] On the 14th of March Brahms' Third Symphony was to be produced here under Brahms' own direction.

CLARA *to* BRAHMS.

LONDON, *April* 1.

Before I leave here I should like to thank you for your lovely letter. I was glad to see from it that you had been pleased with Frankfort. In their own fashion the people there really took a great deal of trouble, and deserve some small recognition. But I hope the account of the brilliant dinner has been exaggerated. For instance, we heard rumours of fish that was not all that it should have been [1] ! ! !—We are now seriously preparing for our return journey, and if everything goes well up to the end I shall not regret my visit. I can give you no idea of the kind of reception I have been given here. It was the same yesterday evening and every evening, whenever I appeared on the platform. One cannot help being pleased by such attachment and appreciation. Thank God, I have had good news from the Herzogenbergs even about her as well. It would have been such a pity if they could not have gone into their little house now. With hearty greetings and best wishes for your journey to Italy, and looking forward to seeing you, Your old CLARA.

CLARA *to* BRAHMS.

FRANKFORT A/M., *May* 6.

I do not want to miss sending you my heartiest congratulations for to-morrow. I need not enter into details. They are always warm and true, as you know. I have long been waiting for news of you, particularly during the critical period of the offer made you by Cologne and your answer.[2] I did not give up all hope for the people of Cologne. There are many things in favour of the post, but I understand your refusal all the same. I could not help thinking that the Rhine would have tempted you, but of course there was no need for you to accept a post for that purpose, you can enjoy it without that.

The Sommerhoffs have left us to-day and gone to Münster a/St. I am very sorry not to be able to get to Düsseldorf to hear your Symphony and the *Parzenlied*, but I would prefer to

---

[1] Eugenie had given a little dinner party in Brahms' honour.

[2] Brahms had been asked whether he would be willing to succeed Hiller.

tell you my reasons some time by word of mouth, or later on. For the present farewell. I hope you will spend your birthday to-morrow in pleasant company, in beautiful scenery and with happy thoughts. The " trio " are shouting their best wishes to you from the next room. Yours ever, CLARA.

We have Ferdinand's three children here with us for two months. His wife has been seriously ill for three. This gives us a lot to do and to think about.

CLARA *to* BRAHMS.

OBERSALZBERG, NEAR BERCHTESGADEN, PENSION MORITZ,
July 13.

Here we are again enjoying the fresh summer air, though I can hardly call it that, for it is only in the woods where I am now sitting that it is bearable. But I mustn't grumble ; for we have been starved of sunshine for so long. And Marie and I needed it badly as, for the last two months, we have been suffering from neuralgia, she in her leg and back, and I in the face. It is a painful complaint, although it only comes on at intervals. Both for the good of mankind and yourself I am delighted that you have found such a charming little spot.[1] I remember the district vaguely, but Fillu knows it quite well and says that it is wonderfully beautiful, while its proximity to a large town [2] makes it all the pleasanter. We had a some-what stormy time in Frankfort latterly ; the children gave us some anxiety, not merely temporary but on account of their future. . . . I often think it is too much for my sorely tried heart to bear. Wherever do we get the strength to go on caring and playing our part ?

There is little to tell you about Frankfort. So far things are going well at the school and we have much to thank Scholz for. In many respects he makes a good Director, but he is very fidgety and seems always to be trying to make us stand out (as regards the other Conservatoires). At the smallest sign from the other side he gets excited, and then I always have to urge him to forge calmly ahead and take no notice of other people. We shall be able to show them what we can do when examination time comes round. We know our own strength

[1] Mürzzuschlag, in Styria, Austria.
[2] It is not very far from Wiener Neustadt.

and we also know theirs ! ! !   But even if they really did do
something good, that need not affect us.   Frankfort is big
enough for two or three good institutions.   I am much more
concerned about the fact that there is so little real ability in
the Raff Conservatoire, for Bülow is not to be regarded as a
teaching force—he hardly ever teaches but only plays to his
pupils, at least so I heard the other day.   I am very glad that
Scholz has got the Rühlschen Verein where he will at least
be able to wave the Conductor's baton occasionally.   Anybody who has done this for years must certainly miss it very
much. . . .

We have an excellent teacher in Frau Héritte,[1] and in other
respects I like her very much.   She is a clever human person.
We agree about almost everything and shall do so all the more
the longer she remains in Germany. . . .   Hiller is not thinking
of retiring.   That was only a gesture made in the first moment
of irritation.   The Herzogenbergs are now busy arranging their
charming house, that is why we have not seen them yet.   Unfortunately all their plans for Wiesbaden next winter have
fallen through.   But they are thinking seriously about it later.
I have my upright piano with me here, so as to keep my fingers
exercised.   I am also working on the instruction course, which
is really giving me a great deal of trouble, because one is constantly starting afresh.   But what I have undertaken I do not
regret.   At all events I now think that the fee, big though it
seemed at the time, is inadequate in view of all the time and
trouble.   Above me here is Professor Lübke.[2]   I am very
pleased about it, as I like him very much and have a high
opinion of him.

And now, my dear Johannes, I will close.   Let me hear from
you soon.   Your old friend CLARA.

CLARA *to* BRAHMS.

FRANKFORT A/M., *Sept.* 29.

I shall not allow the month to come to an end without thanking you for your kind birthday letter.   If I were not overwhelmed with business of all kinds, which is naturally increased

---

[1] Frau Luise Héritte-Viardot, daughter of Frau Viardot, who was
given the appointment in Feb. 1883.

[2] Professor Wilhelm Lübke, the art-historian of Stuttgart.

by my having just returned and having had to get things straight again, you would have heard long ago how delighted I was with your letter which reached me on the 13th. True, it was a *da capo*, but only in the form of address. In any case you know how particularly glad I was to receive your good wishes. We celebrated the day most agreeably. In the morning we were on the Königsee in the most glorious weather, and in the evening we dined with the Herzogenbergs and my sister, and drank champagne. For the last fortnight of our summer holidays we were in Hofreit, where my sister, Cäcilie Bargiel, also spent the whole of the summer. We were only ten minutes' walk from the Herzogenbergs, so we saw a good deal of each other. Their house is charming and, thank God, she is quite well. But she has to be very careful. You probably know that he is going to Berlin to take Kiel's place. I was not in favour of this, but I agree there is much to be said for it, for not only is it a fine post but it is also well paid. Besides which the Herzogenbergs are longing for musical society. Whether they will get it in Berlin— ! ! ! . . . We were not thinking of going to Italy for the time being, but we might go to Florence in April. We are all very much looking forward to your new songs. I wish you would send them to me. Poor Hiller is very ill. He has three dangerous complaints, and every day he has to undergo a painful operation, although he does not guess the seriousness of his condition. Oh, I am very sad when I think about him. He is also very weak and can do nothing. I wrote to him a day or two ago, but I found it hard to say anything to such an invalid without letting him know that one regards his condition as critical. It is really very hard.

Elise returns from Switzerland to-day. They are going to live quite close here (at Wilhelmsbad) until their house is ready, which unfortunately will not be until November. So far everything is going well with us ; work has begun and we are very happy again, although we always feel a little bit holidayfied at first. . . . With heartiest greetings from us all (also from the second floor).[1] Your old friend CLARA.

---

[1] Where Eugenie and Fräulein Fillunger lived.

BRAHMS *to* CLARA.

MÜRZZUSCHLAG, *Oct.* 1.

Let me thank you at once for your long desired and very kind letter, to certain points of which I will now reply. In the first place I find it stated quite clearly in the Vienna newspapers that you are coming to Vienna in January or March. The negotiations (with Gutmann) cannot have been carried very far as you say nothing about them. Quite apart from my own personal pleasure I should advise you to come but for the moment will leave things as they are. With regard to Florence in April, however, on no account change your mind.

I had no idea of Herzogenberg's appointment, but I am uncommonly pleased about it and would certainly have advised him to accept. With regard to Auerbach's Letters,[1] let me earnestly beg you not to allow yourself to be put off by anything,—prolixities, repetitions and vanities, etc. It is well worth while to read this styleless book, but please take a pencil in your hand and underline and mark anything that strikes you. There is a great deal of very fine, beautiful and refreshing thought in it, and one often cannot help liking this diligent, bracing and warm-hearted man.

I cannot tell you much about my plans. I am being terribly bombarded with invitations and I ought really to have a polite refusal form printed. In November Bülow is coming to Vienna with his orchestra and Heckmann with his quartet. I have agreed to do what I can for both of them. I have also engaged myself for the 9th and 12th of December in Hamburg, the 16th in Bremen, and the 19th in Oldenburg, Hanover, etc. But before that I shall have gone off my head ! Surely January the 28th is a jubilee day in Crefeld ? I must certainly jubilate, drink and make music with them. At the present moment it is wonderfully beautiful here and I only wish you could be with me on one of these magical moonlight evenings on the

---

[1] Berthold Auerbach was a German writer who made his name with stories about the Black Forest. He also translated Spinoza and published various novels and other works of some merit (1812–1882). The above mention of him refers to his *Letters to his friend Jacob Auerbach*, 2 Vols., published 1884. In a previous letter Clara says she does not possess them but would be glad to have them and hopes Brahms will bring them himself.—TR.

Semmering. With all good greetings to everybody and with reiterated thanks for all the good and cheerful news, most affectionately yours, JOHANNES.

CLARA *to* BRAHMS.

FRANKFORT, *Oct.* 4.

While thanking you for your kind note I must without further delay tell you all about Gutmann, so that you may be in a position to take up the cudgels on my behalf with the Philharmonic people. Gutmann wrote to me in the summer asking me whether I would care to give a concert in Vienna, and saying that he would like to arrange it and give me a guarantee. I replied that I was not really giving any more concerts, and all that I did was to play at subscription concerts where I only had to perform once or twice. I may perhaps have added out of courtesy (but of this I cannot be certain) that, as there was no chance of such engagements in Vienna, I must decline the pleasure. As I say, I am not quite certain what I told him, but I am quite sure that I never gave him any promise. He then wrote to me the other day to tell me that he had proposed me to the Philharmonic Society, that they had accepted with alacrity, and had commissioned him to invite me. Helmsberger then hoped and he also hoped to induce me to promise them a Schumann evening. I wrote declining. It was impossible for me to take such a long journey and to undergo so much fatigue for one engagement, and as for playing on several occasions—that I could not do, because I had not the time and would require too long intervals for rest between the concerts. All this you know and if necessary can confirm. At all events, Herr Gutmann has no right to give out such notices as he has done, and certainly not to announce that I shall play at Bösendorfer's,[1] which he never even mentioned to me! I would not do such a thing to Streicher—what must he think of me?

It is really most unscrupulous of the man! What can my friends think? It will look as if I had broken my word when all the time I am the most conscientious of mortals. What cheek of the man to offer me to the Philharmonic Society! Just as if they could not write to me direct if they wanted me! I never deal through agents, and in this instance I would not

---

[1] A small concert-hall in Vienna.—TR.

in any case have accepted. Please, dear Johannes, stand up
for me over this business, I beseech you ! We are all delighted
that you are coming into our neighbourhood and we hope
that you will not overlook us. Heartiest greetings from us
all, Your old friend CLARA.

Oh, if only Vienna were not so far away how I should love to
go there occasionally !

CLARA *to* BRAHMS.
(*Dictated*.)   FRANKFORT A/M., *Dec.* 2.

I must resign myself to dictating a few words to you if I wish
to get any news of you. For the last three weeks I have been
almost wholly prevented from playing or writing owing to a
severe attack in my arm. Had it not been for this I should
have been more prompt in answering your last letter and in
thanking you for your intervention in the Gutmann affair.

It will not be long now before you are in this direction and
oh, how gladly would I be present at the festival at Crefeld [1]
if only such functions did not in my case always involve so
much discomfort. In order to feel well I have to exercise a
certain amount of care and when travelling in the winter the
smallest variation in my routine so easily upsets me. But I
hope you will pay us a visit here, and I suppose you will certainly go to Wiesbaden where the Engelmanns now are. But
then for you travelling is not so complicated.

I was furious when I heard that your F major Symphony is
now really going to appear—arranged by Keller ! I think this
very heartless of you, for no one can arrange your things half
as well as you can yourself. And what a pleasure we shall all
lose in consequence ! We certainly had a great treat the other
day when Scholz produced your *Requiem* most wonderfully.
You would have been delighted with it and especially with
number V which my secretary [2] sang really beautifully. I was
pleased on Scholz's account that it was such a success. He
really is a most efficient Conductor.

I am supposed to play in Leipsic next week,[3] but do not yet
know whether it will be possible. I shall wait until the end of
this week and if I am not better I shall of course have to cancel

[1] January 29 and 30.   [2] Marie Fillunger.
[3] At the first concert in the new Gewandhaus.

the engagement. It would be a great blow to me to have to do this, although my heart clings to the old hall, but one gladly gives a helping hand at such a festival in one's native town. Otherwise everything here is jogging along in the same old way. We work and live a very quiet life together. In the School things are taking their normal course and even Stockhausen is said to be doing well and to have many pupils. His course is having a rapid sale. I hope he is earning a lot of money with it. I need hardly say what I should like to ask now, because, more than anything else, I should love a glimpse into your workshop. You write to me about certain songs which I have not yet seen and I also hear a great deal about an alleged fourth Symphony ? [1] Everybody greets you here but especially Your old friend CLARA.

[1] The rest is written with her own hand.

1885

FRANKFORT A/M., *Feb.* 21.

(*Dictated.*)

DEAR JOHANNES,

I am sorry to say that what you have heard is all too true. The burglars seem to have spent the whole night in the dining-room and the other rooms downstairs. We imagine they came in by way of the garden and opened the locks with skeleton keys, which they managed most skilfully, as the locks were not injured. They must have been professional burglars, for they sorted out the gold and silver from the plate with the greatest accuracy. Of course everything has gone, including even my beautiful Leipsic present. They smashed the fine glass decanters against the wall at the bottom of the garden and only took away the gold and silver fittings.

You are right in thinking that even though the loss is great the feeling of insecurity and suspicion is much worse. For years I have been afraid that this might happen, but was always laughed at for my pains. Now from morning till night we think of nothing else but how to safeguard ourselves. We are deliberating whether we should not have a man and a dog in the house and are having special safety locks placed everywhere. The report that my jewellery was stolen too is false, for that I had in my bedroom. But they broke open my writing-desk although they only found a little money there, about a hundred and fifty marks. I had my laurel wreath [1] in my music rack, against which I happened to have laid a picture, so they did not see it.

Please read this to any of my friends in Vienna who may make inquiries—the Fellingers, Franz, Oser. I cannot possibly answer all the letters, there are so many. But thank you for

[1] A golden wreath presented to her at her jubilee.

your kind sympathy.   Thank God we are all well, but you can imagine the state of our spirits !   Ever your CLARA (in her own hand).

On the whole my arm is better.

CLARA *to* BRAHMS.

BERLIN, *April* 20.
(*Dictated.*)
DEAR JOHANNES,

I received your letter just as I was about to leave [1] and you may well imagine that its contents have greatly excited my curiosity about the picture in question.   I presume it has now reached home, but we shall remain here a week longer than we thought, and I did not wish to delay writing to beg you to try to prevent the presentation of the picture to the *Gesellschaft der Musikfreunde,* for if I think it is a good likeness I should naturally like to keep it, and I suppose it is a matter of indifference to the giver whether I or the *G. d. M.* have it.   Everything has gone off very well here.   I shall give another concert on Friday with Joachim and then go back to Frankfort on Saturday.   I shall not go to England, it would be too late now.   With hearty greetings, and most grateful thanks for your letter, Your [2]

P.S.   Greet all our dear friends for me.   As regards electric bells, there are two sides to the question.   What are we to do if they ring, and sometimes they ring when there are no burglars in the house, and what a fright they give you then !

CLARA *to* BRAHMS.

OBERSALZBERG BEI BERCHTESGADEN, *Aug.* 10.

To-day I will send you a greeting from this place and thank you for your last letter to Gastein.   I would have written sooner if the days were not so short and work so plentiful.   We are also being constantly interrupted here and whole days go by on which I can do nothing.

I have just finished one piece of work, which though it has given me a good deal of trouble, has also afforded me great pleasure—the collection of letters which I am publishing under

---

[1] On the 14th of April she went to Berlin where she had promised to play on the 17th.

[2] The signature to this dictated letter was forgotten.

the title "*Jugendbriefe Robert Schumanns*," being his early letters to a few friends and his mother, and extracts from letters to me during our courtship. Härtels are printing them and they are to appear in October, as the copyright in them ends in fifteen months' time. But nobody has any idea of what a lot of work such a compilation involves and how often one has to read and re-read and cross out and put in again, and what a lot of correspondence it has meant in addition with Härtels and with friends one has had to consult about the business side. I know so little about book production that I naturally had to be cautious. . . . But I will tell you all about it when I see you. . . .

I am very glad to say that I am feeling better here than I did in Gastein. This air evidently suits me. If only my stay here had not been curtailed owing to my visit to Gastein ! . . . We have given up our idea of going south, as Hildebrand is coming to Frankfort on the 10th or 11th of September to make a plaque of me.[1] The children have long been wanting him to do this, and so I am gladly making this by no means negligible sacrifice, although I had long had in my mind that I should like to see Meran and get to know it. Please greet the dear Fellingers for me. Eugenie and Fillu are staying in French Switzerland—Sion, Kt. Wallis. Marie sends hearty greetings. She is much better. Yours ever, CLARA.

CLARA *to* BRAHMS.

FRANKFORT, *Sept.* 17.

Thank you most heartily for your kind wishes for the 13th and the exquisite work. I ought also to have thanked you sooner for the Symphony.[2] But we started our journey the day after Frau von Herzogenberg brought it to me and this is the first moment I have had for writing. You can imagine how eagerly we fell upon it. Frau von H. played it wonderfully and more than once we were carried away. I was particularly charmed again and again by the way you developed it,

---

[1] He ultimately made a bust of her.

[2] The fourth Symphony, Op. 98, i.e. the first movement with the beginning of the andante. Brahms had sent the music to Frau von Herzogenberg with the request that she should communicate it, i.e. play it to Frau Schumann.

but I should not dare to judge it without having heard its full effect with an orchestra. Send us the rest soon and let us hear it before long. I shall look forward to it with great joy.

We are terribly busy. Every day we have to read proofs of the letters, which have to be compared with the originals. Then come more proofs, and in addition, new pupils and two hours' sitting a day to Hildebrand. So please forgive this short letter, and with renewed thanks for everything, Your old friend CLARA.

On the 13th I received eighty-four letters ! ! !

BRAHMS *to* CLARA.

MEININGEN. *End of October.*
In the Small Palace.

I came here a few days ago and am practising the new Symphony.[1] On Sunday it will be given at a concert and probably again on the 1st, and on the 3rd in Frankfort. I have worked long and hard at it, thinking of you all the time, and wondering whether it would not perhaps prove a very doubtful pleasure to you. The fact is I am living here in the lap of luxury, I can practise to my heart's content without a concert having necessarily to follow. But as the piece pleases musicians (and does not altogether displease me) I cannot exactly refuse to allow Bülow to travel about with it a bit. The Frankfort Directors cannot object to this while they think with a smile of their great string quartet. What about you ? Are you going to the concert ? May I put up at your place ? If I may, and you are sure that it is convenient and that I am really not putting you out, might I come a few days earlier ? Three seats in the front row, etc. No fuss, but please send me a brief line to let me know whether the whole thing is not a bit of a bore ? ! ? ! ? ?

I should like to have written more but I must go to the rehearsal. I should be so glad if you could find time to write me a few words. With heartiest greetings, Your JOHANNES.

---

[1] The fourth in E minor. This was first produced under Brahms' direction on the 25th of October at the third concert of the Ducal Court Orchestra. It was repeated on November the 1st under Bülow. On the 3rd of November the Duke of Meiningen's orchestra played it in Frankfort.

CLARA *to* BRAHMS.

FRANKFORT A/M., *Oct.* 23.

When I can hear one of your Symphonies played properly, I don't care which it is, the place I hear it in is a matter of indifference to me. I am sorry that the Committee here were again dilatory, but rejoice nevertheless, and you will find your room ready if it suits you. Betty is with us, but she is leaving us the day after to-morrow morning. So we are waiting for you and all we ask is a card to say when you will come. Instead of the three stalls please get three seats in a box in the first tier. We had these places last winter at a Bülow concert, and heard much better than close up to the stage in the stalls.

We have been having an unhappy time. My brother Alwin died the day before yesterday after four months of unspeakable suffering. I feel very miserable, it has meant a good deal to me. I was to have played at the Museum, but have naturally cancelled the engagement. But this is not what I meant by a " good deal." I shall tell you more when I see you. Heartily looking forward to your visit, Your CLARA.

CLARA *to* BRAHMS.

FRANKFORT A/M., *Dec.* 15.

(*Dictated.*)

Here am I obliged to dictate a letter to you when my heart is full to overflowing about your Symphony.[1] It has given me some wonderful moments and its beauty and richness of colour have held me spellbound. I scarcely know which movement I prefer—the first dreamy one, with its magnificent development, its magic pauses and its softly undulating emotional depths (it is as though one lay in springtime among the blossoming flowers and joy and sorrow filled one's soul in turn), or the last, which is so grandly constructed, with its enormous variety, and, in spite of its complicated workmanship, is so full of profound passion, softening down wonderfully towards the middle, only to burst out with fresh power later on ! This passion already lies hidden in the *leit motif* (one can hardly call it a theme). And how one slips into dreamland again with the romantic adagio ! In fact I have grown to love the third

[1] The pianoforte edition.

movement more owing to its exquisite cheerfulness. Oh, if only I could talk to you about it with the score before us ! If I might be allowed to mention something I don't altogether like, I would point to the second motif in the first movement, which seems to me too independent and not welded on to what precedes it, whereas in your works one thing usually evolves so wonderfully out of the other. It is as if you suddenly repented of having been so amiable. Apart from the stiffness of the motif, it also seems somewhat lacking in nobility. The scherzo always strikes me as rather lengthy, as does also the development in the adagio. What seems to me quite heavenly in the latter is the conclusion with the chord of the augmented sixth which then carries us on so wonderfully to E major through a chain of resolved chords of the sixth. I could go on for ever, and yet I must stop, though I am relieved by the thought that I shall have the pleasure of hearing the Symphony again this winter and be able to discuss it with you in person. Kwast and Uzielli played it to me so beautifully after having studied it thoroughly together, that I was able to derive the fullest enjoyment from it. Scholz and Knorr were present at the time and declared that much in it was now clear that had not been so before.

I don't suppose you would mind my lending the Symphony to Kwast for a day so that he can play it to Beckerath in W. In any case I hope you will let me keep it for a little while longer. Perhaps I can get it played to me again—unfortunately I cannot dream of playing it myself.

How glad I am that the letters please you. In those to me we must after all have been more discriminating than I at first thought. There is nothing new to tell you about this place, except perhaps that a day or two ago I heard Bruckner's extraordinary Symphony and am relieved to feel that I at last know how I stand with regard to it. It is a horrible piece of music, nothing more than a medley of scraps strung together with a heap of bombast, and moreover scandalously long. Its reception was a frost. The Wagnerites, who are also followers of Bruckner, said that Müller had deliberately ruined it. But this is a disgusting thing to say, because any impartial person would have been bound to admire the patience with which Müller had studied it and the excellence of the performance.

He had actually had an extra rehearsal of the thing lasting three hours. There was another terrible failure in the same concert. It was quite unprecedented and fell to the lot of the pianist Friedheim, who was hissed and laughed off the stage. I heard the Symphony and his playing only at the rehearsal. His fame as a great executionist had already reached me, and lo, he began Beethoven's E Flat major Concerto like a school-boy playing it for the first time. I have never in my life seen such a thing in a concert hall. The Herzogenbergs are now in Leipsic for the production of his Symphony. I hope it will have a good reception. Now I have been chatting for a long while and have put my secretary's patience sorely to the test. I hope I have not also exhausted yours. Farewell, dear Johannes, and many thanks for having allowed me a deeper insight into your Symphony.

(In her own hand) Ever your old friend CLARA.

CLARA *to* BRAHMS.

FRANKFORT, *Dec.* 30.

(*Dictated.*)

I am afraid I cannot write my New Year's greetings to you myself, but they are none the less hearty for that. It is delight-ful to hear that the New Year will bring you so soon to us. Will you make an excursion to us from Mannheim and Cologne, or will you spend the interval between Mannheim and Frank-fort with us ? You will find your room ready at any time. I don't suppose you will go back to Vienna first. Many thanks for your kind letter, but it told me nothing about where you spent Christmas. You could not have been serious when you thought that we were going to have a jolly time. Were not our thoughts, mine at all events, the whole evening at Ferdi-nand's, where, in spite of the tree, things must have looked dreary enough. It is impossible to be cheerful with such thoughts. And you could not have imagined me at the piano because of my bad arm ! You must have been very absent-minded, my dear Johannes, when you wrote that letter—I was in the depths of woe ! And now I suppose I must return the Symphony. I don't like doing so, but of course am sending it at once.

I had lent it to Kwast, who wanted to play it to the Beckeraths yesterday, and I have written to him to send it back to me immediately. I am very pleased with the songs.[1] If only I were in a position to play them myself ! For the last few days the pains have not been so severe, and I am feeling more hopeful again. If I could play on the 22nd here instead of on the 5th of March, I should so much prefer it, for I am particularly anxious thoroughly to enjoy the Symphony [2] for the first time.

So farewell for to-day. May all good wishes accompany you into the New Year and all through it. . . .

(With her own hand) As ever, Your CLARA.

[1] Op. 96, 97.
[2] On the 5th of March Brahms conducted his fourth Symphony with the Museum Orchestra.

1886

FRANKFORT, 14*th May.*

DEAR JOHANNES,

Just a word to-day about your beautiful songs. I have very
much enjoyed them, although I have not yet heard them, but
only been able to read them as Fillu has a very bad cold. I
like all the songs in Op. 96, and think the second one particularly fine and full of feeling (the transition from minor to
major is delightful). And oh, how the third moves one with
its cry of despair at the end! The fourth is wonderful in
its massive harmonies.

Of Op. 97 I like more especially the first which is quite
original. How magically the notes of the nightingale strike
one's heart-strings. It is a pearl of poetry! From the musical
point of view, I also like the introduction, but the text says
nothing to me. Many thanks for this new gift! Now let me
turn to something more prosaic. May I send you all I have of
the Schumann edition? It is accumulating here and must go
to you sooner or later. And then you wanted two operas—
Echo and Narcissus, but what was the other? I have forgotten.

I wish you would decide to send me the letters so that I may
look them through.[1] I[2] should then be able to destroy a good
many of them and select a few to be kept. Do please make
up your mind to do so! You must realize that your letters
are on a somewhat different footing. If I were to die they
would fall into the best and most careful hands. . . . We are
in the throes of the examinations, and having concert after
concert. I have not yet received the Symphony and am much
looking forward to it. Is it coming arranged for four hands?
(Eugenie.)

[1] Letters from her to Brahms.
[2] From this point Clara dictates.

And now farewell. Answer me soon, and also let me know when you are leaving Vienna and where you are going. (In her own hand), I shall have to take the waters somewhere before going to Obersalzberg. To my intense relief the doctor told me that there was nothing organically wrong with me, it is all nerves, etc. With heartiest greetings, Your old friend, CLARA.

CLARA *to* BRAHMS.

OBERSALZBERG, *Aug.* 24.

DEAR JOHANNES,

Herewith I return Billroth's letter with thanks. Glad as I am to see from it how much you have accomplished, I cannot pretend that it gave me as much pleasure as the works themselves would have done. When in one of your bad moods [1] you wrote to me that you thought you had very often been a nuisance to me with your compositions, you must have forgotten that as an artist I am never able to send you superficial criticism of your work, and any opinion is bound to be superficial so long as one is not completely familiar with a particular work. But circumstances are often too strong for one and a speedy judgment is not always possible, as for instance when one only receives a manuscript score and is as little skilled as I am in reading it, and can only get an inadequate idea of its musical effect by merely looking at it—or when you send me a symphony written for two pianos, with the parts written one above the other and do not send the second piano-part, so that I cannot try it—or when I have pains in my arm and somebody has to be found who can play the thing to me. Sometimes too you send me songs written in different keys which greatly increases the difficulty of learning them for me. Moreover, I

---

[1] In her Diary Clara writes on August the 23rd : " Letter from Brahms, evidently written in a bad mood. He says that I have asked him about his life and work, but that during the last few years he has been under the impression that he has been a nuisance to me with the works he has sent me in MS.," etc., etc. Brahms must have been provoked to this outburst by the apparent lack of sympathy shown towards the fragment of his fourth Symphony, though in the end his displeasure was directed more towards Frau von Herzogenberg. There is reason for supposing that a feeling of distinct hostility to Clara prevailed in Brahms' circle.

am not always mistress of my own time and my own strength, and cannot, like Frau von Herzogenberg, bury myself in a work for whole days at a time. In short there are a hundred and one reasons why there should occasionally be some delay in sending you my comments on things you have forwarded to me. I am not offering all these explanations in order to excuse myself, for, as far as I am aware, I have never been guilty of any carelessness or indifference towards you. But one cannot pass over in silence an unjust reproach except in the case of people one does not care about. . . . As ever yours, CLARA.

CLARA *to* BRAHMS.

FRANKFORT, *Nov.* 4.

Why are you sending me nothing more ? Do you wish to leave your old friend quite out in the cold ? That would be a crying shame ! And I beg you most urgently to send me anything which you can spare for a little while. The new Sonatas with violin and violoncello [1] I should be able to play almost immediately—the first with Joachim, who will be here in three weeks, and the second with Hugo Becker ; and in any case I would be able to start practising them at once. I hope I shall not have to wait in vain for the beautiful things which in the old days you used to send me.

Yours affectionately, CLARA.

CLARA *to* BRAHMS.

FRANKFORT, *Dec.* 7.

Everything was certainly not in order—your last letter but one wounded me so deeply that all I could do was to send you a card telling you what was absolutely necessary.

Not only did you definitely refuse my request but the very tone in which you did so was offensive. But I see from your last letter that you yourself felt you had hurt me, and after such kind words I cannot keep up the quarrel with my old friend any longer. But let me beg you, my dear Johannes, never to write when you feel out of sorts. For every unkind word, which in you is but the expression of the moment, impresses itself on my memory. Age robs one more and more of every joy ! How much do I not have to give up now because

[1] Op. 100, 101.

my bodily strength no longer allows of it ! And in addition I constantly have fresh anxieties which are very hard to bear. But my heart is just as strong as ever in its love for my children, my friends and my art, and cannot suffer any loss in these relationships without pain.

But enough of this, and let us turn to your concert about which I have spoken to Hanau. The Committee are quite ready to arrange a special evening and would be glad to hear when this could be. But in any case you would come here a day or two beforehand, wouldn't you ? You will always find your room ready. It is the room with the balcony which we have arranged as a guest's room. Let me have a card a day or two beforehand to say when you are coming so that we may have everything comfortable for you. As regards the programme, don't you think that three new things are a little too much even for the most intelligent audience ? Wouldn't it be better to have at least one old work (the quartet in A major or the quintet in F minor in between or at the end ; you might perhaps have the new songs also, or the choral quartets) ? But we shall be able to settle this better by word of mouth.

As to your copy of Robert's works, so far I have only been turning it over in my mind, and everything is still at your disposal. Now in conclusion, let us hope we shall soon meet. Awaiting to hear about your final arrangements, with affectionate greetings, Your CLARA.

1887

CLARA *to* BRAHMS.

FRANKFORT, *Jan*. 13.

DEAR JOHANNES,

It was not only your words that offended me but your deeds. The fact that at the moment when you were playing your new pieces you did not send them to me was natural enough, although in the past you often had a thing copied for me, for instance, at the time of the first Sonata with violin. If you had wanted to do so, however, you could certainly have sent me one or the other after a while, for I should in that case have scrupulously observed any condition you chose to impose. But in the same letter you say, " I have written to Frau Kwast (who begged me for my MS. for her husband's musical evenings) and told her till I was sick and tired of it that I could not do anything for her, and now it would seem as if you were distressed because Kwast cannot help himself to things which, all the time, are lying quietly at your place ! ? "

I should have preferred to pass this over in silence. But as you again return to the subject of Kwast I must tell you that there was no need for you to worry about how we settle matters among ourselves here. To speak quite frankly, it would never have occurred to me that it was necessary for me to apologize to him for having received a MS. from you before he did. He is not an intimate friend of either of us, and as for placing him on the same artistic plane as myself, such a thing surely never occurred either to you or to me.

I am very sorry that the Brahms evening is not to take place, and so are many others. I suppose you have good reasons for this. But it certainly looks somewhat capricious after you had proposed the evening yourself ; for in my opinion, it might have been just such another night as we had in Pesth, where, in addition to two new works, you performed one that was already well known. . . .

With affectionate greetings, now as ever, Your old friend, CLARA.

CLARA *to* BRAHMS.

FRANKFORT, *April* 24.

DEAR JOHANNES,

I am a little late in answering your letter, but I hope this will reach you in Vienna. I received your kind parcel four days ago, but at the same time a piece of news reached me which was such a terrible shock to us all that we have not had a moment's peace of mind since. Elise had gone with her children to pay a visit to their grandmother (her husband's mother) in Zurich. She had done this to give them a surprise and her husband was of course with her. But when they got there her only daughter, a darling, gifted child of four, developed diphtheria and died the day before yesterday. For ten days they nursed the child themselves and everything possible was done. How my son-in-law will bear it I do not know. Elise will show more fortitude. If only we could do something for them! But they are so far away and so much wrapped up in their grief, that we have not yet had a word from them direct, and all we know is that the funeral is to-day. Oh, what will our next meeting be like! The poor parents! I know you will sympathize and will forgive my delay in thanking you, both for the letter and for the MS. which I was so glad to receive.

Of course I ask you for the other letters. But I also beg that I may be allowed to keep just a few of yours. They are quite safe in my hands and were I to die suddenly the children would return them to you at once. Wishing you a pleasant journey and a holiday in Thun which will do you a lot of good, I am, with affectionate greetings, Your CLARA.

BRAHMS *to* CLARA.

THUN, *May.*

The way you are treated by Fate is really too cruel! Deeply as I sympathize with you, I cannot bear to form any clear picture of your grief. I cannot even speak to you further about it. For in addition to this stunning and terrible blow you have

so many other sorrows which pursue their sad course uninter-
rupted. My one comfort is that I feel your fine nature has
not allowed you to become insensitive to any chance ray of
sunlight which either life or your art may bring you. But
please tell the Sommerhoffs how deeply I sympathize with them.
When I was again among the glories of Italy this year there was
no one about whom I thought more or with greater yearning
than yourself. How I wished that you might have as much
strength for this highest of joys as you have for your art. I
know of nobody more capable than you of enjoying all this to
the full, if only you had the bodily strength for it.

We were everywhere favoured by the most gorgeously mild
spring weather. Our tour would have been too much for you,
but if you had spent the beautiful weeks say in Florence I don't
suppose anything in the world could have been more enjoyable.

Our itinerary took us through Verona, Vicenza, Venice,
Bologna, Florence, Pisa, Milan and back through the St. Gotthard here. Not a day passed which was not full of the most
beautiful experiences. My companions were Simrock and
Kirchner. It was a nice idea of Simrock's to let Kirchner see
Italy at last. Twenty years earlier the experience might have
produced good fruit. In Italy I find that travelling companions are both pleasant and necessary to me, even if they do
not always increase the enjoyment or leave it unimpaired. I
am now enjoying my second early spring here and feel very
happy. I do not like the idea of having to go to the musical
festival in Cologne at the end of May, but I suppose I must keep
my word to Wüllner, and I could even look forward with pleasure to the beautiful trip on the Rhine if the thought of a short
visit from me were also pleasurable to you.

Simrock has just published a catalogue of my works. If he
should send a copy to you I need hardly tell you that I did not
ask him to do so. On the contrary, I prevented it as long as
possible. I could not, however, forbid it.

And there is another matter I was on the point of forgetting
—it is much more important that my letters should be sent
back than that yours should. You can always have the latter,
as can also your children—although I do not believe in the
contingency arising. But in case of my death, my letters have
no one to go back to. That is why I most earnestly beg you to

return them to me, and when I say send them quickly, please
don't think it is because I am in a hurry to despatch them to
the bookbinders !

There is sad news about Franck and Herzogenberg.   The
former seems to be in a bad way, but there is still room for hope
in the case of H.—unfortunately there is an entirely similar
case here in which all hope is gradually being abandoned.   And
now to conclude with affectionate greetings, Your JOHANNES.

CLARA *to* BRAHMS.

FRANKFORT, *May* 27.

Only the very pressing correspondence of weeks could have
prevented me from answering your dear letter before ; besides
which I also knew that the festival in Cologne was only fixed
for the end of June and not as you erroneously wrote for the
end of May.

First of all let me thank you for your words of sympathy.
The blow was a hard one, particularly hard in view of certain
circumstances which I will tell you about some day.   But you
are right when you say that still harder things come to one
through human beings and unhappy conditions.   We are
suffering from such things at the present moment and they are
depressing me most dreadfully.   I refer to the complete dis-
persion of Ferdinand's household, the placing of all his children,
some of whom must be confided to the care of men, and the
treatment which Ferdinand is now to undergo.   For weeks we
have spent hours every day in writing to Ferdinand, the doctors, and the children's teachers.   In the midst of all these
difficulties, however, we have had some compensations.   But
more about these and a good many other things when I see
you.

Above all let me say that we are greatly looking forward to
seeing you, and as soon as you can fix the date we shall be glad
to know when you are coming.   Could it not be before the
festival ?   But do whatever suits you best.   We shall be here
in any case until the beginning of July.   I have already practised your new pieces most diligently, and am particularly
delighted with the trio.[1]   If only your things were not so often
beyond my physical strength !   This is so painful to me, for I

[1] C minor, Op. 101.

know that I understand and feel them better than most people, and yet am obliged to give in. Yesterday I had another bad attack in the arm, but did not wish to delay any longer before I wrote to you. Many thanks for your fine description of your Italian tour. Oh, this body of mine which prevents me from enjoying any treat of art or nature ! Farewell then, and let us hear from you soon. Your old friend CLARA.

BRAHMS *to* CLARA.

THUN, *July* 7.

My copyist has finished the Variations and I gladly take the pen from his hand in order at last to send you my heartiest greetings and thanks. It was with the most extraordinarily pleasant feelings that I travelled along the Rhine the other day. The journey was its own best reward, and Cologne had no need to make any effort on my account. I wished for nothing more. And now, if the truth must be told, let me say that everything went off in the happiest and most delightful fashion. Wüllner did his work excellently, and everything was much more successful than one expects at these festivals. The company about me, both young men and girls, were fair to look upon and jolly, and ultimately at Rüdesheim we sampled as much of the best wine as we possibly could. I had the best of grey skies for Cologne, and here once more I have the best of blue ones, and you may be sure I am making the most of it. Yesterday afternoon, for instance, I walked for four hours to visit our friend Widmann,[1] who has settled down here on the Lake for the summer. This morning I got up at half-past four, walked for an hour and a half, and then returned home on the steamer. At the present moment I have the feeling that you could also do the same with great ease and pleasure ? !

I have written to my copyist and told him to leave the Variations at his place for the time being. Do you want them yourself or can you suggest anything else ? Let me have a word to say. And now a thousand thanks to you and the girls for the delightful days in Frankfort. I hope to be able to repeat them in the autumn. Let me know some time when you are going to Berchtesgaden, and with most affectionate greetings, Your JOHANNES.

[1] J. B. Widmann from Berne.

CLARA *to* BRAHMS.

FRANZENSBAD, LOIMANN'S HYDRO, *July* 23.

If you do not like to leave the Variations so long in the care of the copyist, have them sent to Herr Emil Ladenburg, 14 Junghoffstrasse, Frankfort a/M. (to await Frau Schumann's arrival). You must let me have the bill for them some time. I had already heard a good deal about your fine reception in Cologne, but I was doubly pleased to have the news confirmed by you and to hear that you had been satisfied with everything, introduction and finale. And now you are once more enjoying the beauties of nature with full mental and bodily vigour. What a happy existence ! And soon Herr Wendt is going to join you, which will be sure to give you great pleasure. Unfortunately we never see him now, although I like him so much. In fact how seldom does one meet anybody at all who gives one any pleasure or who lifts one above the daily routine. At the present moment I am living immersed in your letters—a melancholy pleasure ! Words cannot describe what stirs the soul when one dips deeply once more into times long since gone by. In giving you back these letters I feel as if I were already taking leave of you. In reading them I become abundantly convinced that it would be a crying shame to destroy them. You ought to compile a kind of diary out of them for they contain almost the whole of your career as well as innumerable interesting remarks and opinions which are invaluable for a biographer. Please do that first and then destroy them afterwards. For what seemed good and at times sad to ourselves belongs to us alone, nobody need know anything about it.

Our poor Ferdinand is very ill. Marie has visited him in Teplitz, and all he can do is to walk from his bed to the sofa with the help of two sticks. He wants to leave Teplitz and go to an institution in Thüringen in order to get rid of the morphia habit. He has already tried again and again, and Marie says the struggle was terrible to behold. It really is shocking that there is no law against such crimes on the part of doctors.

Have you ever written to Durant about your author's rights ? I have just received 1,200 marks [£60] for the last year (more than ever before), and on receiving it I was really grieved to think that you allow such a source of income to lapse. Surely you can find someone who would draft the inquiry for you in

French, and all you would have to do would be to copy it. And now to conclude—we are leaving here on the 6th of August for Obersalzberg (Pension Moritz) and shall stay there as long as the weather remains good. I shall be so glad to see the Herzogenbergs again, but I hear that he has improved very little. It really is very sad. . . . Farewell, dear Johannes. May you enjoy the summer. Go on creating for your own and other people's joy and let us hear from you again. Your faithful old friend CLARA.

BRAHMS *to* CLARA.

HOFSTETTIN, *August.*

By now you will have arrived at your beloved Berchtesgaden, strengthened, refreshed ? This time it does not seem to me at all necessary ! Aye, what I imagine is that you descend daily from your great hill and proceed to call on one friend after another.

But we are behaving in a remarkable manner about our letters ! I have always secretly meditated an exchange but did not dare to utter the word. I then sent your letters, but had not the courage to look into them and read them beforehand, because I took it for granted that if I did I should not be able to send them away. But you are a regular fraud. You start the whole ball rolling, send nothing, and go on reading—I will wait a little longer though. Herr Wendt is here and sends his heartiest greetings. But you have a most exceptionally amiable sister ! Why not exchange ?

I have at last taken measures with regard to the French author's rights. This is what happens when one has no family. What I spend myself, and the large amounts I spend on others, I earn on the whole very easily, and have no need to trouble myself about fresh sources of income.

The Herzogenbergs send you hearty greetings ; unfortunately he is by no means better, and his case seems to be the same as that which I met with in an acquaintance here ; I will tell you about it.

As to myself, I can tell you something funny, for I have had the amusing idea of writing a Concerto for violin and cello.[1] If it is at all successful it might give us some fun. You

[1] Op. 102.

can well imagine the sort of pranks one can play in such a case. But do not imagine too much ! I ought to have handed on the idea to someone who knows the violin better than I do (Joachim has unfortunately given up composing). It is a very different matter writing for instruments whose nature and sound one only has a chance acquaintance with, or only hears in one's mind, from writing for an instrument that one knows as thoroughly as I know the piano. For in the latter case I know exactly what I write and why I write it as I do. But we will wait and see. Joachim and Hausmann want to try it. Joachim suggests Cologne as the proper place for it, and I Mannheim and Frankfort. Now with affectionate greetings, and heartiest remembrances to Marie, the Herzogenbergs, Franz, Fräulein Wendt, and whoever else is swarming round you—I suppose only Franck's house is standing empty ? Yours always, JOHANNES.

CLARA *to* BRAHMS.

OBERSALZBERG, *Aug.* 25.

A task to which I have been devoting the whole of my writing powers (the diary which was much in arrears) prevented me from writing to you sooner, as I should like to have done, to tell you how happy I am at the prospects which you hold out to us. Surely this wonderful combination has never been tried before ? I discussed it a good deal with Joachim who paid me a visit the other day, and we are tremendously pleased about the work. My idea is that one who has written such Symphonies, such Sonatas for violins and violoncellos must know these instruments to their inmost core, and must be able to conjure unsuspected harmonies from them. I hope Joachim will propose the work for the Museum, where he is engaged for November, and then Hausmann will come from Berlin. He intends to do so and will soon write to me about it. We are now wallowing in the most gorgeous weather after having had a few horrible days. Unfortunately, in spite of being pretty well, I am still limited to quite short walks. You think I am stronger than I am. I only wish it were so ! We have already seen a large number of acquaintances here and I am particularly glad that Julius O. Grimm should be in Berchtesgaden with his daughter, while his wife is taking the cure in Tölz. We often see them. Fräulein Wendt has unfortunately gone. It was very pleasant with her and her friend. Every evening after dinner they used to come to us with a lantern from their boarding-house, which is ten minutes' walk away, and then we played whist or talked.

We saw the Herzogenbergs before we came up here and found him seriously ill. They have gone to a sanatorium now which they hope will cure him. This illness is a hard trial; but I do not give up hope yet. He is a vigorous man and was always healthy. I shall soon see them again, as I will visit them from Munich. Friends of the Francks are staying at his house, but I heard some mention of the house being sold. I also see Frau Franz occasionally up here. She is always the same amiable and loyal friend and her children are charmingly brought up, agreeable and unassuming. We have good news of Eugenie in Mayens. As for Ferdinand I have little hope ; things are still very bad with him. But with regard to his two eldest boys I believe we have found the right thing in Schneeberg. They enjoy the advantages of a small town, woodlands, meadows, and a garden with their own little flower plots, a pool in which they can swim daily, parties, etc. They write very happy letters. I believe that Ferdinand cannot yet reconcile himself to the fact that his sons are not to be educated in Berlin. . . . Gade [1] gave me a pleasant surprise by sending me a most delightful photograph of himself together with a nice letter full of kind things, which took me back to days long since gone by.

My arm gives me painful warnings. I must stop. I hope you will thoroughly enjoy the autumn, and let us hear from you soon. Your old friend CLARA.

BRAHMS *to* CLARA.
(*Postcard.*)

Sept.

On September the 18th we would like to have a piano rehear-

---

[1] Niels Wilhelm Gade, Danish composer (1817–1890), at one time violinist at the Chapel Royal, Copenhagen. When Mendelssohn died Gade became the director of concerts at the Gewandhaus, Leipsic, but returned to Copenhagen in 1848 at the time of the Schleswig-Holstein rebellion.—TR.

sal at your house. Would you be so kind as to let me have
your address so that my copyist in Vienna can send the music
there ? The Variations by Robert Schumann will come with
them. I need hardly tell you how very much I am looking
forward to the morning at your house. But do not expect too
much ! It is a very modest piece in every respect. It is very
wise to allow you time to read and enjoy all the friendly greetings you have received for the 13th, for let us hope that our
arrival will mean a second little celebration of the date. Most
affectionately yours, J. B.

CLARA *to* BRAHMS.

MUNICH, *Sept.* 11.

I am writing to you in great trouble. Just think, I must
stay here for another week on account of Ferdinand. He
refuses to remain in the institution where he now is, and I am
going to bring him here to the establishment that Herzogenberg
is in. We were just on the point of going to Baden-Baden
when a letter arrived from Ferdinand which seemed so desperate that, at his request, I consulted a doctor here. To cut
a long story short, he is to come here, and if all goes well, as we
have arranged, he will probably arrive on the 16th or 17th, in
which case, we could not leave here before the 20th or 21st.
He had already told Marie in Teplitz that he had a terrible
longing to see me. So how can I go away a few days before
he arrives ? I feel convinced that I must stay provided he
comes this week. At all events I will go to Baden-Baden from
here and, if the weather is fine, enjoy the air for another week
or more, and try to recover from the horrors and trials of these
last few days before I return to Frankfort to take up my work
again. . . . Forgive this dreadful letter. I am writing in a
turmoil, as you may imagine. I shall let you know at once if
there should be any change in my plans, but I don't think there
will be. We shall have to remain here for this week at any
rate. I need hardly tell you what a disappointment it would
be for me if you were unable to postpone the delightful though
belated celebration of my birthday. I am too deeply agitated
to write any more. I am informing Joachim as well. Farewell and don't forget your old friend, CLARA.

Herzogenberg is very bad.

BRAHMS *to* CLARA.

THUN, *Sept.* 11.

This is to send you my heartiest greetings for September the 13th. As I am to sing and deliver verses and variations on this beautiful theme in a day or two I shall not try to do so to-day. I really meant to be there on the day (i.e. the day after to-morrow) but I have not heard that you, or whether you, are there already,—that is to say, whether our rehearsal can take place at your house. As nothing has come from you I may get a telegram from Joachim saying that both you and the rehearsal will be elsewhere. I don't know whether you have received my card (sent to B.).

Hausmann too would like to know where you are staying, so that he can arrange accordingly. My copyist is sending you the music from Vienna for me without any precise address. I hope it will arrive. The two pianoforte variations are also in the parcel.

Do please let me have a card at the Bär Inn. I intend putting up there on the 16th or 17th. The Prince of Hesse has delayed me very seriously and I must now quickly dash to the station to catch the train to Berne for the evening function. So please send me news at the Bär. It would reach me too late here. Wishing you the happiest of birthdays, and with most affectionate greetings, looking forward enormously to next week, Your JOH.

BRAHMS *to* CLARA.

THUN, *Sept.*

. . . I hope that we three will reach there [Baden-Baden ?] on the 21st, and even if our pleasure does not last very long, I am delighted to think how happy you will be when we start tuning up. Naturally I wrote at once to J. and we ought to think ourselves lucky if H. is not already on the way. I was also just on the point of going off, because I wanted to break my journey on the way to you. But I waited for some sort of message. Thank goodness I waited long enough !

I am extremely sorry to hear your news, and that you have had such a sad time in Munich. And so Herzogenberg is also " very bad." Greet them affectionately for me and may your last days there bring you some sort of solace. What a sad conclusion to a holiday !

If you make any definite alteration in your plans or have anything new to say about them, let me have a word by card as early as possible, so that I can let Hausmann know. I hope our arrangement to meet in Baden will stand, for I am looking forward to it tremendously.[1] Your JOH.

[1] For details about the meeting and the happenings in Baden-Baden see *Life*, Vol. II, pp. 391–392.

1888

CLARA to BRAHMS.

STUTTGART, *Jan.* 12.

DEAR JOHANNES,

I was not able to find time in Frankfort to thank you for the beautiful copy of " Old England." I am right, am I not, in thinking you meant to make us a present of it ? As I was on the point of leaving home I could only just glance at the fine engravings, but now we want to read it. I have played here and thoroughly enjoyed the youthful ardour with which Klengel has practised everything. Your E minor Symphony was given here for the first time—and excellently. We are going back to-day but I did not want to wait any longer before thanking you, because the moment I reach home I am bombarded on all sides. With affectionate greetings and thanks, Your old friend ᴊLARA.

BRAHMS to CLARA.

VIENNA, *Middle of January.*

DEAR CLARA,

I sent you that book in the hopes that if your visit to England did not come off this year, it might prove some small compensation. Twofold thanks for your greeting from Stuttgart,[1] for it afforded me a twofold pleasure—I was pleased for myself (and for my Symphony) and also for you, to hear that you are so well and lively, and that you are able to give both yourself and others so much enjoyment. During the holidays I travelled about a good deal. I was in Pesth before Christmas, in Meiningen on Christmas Eve, and in Leipsic for the New Year. But I should have been particularly glad if you could have enjoyed things with us in Meiningen. You would have been delighted with everything from morning to

[1] She had played there on January 10.

122

night. You would have duly admired the Christmas trees (mine too) and everything connected with them. But how many other things would you not have enjoyed—our amiable and excellent hosts (the Duke of Coburg as guest), the theatre and the orchestra, and, in addition to everything else, such beautiful winter weather for our leisure hours as I have never before enjoyed ! The trees were covered to their tiniest twigs with snow. One never got tired either of the landscape or of walking about. . . .

Leipsic was also as pleasant as possible, except that one could not forget the sad plight of the Herzogenbergs. It was very charming of Fillu to have given up her holidays to the poor things, but I fear that she will scarcely have brought comforting news back with her. I suppose you know that the poor Francks lost their only child on Christmas Day. His condition is hopeless, otherwise I have only good news to give you of all our friends here, and your good news from Stuttgart will give particular pleasure to the Swabian, Frau Fellinger. With most cordial greetings to all from Your affectionate JOHANNES.

CLARA *to* BRAHMS.
(*Postcard.*)

FRANKFORT A/M., *Feb*. 9.

There are just a few things I want to know. First, do you know a Herr Moritz Brichte in Vienna ? Is he a man of honour, an artist, or what ? Secondly, do you know a musical encyclopædia begun by Hermann Mendel and continued by Dr. August Reissmann ? There are one hundred and eleven serial parts published by Robert Oppenheim in Berlin (1879). It has been offered to me to buy and Marie would like to have it if it is good. Please send me your answer on a card. I am being so heavily bombarded with offers from England that I shall probably go there for a few engagements after all.[1] With affectionate greetings, Yours, CL.

[1] On the 20th of February she set out on her nineteenth and last concert tour in England. She gave six concerts there, the last one on the 31st of March. On the 5th of April she was back in Frankfort.

BRAHMS *to* CLARA.

VIENNA, *Feb.*

I don't know any Herr M. Brichte, but I will make casual inquiries about him. I would naturally be pleased to do anything for you if you will simply tell me what his business is or send me his letter. If it is a begging letter you must surely be aware that in a large town this sort of thing is a genuine industry.

Don't buy Reissmann-Mendel. The book is bad in itself and in addition you would be particularly annoyed by it if you lighted upon such articles as the one about Spitta [1] and other details about the *Hochschule*. The best Encyclopædia of Music is by Koch, newly revised and published by Arrey von Donner (Heidelberg, 1865). This is an excellent book, which you would be able to read to your heart's content, and in which you will always find your questions answered instructively and thoroughly. But there are no biographies in it and I should think Marie would like to have articles about living artists ? In that case I would suggest Hugo Riemann's Encyclopædia. It is most highly thought of and is said to be good and reliable. It consists, moreover, of one volume only and not twelve !

It has not occurred to me even in my dreams to go to Stuttgart. But if you are going there and I happen to be in Thun I shall certainly come. At present I am of course making plans for the spring in Italy. I am thinking of going there with Widmann from Berne, perhaps to Sicily. But I leave this to Widmann, for it is all the same to me where I go in Italy ; one part is as glorious as the other.

At last I was able to write the Herzogenbergs a few lines yesterday. I think of them often and affectionately, but it is so distressing in such a case to have to say anything or ask questions. On the same principle, there is much in your life about which I do not ask questions; but that I think about it you must surely know, and if there is any change for the better, you must not fail to inform me. I send you all my good wishes for the English tour. Billroth is making plans

[1] August Philipp Spitta, writer on music. He wrote a biography of Bach, and became in 1875 Professor of the History of Music at Berlin University.—TR.

for Spain and Egypt, but my Italian plans please me best,
and I envy neither of you.   I hope Marie's hand is better,
and that all goes well in the house.   With most affectionate
greetings, Your JOHANNES.

BRAHMS *to* CLARA.

VIENNA, *End of Feb.*

Please do not be cross with me, but I had to laugh most
heartily at your good nature and at the childishness of your
Vienna affair.   All the man wants is autographs, and that's
all there is in it.   I could tell you of many other tricks by
means of which these people try to get what they want.   They
will be played on you too, but you let the people catch you.
The tale about the Schumann Society is of course all a hoax.
If it were true it would be very sad.   God knows we don't
require any society to promote the cultivation of Schumann's
music, nor does one want to encourage people in any kind of
one-sidedness however desirable !   It is just possible that Herr
Brichte occasionally, or frequently, plays Schumann with one
or two female relatives—but they have evidently constituted
themselves into a Schumann Society, for the purpose above-
mentioned.   If the Society had members, even only from
across the way, Herr Brichte, like all good Germans who found
societies, would have had something printed and sent out a
circular.   At all events he would have had something printed
at the head of his notepaper.   Perhaps the affair will look a
little more suspicious and delicate when I tell you that Dr.
Br. is the agent of Princess Wittgenstein (of Liszt fame) whose
patrimony he has charge of.   From this it is not difficult to
see that by virtue of his post he has come into the possession
of the handwriting of the most modern masters and has made
a hobby of it.

My book criticism has enabled me to find in Frl. Marie a
worthy and serious teacher.   For their quantity of volumes,
go to Mendel and Reissmann ; but Koch-Donner is more difficult to read and is worth while.   I have taken the liberty of
purchasing Donner and also Riemann and hope that Marie
will have no objection to finding them awaiting her in Frankfort.   I should, however, like to know whether Marie has
Donner's history of music.   I seem to remember having given

it to her once. I send you my best wishes for your stay in
England as for all times and places, and with affectionate
greetings, I am, Your JOHANNES.

CLARA *to* BRAHMS.

LONDON, *March* 21.

I have so much to thank you for, and yet I have been quite
unable to find the necessary peace to write you a decent letter.
In the first place, allow me to thank you most heartily for the
prompt reply to my inquiries, and for the books, which were
such a pleasant surprise to Marie. She will, of course, write
to thank you herself.

I would send Brichte's letter herewith if I had it by me. I
was not so childishly trustful after all. For if I had been I
should not have asked your advice first. In such matters I
am certainly much more cautious now.

I have nothing new to tell you about England. I have had
the same friendly reception which always touches me, and it
gives me great pleasure. No one in Germany has any idea of
the kind of enthusiastic outbursts that are to be witnessed
here. People are always asking me about you, and your
things are constantly being played. Yesterday I had the joy
of playing your Trio at the Popular, accompanied very beautifully by Mad. Neruda and Piatti. Joachim left me in the
lurch over this, because he had to go off suddenly to a funeral
in Berlin, but Mad. Neruda sprang into the breach and played
with great warmth and beauty. One has to sweep Piatti
along with one, which I succeeded in doing, and once again
enjoyed the magnificent piece more than anybody else. I
make so bold as to say that my feelings while playing could
only be equalled by yours when composing it ! ! !

I wonder whether you are in Italy already ? From all
accounts the weather is very bad there, so I hope you have
waited a bit. We expect to be back on April the 5th. Thank
God I have made so much money that I shall not have to
worry over any expense connected with Ferdinand this summer, and this will, I hope, enable me to have a really happy
and beneficial holiday. Let us hear from you soon, and with
all good wishes for your journey, Your old friend CLARA.

Brahms *to* Clara.

Vienna, *April.*

I should love to be with you for a little while when you return happy and contented from England. You have had many pleasures to help you to endure the strain, and the result is certainly most satisfactory. But what I am particularly pleased about is that you are still so kindly disposed to my Trio. Enclosed Robert Schumann's *Jugendlieder.* When you want to show a singer a special favour you can honour him with the wonderful one out of the F Sharp minor Sonata.

But a much more valuable possession to me is the first version of the D minor Symphony.[1] I have now added the finest copies to the printed score and bound them together. Unfortunately it will not suffice for your pleasure and understanding if I send them to you. Everyone who sees it agrees with me that the score has not gained by being remodelled ; it has certainly lost in charm, ease and clarity. Unfortunately, however, I cannot make any thorough trial anywhere. In Cologne the hall prevents me.

Joachim had the score with him the whole of last winter. But in spite of his own, Herzogenberg's and everyone's conviction regarding its excellence, his interest was not great enough to make him try it. Discuss it with Müller some time. He certainly revels in the work and at the same time finds it extremely difficult to learn. But in this new (or rather original) version he will find no difficulty, only joy, and I would give a good deal if only you could hear it, just as a change, and a refutation of the usual methods of instrumentation. And Müller, who always practises a thing so painstakingly and industriously, is precisely the man with his excellent quartet and the beautiful hall at his disposal. . . .

At the end of this month I am going (with Widmann of Berne as you well know) *via* Bologna, Rimini, Ancona, and Loretto to Rome, and *via* Viterbo and Florence back—whither ? At Billroth's we had a very pleasant evening with the *Zigeunerlieder* [2] for quartet with piano, sung by myself. They are a

---

[1] Schumann, Op. 20, composed in the summer of 1841 and first produced in the Gewandhaus in the December of that year. It was re-scored in 1851 at Düsseldorf.

[2] Op. 103.

kind of Hungarian love songs, and beautifully sung as they were and in such jolly company, you would have found listening to them a delight. Otherwise they might seem to you a little too rollicking. But you would like to have heard one or two choruses at Faber's. If only Stockhausen had a fine quartet I would come and have them sung to you.

I shall probably go. to Thun again. It is very beautiful there and I shall not have the bother of looking for rooms. But now let me release you at last, and with most affectionate greetings to you all, remain ever yours, JOHANNES.

CLARA *to* BRAHMS.

FRANKFORT A/M. *April* 12.

Just as I was sitting down to write to you there came the news of Beckerath's death. I am very much upset. He was a noble man, and I can so thoroughly sympathize with what his poor wife is now enduring. Many thanks for the kind letter which welcomed me home and for all the nice things in it. I shall speak to Müller about the D minor Symphony as soon as I am able to go out again, for as a matter of fact I have brought back a severe cold from England, and have to keep to my room as long as the weather does not improve. It is snowing again incessantly. It has really been a most appalling winter and, according to the Hanaus, who have just returned from there, the weather is also bad in Italy.

But please tell me, how do I manage to come by the score and parts of the D minor Symphony ?

What a magnificent journey you have before you ! How glad I should be to hear from you occasionally when you are there ! This month we are opening our new school buildings. Everything has already been moved there. I have not been able to see it yet, but shall play in the concert, in the quartet, giving your A minor Sonata, which I grow to love more and more. Farewell, and may you have a successful journey, which in that case must be a happy one. Everybody here sends you greetings. Marie has just taken Julie [1] to the *Luisenstift* [2] in Berlin, an excellent institution. The Empress got me a free scholarship there for her. She had spoken to

---

[1] Clara's granddaughter, her son Ferdinand's child.
[2] A charitable institution.

me about it during the summer at Ems.   But the parting
was hard.   Your old friend CLARA.

BRAHMS *to* CLARA.

VIENNA, *May* 5.

My journey is postponed again, but I think I shall leave
next Sunday and reach Verona at eleven o'clock on the evening of the 7th.   As you know I am travelling with my dear
friend, the poet Widmann of Berne.   Literally at the eleventh
hour, therefore, I shall be able to celebrate my birthday, for
I expect to find him there, and he will have the glass ready
in his hand !   As to the *Zigeunerliedern*, for the moment the
matter is off.   Simrock is here and I have allowed him to get
them out of me.   I should have liked you to see them beforehand, as usual, but it is perhaps better so.   In any case playing them through is not enough for you, and an experiment
with Stockhausen and the quartet would in all probability
have failed.   But remember me to Frl. Fillunger and tell her
that the songs will be ready, and will be delighted to be taken
by her on a journey to England in the autumn.   I do not think
that these rollicking and unpretentious pieces would altogether
please you, but you would have really enjoyed hearing them
sung, as they were the other day, at the *Tonkünstler-Verein*
by a really excellent quartet. . . .   With most affectionate
greetings, Your JOHANNES.

BRAHMS *to* CLARA.

THUN, *June.*

I received your kind birthday greeting while I was still in
Vienna and have since made the most beautiful of Italian
tours.   But the last is always the most beautiful. . . .   In
Widmann I had above all the most delightful of companions
and throughout the tour we again enjoyed glorious weather.
During the whole time we only had one little storm, and that
was just before leaving Rome, which cooled the air nicely for
the journey.   If you were to take your Gsell-fels, or whatever
other guide-book you use, in your hand I should only have to
tell you the names of the places we visited, and you would
be able to read about everything that I enjoyed.   I was able
to celebrate the last half-hour of my birthday in Verona.   Then

came Bologna (exhibition), Rimini (on the Adriatic), whence
we were able to visit the little republic of S. Marino, Ancona
(with an excursion to Loretto), Spoleto (with a visit up to
Montescasa [?]), Ferni (waterfall), Rome. Here we made the
most delightful excursions into the neighbouring country.

Richard Voss, the writer, lives at the Villa Falconieri at
Frascati (you may perhaps know Paul Heyse's last novel which
was written at the villa and was named after it). We went
to the old Greek theatre, etc., with Voss. Then Tivoli (again a
waterfall—but what a waterfall!) and then to the shores of
the Tyrrhenian Sea, to Porto D'Anzio and Nettuno. A few
days in Florence and then through the St. Gotthard. Here we
made a beautiful finale by getting out at Göschenen, staying
the night in Andermatt and then, for six or seven hours in
the morning, walking down the gorgeous Reusstal to Ersfeld.
Then to Berne and the day before yesterday, I alone here.

This is hardly a description of a journey, but with a guide-
book in your hand you can amplify it, and at the same time
think of two strong, hearty and impressionable fellows, who
throughout the whole journey enjoyed every minute of the
time, and had not a moment's annoyance. For instance, the
only insects they saw were the most beautiful glow-worms!

Although we never had to suffer from the heat I am nevertheless enjoying the coolness of early spring here. I hope
things are going well with you and that you are happy reeling
from one festival to another. What with openings and jubi-
lees,[1] I suppose the next thing will be a Raff monument. I
also hope you may have a nice quiet rest in the summer at
Berchtesgaden and wherever else you may go—why can it not
be Thun! With heartiest greetings to you and yours, Your
J. B.

CLARA to BRAHMS.
(*Dictated.*)

FRANKFORT A/M., *June* 8.

I was delighted with your letter, and above all to hear that
your journey had gone off so splendidly. . . . There is not
much news to give you about us. You already know that

---

[1] Held on the 28th of May to celebrate Stockhausen's forty years of
artistic life.

unfortunately I have been suffering a good deal with my rheumatism and long to be away, although I shall be sorry to leave our nice balcony and garden. I should like you to see the latter at this time of year, with all its fresh young green and its roses just blooming. Next week we shall be having a lot of music here. This time we have six examination concerts ; but there are one or two pupils who are a great joy to us, one in particular, who plays all your things in such a way that I very often listen not only with pleasure but with real emotion. This sort of thing makes up to one for many disappointments.

And now farewell, my dear Johannes. For the good of all I hope you will enjoy the summer very much. Everybody here greets you affectionately, and I above all, Your old friend Clara.

P.S. I was unable to write myself owing to rheumatism in my arm.

Brahms *to* Clara.

Thun, *June.*

. . . With the idea of seeing you there I had almost allowed myself to be lured to Stuttgart, but apparently I was right to be doubtful about it. You do not appear to be going there at all. But surely you are not holding the six examination concerts instead of it ! Good God, to think of all the bowings and scrapings connected with such functions ! Can't you get off with only one or two of them ? . . . Who is the excellent pupil of whom you write with such warmth and affection— surely not an Englishman ? I can well imagine your garden and how pleasant and beautiful it must be. How much I should like to have breakfast with you in it one of these days. With affectionate greetings, Your J. Br.

Clara *to* Brahms.
(*Dictated.*)

Frankfort a/M., *June* 14 (?).

I am not going to Stuttgart, but must go instead to Köstritz to see the doctor who is now looking after Ferdinand and consult him about the matter. Then I shall go on to Schnee-berg to see my niece and the three grandchildren who are living there. From there I shall go on to Franzensbad from

the 1st of July to about the 4th of August.   Perhaps you will
send me a card there occasionally.   It would please me immensely.   It was extremely hard for me to have to cancel
Stuttgart because I was very much looking forward to a few
pleasant days at the Pfeiffers, and also hoped to hear the *Peri*
performed again by good artists.   But after all I should have
had to pay for it with the *Parsifal* overture—what a combination !   By the time the *Peri* came to be performed I should
have been half dead !

I shall hardly be able to miss one of the examination concerts, first of all because the Director has distributed my own
pupils' performances over five concerts, and if I am to offend
nobody I must attend them all ; and secondly, because I also
feel in duty bound to show a little interest in the efforts of
my colleagues in the institution ; otherwise, as a rule, I avoid
the rehearsal evenings.   The young man about whom I wrote
to you is an Englishman after all, but one whom, if you knew
him, you would like.   Last night he played your Rhapsody in
B minor magnificently, and afterwards Liszt's Variations on
the *Hexenthema*.   He played both better than any of these
new virtuosos would have done. . . .

You will see from this dictation that I cannot write myself.
For weeks I have again been suffering acutely from rheumatism,
and could not be present at the opening of the new Conservatoire buildings the other day, which was a great disappointment to me.

Simrock has sent me the score and pianoforte arrangement
of your Concerto, which has pleased me very much.   So now
farewell.   I hope you are enjoying all the glories that surround
you.   May something glorious spring from it—a mating of art
and nature !   Your old friend CLARA.

CLARA *to* BRAHMS.
FRANZENSBAD, LOIMANN'S HYDRO, *July* 11.
You have perhaps been wondering why I have remained
silent so long regarding your dispatch of the double score [1] to
Müller.   But what a number of events have crowded into these
last few weeks !   What with preparations for our holiday,

[1] This appears to refer to Rbt. Schumann's D minor Symphony,
mentioned in Brahms' letter of April, 1880, *ante.*—TR.

excursions of all kinds and all manner of troubles, worries and sorrows, I have only to-day found sufficient peace of mind to thank you. We have been extraordinarily interested in the double score. Müller went through it with me bar for bar and was able to convince me that he had studied it carefully. But he seemed to think that the re-scored version was more brilliant and more effective, and found only a few passages in the andante and the scherzo more beautiful in the earlier version. He is not in favour of producing the first instrumentation, but, if I had the parts, he would gladly have the symphony played to me at a rehearsal. But to have the parts all copied out for this purpose seems to me an expensive business, so I shall have to resign myself to not hearing it, because I could not charge the Governing body of the Museum with all that expense just for one rehearsal. I am convinced that Müller has gone through the double score with great interest, but he could not agree with your view that the first version was more beautiful, and said that he would so much like some day to discuss the matter with you with the score before him. What shall I do with it ? Shall I—as I should prefer—keep it until you can fetch it yourself ? Do write and let me know. We have now settled down here into the same old watering-place routine. If only we had better weather so that we could be out in the open more ! The present weather is very bad for my rheumatic pains which are giving me great trouble.

I found Ferdinand looking well, but still only able to move about with great difficulty on two sticks. The doctor says that it is hardly possible that he will ever be able to resume his old activities again. Although I had always feared this it came as a great blow, and I cannot for the life of me, see how the poor fellow is to end his life. It is a desperate situation. I am now arranging for his wife and the two youngest children to move to a small town where living is cheap (as for him, he cannot go into the bleak atmosphere of Berlin and must in any case remain for some time longer under medical supervision). We found the three boys in Schneeberg lively and most lovable, but we are greatly preoccupied about their future. They must earn their living as soon as possible, for how could I afford to enable them to study, or how could my children do so after my death ? I can hardly afford what they cost me now. Their keep runs me into 2,000 marks [£100] a year for the three alone, and in addition I cannot reckon on less than 500 marks a month for Ferdinand. I have often wondered whether I could not sell my house and find a cheaper one, but I should hate to do this. I may have only a few more years to live and it is dreadful to have to retrench now. The children are constantly begging me not to do it ; but all this quite between ourselves, dear Johannes.

In addition to the above, I have now had another great blow. Fancy, Marie Wieck has just published a book under the name of Dr. Kohut for which she has paid him 300 marks and which she calls " *Friedrich Wieck und sein Leben und Kunstlerbild*," [1] and in it has given to the public a number of letters from me to my father and from Ernestine v. Fricken to me. And she has done this without asking me and without my even knowing that the letters were in existence. Isn't it most exasperating ? I might have had the book suppressed at once, but that would have led to litigation and to painful scenes with Marie and my mother, and although they have deserved it, I should not like this. The publisher has begged me most earnestly not to insist upon suppressing the book, and has promised me not to publish a second edition. My mother has also implored me in the same strain, constantly reminding me of her eighty-three years in so doing. . . .

But enough, I have bothered you too much about it already ! Though you can imagine how the matter is occupying my mind. . . . My arm warns me to stop. Farewell, dear Johannes. Let me hear from you soon. I shall remain here until the 4th of August, and then go to Pension Moritz, Obersalzberg, near Berchtesgaden. With affectionate greetings from the children and myself, Your old friend CLARA.

BRAHMS *to* CLARA.

THUN, *July* 24.

I was delighted by the very sight of your letter. " So much written by her own hand," thought I, " must mean that her rheumatism is better, and we ought to be pleased." Nevertheless I delayed answering your dear letter, for I had something on my heart and in my thoughts which I found it hard

[1] *Friedrich Wieck* : *His Life and Art.*

to tell you. But after all it cannot be helped. So summon up all your goodness of heart and your friendly feelings for me and listen, and then be kind and say " Yea." I feel the deepest concern for everything connected with you, as well as for all the anxieties and cares which cannot be excluded from a life so full as yours has been—but of which you have certainly had too great a share.

I do not take an exaggerated view of those smaller cares which are financial, but it annoys me that you should have such cares when all the time I am rolling in money which is no use to me and out of which I get no particular pleasure. But I cannot and do not wish to live any differently. It would be quite useless to give my relations more than I already give them, and when my heart bids me to do so I can help others to any extent and do them good without feeling it. After my death, however, there will be no obligations to fulfil and no particular wishes. In short the position is a simple one. All these days I have been turning over in my mind how in the world I could set about sending you a certain sum, whether I should do so as a rich artistic friend by means of an anonymous letter, or whether I should make a belated contribution to the Schumann Fund. But I should be unable to do either without drawing somebody so far into my confidence that he would be bound to guess the truth. If, however, you take me to be as good a man as I am, and if you are as fond of me as I should like you to be—then the second stage of the transaction would be quite simple and you would allow me without further ado to disburden myself of some of my superfluous pelf in order this year to contribute towards your expenses for the grandchildren the sum of about 10,000 marks [£500].

Simrock has again taken a whole heap of choral pieces, quartets and songs. But I shall not even notice the handsome fee that all this means. It simply slips silently and uselessly into the Reichsbank. Now just think how much pleasure these works and the fee would give me if you were just to send me a good clear " Yea " ! But as there are two sides to every question, I may tell you that in the event of an unfavourable reply I have made up my mind to instruct Simrock to pay the sum into the Schumann Fund. I shall deal with the rest of your letter in a few days. For the present I will only say that with regard to the Wieck affair I am in favour of the most complete silence. I should think the book would be so bad that it will hardly see the light of day. I cannot imagine what would have to be done to me to provoke me to make a public protest.

Apparently dear Frau Röntgen is just dead. Julius was with me a little while ago when a telegram came summoning him to Leipsic. As I say I shall write more later on. All I ask for to-day is that you will send me a friendly card and on it the one happy word for your then most happy JOHANNES.

CLARA *to* BRAHMS.

FRANZENSBERG, *July* 27.

What can I say to your friendly offer ? I could not help being deeply moved while reading your letter. Words sound so inadequate compared with what one feels at the moment, and all I can do is to press your hand affectionately and acknowledge that the assistance you offer has given me a sense of relief to which my heart has long been a stranger. But I cannot accept your dear offer for the moment ; it would not be right for me to do so, unless the need were really urgent. Thanks to what I earned in England last year and this, I have still a small sum available which will suffice for the present year, and in addition I have Elise who is giving me substantial help by defraying the expenses of educating one of the boys (her god-child). Moreover, I am still negotiating about the sale of Robert's MSS., and some settlement must be reached soon. So that for the time being there is no need for me to break into my capital. What I am chiefly troubled about is the future. For the prospects of earning money by giving concerts must grow ever less, while my expenses for Ferdinand's children must go on increasing. So this is my conclusion—as I do take you to be as good a man as you are, and since I am as fond of you as you would like me to be, I promise you to appeal to you without hesitation as soon as my anxieties become sufficiently pressing. Are you satisfied with that ? I hope so, and beg you to rely on this promise of mine and take no further steps. I shall close for to-day ; I am too much moved to be able to chatter. But this I shall do soon when we are in Obersalzberg, which we hope to reach on the 6th of August.

The children have asked me to tell you how much they appreciate your deep friendship for me. And so with the most affectionate greetings from three grateful hearts, I am Your faithful old friend CLARA.

BRAHMS *to* CLARA.

July.

I don't mind saying that I awaited your reply with some anxiety, and therefore immediately felt comforted and grateful to you. You decline my offer in such a friendly way that I suppose I must be pleased with you though I am not so pleased with myself. I ought to have managed the thing more cleverly, for here I remain shining with gold plate as I did before ! But seeing that you look at the matter so amiably and that, moreover, you must be in constant fear of my committing some blunder, you might just as well extend your kindness by sending me a hearty " Yea " ! ? ! ?

All this time I have been wanting to write to you in greater detail about the Symphony, but I hope to be able to discuss it with you some time with the score in front of us. You might keep this for the time being, although Wüllner was here the other day and begged me to let him have a look at it. Of course W. has more insight and better judgment than Müller. Unfortunately I do not like the Gürzenich for the production of the piece, and I don't expect that you would attend a rehearsal there. But perhaps you will see that the score is sent to Wüllner at your convenience. I hope you will be very happy once more in Berchtesgaden. There are two houses there which will always make you sad to look at ! I have not heard from the Herzogenbergs direct for a long time—I suppose one cannot expect any comforting news from that quarter. I hear that they are going to Baden-Baden later on. If you should see them there, please greet them most affectionately for me. I would write to them more often, but it is so dreadfully sad always to have to begin with the same questions in a minor key. But I have very little hope, and I am very unhappy at the thought of the worthy couple.

I shall probably be back in Vienna very soon. I should like to spend a few days in Berchtesgaden on the way, but this must depend upon circumstances. In any case you might send me a card to say whether I can stay at the Pension Moritz with you. I believe Frau Franz has actually invited me to stay with her, but I am not certain about it. Is her house very far from yours ? With affectionate greetings to you and the girls, ever Yours, JOHANNES.

CLARA *to* BRAHMS.

BADEN-BADEN, *Sept.* 25.

During my first few days at home it was impossible for me to find time to thank you for your kind birthday greetings, and that is why I do it from here. I am very much surprised that you should have returned to Vienna so soon, particularly as we are having such heavenly weather now. We often think of the September of last year ! This year everything is so quiet in the drawing-room—for we have no piano. But pupils enough are waiting for us at home. When we start there again it will be a very different story ! ! !

Please, dear Johannes, write and tell us exactly when and where you are coming into our part of the world. You will surely come to see us ? We return on Thursday, and then Eugenie will go to Munich to meet Ferdinand and take him to Meran for the winter. In this way he will at least enjoy a little warmth and will also be able to consult Oertel who is there.

I have nothing fresh to tell you. Everything pursues its normal course. So farewell, and awaiting a card from you soon, or better still, a letter, Your old friend CLARA.

BRAHMS *to* CLARA.

VIENNA, *Oct.* 3.

Do not be angry with me if I return to my old request. In the summer you refused my proffered assistance so kindly that, now we are both at home, I venture to ask you again. I ought perhaps to have set about the whole business more cleverly, but I am still at a loss to discover how.

If I wished to hide my identity in sending it I should have been obliged to get somebody to write the address, etc., and his suspicions would naturally have been aroused. So please consent, and let me lay 15,000 [1] (this includes simple and compound interest !) most respectfully at your feet. All I most earnestly beg of you is to send me a card to say it is lying there, but nothing more.[2] I know and think with pleasure on the conscientious way in which you are wading through your vast heap of birthday correspondence, and I can see it daily melting away beneath your industry. I also often like to think of you enjoying the beautiful autumn days and delighting in your comfortable house and charming garden. With affectionate greetings to you all, and begging you not to be angry but to take the thing quite kindly, Yours ever, JOHANNES.

CLARA *to* BRAHMS.

FRANKFORT A/M., *Oct.* 9.

The money is here and I stand before it not knowing what to do ! Give it back to you—how could I behave like that to a magnanimous friend ? Keep it—I cannot tell you what I feel about doing that, except that by taking it I show a trust in you which I would certainly not show to anyone else in the world !—

For the time being I shall put the money by and regard it as capital to be broken into and used for Ferdinand and his family without my having to feel that I am robbing the other children. This gives me a real sense of relief and I press your hand affectionately. There is sadness in my gratitude. I cannot tell you all that stirs my soul.

Shall we soon be seeing you here ? You hinted at so many things in your birthday card. If you have any engagements in this part of the world you will be sure to come and see us here, won't you ? . . . Farewell, dear Johannes ; let us hear from you soon. Ever your old friend CLARA.

---

[1] £750.

[2] Clara writes in her Diary : " We were taken completely aback. What was I to do ? Was I to send it back to a friend of so long standing ? That was impossible. I had to keep it and to thank him for it. There was nothing else to be done." See *Life*, Vol. II, p. 398.

CLARA *to* BRAHMS.

FRANKFORT A/M., *Oct.* 16.

I must send you a short but hearty letter of thanks to-day for your *Zigeunerlieder* which I at last heard yesterday most perfectly performed at Stockhausen's. Everyone sang with genuine enthusiasm—Fillu's voice and temperament suit the songs admirably, and I enjoyed them immensely. If only I could have heard them again to-day so as to get to know one or two of them more thoroughly and pick out my favourite. Thus the parcel from Simrock has been a double pleasure to me—I have just received everything, even the precious portfolios of songs. Unfortunately, however, the singing parts to the *Zigeunerlieder* are missing. Could you have them sent to me ? I should be glad if they could be sent off to-day. You have done so much, I know, to let me have these songs, that I am deeply grateful to you. Unfortunately I have no time for a chatty letter. Your old friend CLARA.

BRAHMS *to* CLARA.

VIENNA, *Oct.* 19.

The whole of the time and especially to-morrow all my thoughts will be with you. But what I should have liked above all would have been to celebrate your rare and beautiful festival [1] with you myself. I cannot help imagining the crowds of people, the many festive dinners and speeches, and though I am so far away, I shall be full of happy thoughts of you. All these things, however, I would gladly forego, but what is harder for me is not to be a silent spectator and listener, or, best of all, to follow you and your thoughts, instead of being alone here and forced to carry them silently in my mind. But you, great woman and artist that you are, must be rejoicing at the thought of the beautiful experiences you will have to-morrow, and blissfully calling to mind all the wonderful things which have brought you and your husband so much love.

Many thanks for your last letter and the one received to-day. I wrote to Simrock at once to send you the parts—I only hope you will use them. If Fillu is in the right mood she ought to sing the songs very well. . . . Yes, there is for instance

[1] The Diamond Jubilee of her artistic career.

also a little violin sonata [1]—but if it reached you what a
flood of letters I should immediately receive from Frankfort
and not merely from Myliusstrasse. So I hope that I shall
soon be able to start on my famous autumn travels, when
I can take it with me. Then I too should be glad to hear
the *Zigeunerlieder*. They must have been very beautifully
sung to have won your favour! With most affectionate
greetings, and best wishes for this and all other days, Your
JOHANNES.

BRAHMS *to* CLARA.

VIENNA, *Nov.* 2.

The violin sonata which I mentioned the other day I have
sent to the Herzogenbergs and I have received such an un-
expectedly kind letter about it, that I am now wondering
whether it might not please you too. I should like to take
it for granted that you wish to see it, and if you have the
time to do so, write to the Herzogenbergs so that they may
send it to you at once. Perhaps you would like to try it
with Koning or, as I hear that you are going to Berlin, with
Joachim when you are there. The Herzogenbergs have a
good legible copy together with the violin part. Forgive
me for not having sent you the sonata first, but you will
never believe my chief reason for not having done so. The
truth is I can never do a piece the credit of believing that
it can please anybody. I feel the same about this one, and
that is why I doubt very much whether you will agree with
Frau Herzogenberg's letter. If, however, the sonata does
not please you when you play it through, do not try it with
Joachim, but send it back to me. I hope your festival went
well and that you enjoyed it. I thought of you a great deal.
With most affectionate greetings to all, Your JOHANNES.

CLARA *to* BRAHMS.

FRANKFORT, *Nov.* 4.

Your letter of yesterday is a severe reminder of my debt
to you. Forgive me if I only thank you for your previous
letter to-day. You are well aware of all my responsibilities
and that I no longer have time for anything! In the first

[1] The D minor Sonata, Op. 108.

place let me tell you how very much I am looking forward
to the sonata and please urge Herzogenberg to send it to
me at once. It would be splendid if I could play it with
Joachim in Berlin ! If only it is not too difficult for me to
learn it before I go !

Everything here is over, and glad though I am that it is
over, I would not have missed a moment of it ! Unfortunately new troubles have again befallen me and this time
through Eugenie, who, as the result of Franzensbad, is not
at all well. It was too damp and cold there and she ought
never to have tried the cure. And now Ferdinand is giving
me fresh anxiety. On Oertel's advice he is being massaged,
but he writes that he is being brutally ill-treated, and that
ever since the massage began he has been quite unable to
walk. So I want to ask you a favour. The doctor in question—Dr. Schreiber—is well known in Austria and has a summer institute near Aussee. Could not you ask Billroth whether
he thinks he is reliable ? If this report is unfavourable you
may of course rely on my discretion. All I want is to see my
way clearly, as one cannot always believe the patient himself.

Antonie Speyer has recently sung all your new songs to
me, with some of which I am quite delighted—for instance,
numbers one, two and three in Op. 105, then in Op. 106, my
songs, and also *Maienkätzchen*. But many of them I must
hear often again. *Auf dem Kirchhof* [In the Churchyard]
is, in my opinion, very interesting, but too dreadfully sad !
To-day we are again going to hear the *Zigeunerlieder* at Stockhausen's (he is giving a song recital) which I am much looking
forward to. . . . I must now close and beg you, dear Johannes,
to let me have the Sonata quickly ! With affectionate greetings, Your old CLARA.

CLARA *to* BRAHMS.

FRANKFORT, *Nov.* 5.

I feel I must follow up my letter of yesterday with another,
as I must unburden my heart of the joy your *Zigeunerlieder*
have given me. I am quite delighted with them. How
original they are and how full of freshness, charm and passion ! How wonderful the voice progression is, so graceful
and interesting ! Their feeling is so varied that in spite of

the incessant 2/4 time one is not conscious of any monotony.
I will now tell you how it was that I did not enjoy them as
much the other day. While they sang with vivacity and
ease, Fillu and Kaufmann bewildered one so much in Stockhausen's small room that one could not enjoy the songs.
They were sung too loudly throughout. But yesterday in
the large hall everything went off much better; they had
studied the songs a little more and did greater justice to the
piano parts.

The enthusiasm was great and many of the songs had to
be repeated. Fillu sang with so much ease and spirit that
everybody said they had never heard her in such good form.
But you have probably had news of it all from Stockhausen
by telegram? Let me press your hand, dear giver of joys.
With heartiest greetings, Your old friend CLARA.

BRAHMS *to* CLARA.

VIENNA, *Nov.* 6.

Here is the report from Billroth. It is unfortunately not
favourable, and so you will have fresh anxiety. I have to
thank you very much for your dear letter. I was charmed
to hear that the *Zigeuner* had afforded you so much pleasure.
Please greet Frau Speyer for me and thank her for having
won your approval of my songs. . . . You would have
received the sonata a few days earlier if you had sent a card
direct to H. Please do not hesitate to say so if it does not
please you. The Herzogenbergs were somewhat starved and
were therefore easy to please. She has probably not played
with the violin for a long time. If you approve of it take
it with you to Berlin, but not otherwise. The Duke of Meiningen and his party are here and they want me to promise
faithfully to spend Christmas there. Joachim will be there
about the beginning of January and if I am anywhere in the
neighbourhood I shall come on to Myliusstrasse, which I
shall look forward to very much. I hope the Herzogenbergs
will not keep you waiting. Affectionately yours, JOHANNES.

CLARA *to* BRAHMS.

FRANKFORT A/M., *Nov.* 23.

I must let you know with my own hand how very much

I enjoyed your sonata last night (Elise and Koning played it to me).[1] There was only one shadow to mar my joy— I could not play it myself. What a wonderfully beautiful thing you have once more given us! What warmth, what depth of feeling, how thoroughly interesting from beginning to end! I thought the organ-point in the first movement magnificent; how beautifully it recurs at the end. I marvelled at the way everything is interwoven, like fragrant tendrils of the vine. I loved very much indeed (but what did I not love very much indeed?) the third movement, which is like a beautiful girl sweetly frolicking with her lover —then suddenly in the middle of it all, a flash of deep passion, only to make way for sweet dalliance once more. But what a melancholy atmosphere pervades the whole! The last movement is glorious, so full of varied emotion, one can really revel in it!

I am thinking with longing of the time when I shall be able to play it myself. Oh how hard such periods of privation are! I do not know what will happen about Berlin. For the time being I cannot think about playing, but on the advice of my doctor I have not yet cancelled the engagement. I shall work at the sonata as soon as I am able to do so. Elise played it remarkably well, by the by. I shall write to you as soon as anything is decided. Oh, and another thing—I hear from the Museum Committee that they want to have a private chamber concert if you come. If that is so please do not accept for the 27th to the 29th of January, because Fillu has to go to Münster on the 28th and so would not be able to sing the *Zigeunerlieder* here, which would be a terrible disappointment to her, besides being in any case a great pity, because no one here sings them anything like as well.

My arm is hurting me, but I could not dictate a letter about the sonata. Farewell. Thank you for everything. Your old CLARA.

[1] In a letter written on the 14th Clara told Brahms that although she had received the sonata, she could not play it owing to neuralgia in her arm.—TR.

CLARA *to* BRAHMS.

FRANKFORT, *Dec.* 4.

I have just heard that you have refused for the 28th, but the news has come to me at third hand and I don't know whether the entertainment has been postponed. Have they sent you no invitation to conduct your C minor Symphony ? It is on the list for this winter. The whole thing is such a muddle [1] ; we know nothing for certain and cannot find out, because everybody is completely taken up with great preparations for a charity concert for which rehearsals have been held every day for weeks, etc., etc. Please let me have a few words to tell me how matters stand ; but be quite clear, dear Johannes, so that I may know what I have to look forward to.

Unfortunately (forgive the accident with the ink) owing to my pains I have been obliged to cancel Berlin and shall probably postpone the concert to January. That is why I am most anxious to know when you are coming here. Thank God I have so far improved that I can at least play again. I have spent some happy half-hours just lately (I cannot stand anything longer) with your wonderful sonata, and at the end of the week I shall play it to one or two of the musicians here. To-day I had a rehearsal with Koning and we revelled in it. But it is a difficult piece and the last movement is particularly tiring for me because one is obliged to let oneself go to the end.

How wonderfully happy such beautiful music often makes me feel for hours—it is a real stroke of good fortune, for our misery is great. So farewell, dear Johannes. Let me have a cheering word from you soon. Your old CLARA.

Forgive my shocking writing. Writing is becoming so hard for me.

CLARA *to* BRAHMS.

FRANKFORT, *Dec.* 9.

According to your card I take it that I may keep the sonata. Yesterday I played it at my house to a large number of musi-

---

[1] The German word is *Schwüle*, which means stifling heat, and figuratively, anxiety. As this could not have been intended, and the editor queries it, I have made the above guess at the writer's meaning.—TR.

cians and they were all enthusiastic. And yet no one can have had such joy over it as I had, for it was a twofold pleasure, first there was the work itself, and secondly I was so happy at being able to play it myself ; for only a few days previously I had had such a severe recurrence of pain in my shoulder that I was afraid I should be obliged to cancel the evening. I believe it was my fear of not being able to play after all that brought on the pain. If I had anything left to wish it was that Joachim might have been there, and that was certainly—a good deal ! . . . But I hope soon to have the pleasure of playing it with J. and that is what I joyfully look forward to every time I think of the sonata. . . . If only I could write to you about everything, but soon I shall be seeing you, and it will be so much easier to talk than to have to bring on the pain in my arm ! I am waiting for your reply about your arrival here and the Museum. It would be splendid if you were to conduct your D minor Symphony here. Please do ! And now adieu ! Shall I sing the praises of the dear composer—surely they can be taken for granted ! Your old friend CLARA.

BRAHMS *to* CLARA.

VIENNA, *Dec.* 14.

I hope you will be satisfied and that it will be sufficient if for the moment I tell you that I expect to be able to come on the 11th of January. As soon as I can let you know anything definite I will certainly do so.

But why is it to be a Brahms evening this time ? Neither for myself nor for anybody else is this either necessary or desirable. At all events the brutal clarionet quintet would not do. I hope for the first item they will choose some beautiful chamber-music piece ; for the second, a ditto song (*ensemble*), for the third my sonata, and for the fourth the *Zigeuner*. If you have the time and your arm allows of it, you would do me a great pleasure if you played the sonata now with Heermann. At any rate I am invited to play with him, and it would be a good thing if he had some previous acquaintance with the piece and knew a little bit about it.

Besides, if by any chance I were not to come to Germany, it would not be such a dreadful misfortune either for Frankfort or for the evening in question. In the end you would play the sonata in my stead, and I alone would suffer the extreme annoyance of not being able to listen to you. With heartiest greetings, Your JOHANNES.

CLARA *to* BRAHMS.

FRANKFORT, *Dec.* 17.

Enclosed I am sending twenty florins and beg you to be so kind as to buy cigars for Ferdinand's Christmas present with them. They are frightfully dear and bad in Meran. Choose a mild brand and not too good, as Ferdinand does not care so much about quality as about quantity. Not knowing much about it I would suggest that you should pay from ten to twelve pfennigs apiece and have them sent direct from the shop to Herrn Ferdinand Schumann

Villa Regina, Ober-Mais, Meran, South Tyrol.

I should think if they were sent off on Saturday they would reach him exactly on Christmas Day. If they should cost one florin more or less it doesn't matter, I cannot say exactly what they will be.

Your short note was distressing. We were again at a loss to know what to do and I have now placed everything in the hands of Dr. Spiess. Let us hope that the matter will be arranged to everybody's satisfaction. I gave Heermann his part for the sonata and will practise it with him in a day or two. Adieu for to-day, we are frightfully busy. With heartiest greetings and best thanks in advance for all your trouble, Your old friend CLARA.

BRAHMS *to* CLARA.

VIENNA, *Dec.* 22.

Just a line to wish you all very briefly but very heartily the happiest of Christmases. . . . I suppose I am not expected to go on answering ever further letters from the Museum Directors ? I wonder whether you would be so kind as to discuss with one of these gentlemen what I have already written to you. We cannot begin with the sonata, and the E minor Quintet is not suitable for the programme. It seems to me that the best thing would be a fine string quartet or quintet to begin with, then a song solo or quartet, then the sonata, and last of all the *Zigeuner*.

The cigars, which I did my best about, were sent off to Ferdinand yesterday evening, but if, in spite of everything, he should not be satisfied with them, don't be surprised. For I think there must be some misunderstanding behind it all. Where he is he has the same Austrian cigars as we have here, and he probably does not care for them very much. The brands are the same here as there, but it is just possible that the quality here is better. But there, let us hope that he won't take it too much to heart! I have sent him three different brands, two hundred and fifty cigars in all, and in addition to that he has beautiful scenery.—What more does he want?

I have just read in an essay by Kalbeck (which by-the-by is very fine) that your husband had made a note of the title "*Deutsches Requiem*." This is something quite new to me and I don't suppose you knew it either, at least you never mentioned it!?

But now *au revoir!* From the New Year onwards my address is Meiningen, but a little later on, 32 Myliusstrasse, which is very much being looked forward to by Your JOHANNES.

1889

BRAHMS *to* CLARA.

MEININGEN, Jan. 5.

DEAR CLARA,

I intend to reach Frankfort at 8.15 on Monday evening.
I suppose there will be a bit of supper left for me ? I shall
be ready for Heermann at any time on Tuesday either at
his place or yours. If you see him will you please ask
him ? Ditto for Stockhausen's quartet. Joachim left
yesterday evening, that is earlier than he had intended.
It was all owing to a telegram announcing the death of
Frau Franz Mendelssohn whose funeral he wanted to attend
to-day.

Oh how I wish you could have spent the last few days
here with us ! You would have loved it. At the concert
d'Albert played my D minor and Joachim and Hausmann
my Double Concerto. Both went excellently. Yesterday
at a rehearsal Joachim played Beethoven's Concerto and mine
quite magnificently. During his stay he also gave us the
Chaconne, the F major Suite by Bach and my new sonata,
trio, etc. In short it was a very mixed but sumptuous menu.
I believe the guests here enjoyed it very much and you would
have done so too. The only thing that makes it difficult
for you is the tiresome journey. Otherwise I would always
try to entice you to come. (I think it is rather amusing
that the Duke could not make up his mind whether to send
Hausmann an order of Knighthood of the First or the Second
Class, and that I was able to help in getting him the former.)
But on Monday evening we shall be able to talk. So addio
for to-day, and with most affectionate greetings to all, Your
JOHANNES.

CLARA *to* BRAHMS.

FRANKFORT, *March* 4.

DEAR JOHANNES,

It passes my comprehension why I have heard nothing from you since you left.[1] You only gave me one sign of life and that was through the Press. I thank you for this, but it does not suffice me, although I read it with great interest. Hanslick writes delightfully about the sonata which, as Joachim must have told you, I played with him twice running before a company consisting chiefly of musicians.[2] I was very sorry Joachim had to leave, otherwise we would have given a chamber-music evening where we should certainly have played the sonata, which I should have enjoyed very much ; and Joachim could so easily have stayed, when lo, the affair of the Crown Prince intervened ! In an hour I shall be going to Leipsic for a concert and hope to be back here on Saturday. But tell me, dear Johannes, are you put out with me about anything, or perhaps a letter has been lost ? Everybody here greets you affectionately, but above all Your old friend CLARA.

LEIPSIC, *March* 7.

Here is another greeting from Leipsic. My letter was left in my writing-case through some oversight and came along with me here. Meanwhile I have definitely heard that you were in Berlin for the Jubilee, and I am heartily glad for Joachim's sake—I should have been delighted to have been there too, but the day for such things is past. . . . I am playing here to-day. Yesterday at the rehearsal there was great enthusiasm. I hope I shall play as successfully again to-day. Addio, and please let me have news soon. I hope to be back in Frankfort on Saturday.

BRAHMS *to* CLARA.

VIENNA, *March* 15.

I wish I could convince myself that a letter had been lost. Unfortunately I remember only too well how often during all this time I have wished and even made up my mind to

---

[1] Concerning Brahms' stay in Frankfort (Jan. 7–12) see *Life*, Vol. II, p. 400.

[2] This was at Levy's in Berlin.

write to you. So many things of more than usual interest
have occurred about which I have wanted to talk to you,
and now I envy you your diary. I have not the smallest
note to remind me of any particular day or of what it might
have meant or brought to me. I was positively ashamed
yesterday when I found your kind letter awaiting me here.
That is all I wish to say for the present apart from thinking you for it, and to-morrow it is to be hoped that I shall
be able to tell you more, even if it is only quite briefly. I
heard of your trip to Leipsic in Berlin. Your host gave me
his blessing and a part of my audience went off to Leipsic—
Fräulein Wendt and her friend.

But you and your present biographers are mistaken when
they think that this was the first time you did Chopin's F
minor Concerto the honour. For you also played it in Leipsic,
for instance on the 14th of March 1852.[1] If, as I say, I am
able to write to-morrow, as I hope, I shall have to begin with
Frankfort and say how delightful it was there and how happy
and pleased I was as I looked back on it during my journey.
For to-day let my affectionate greetings suffice, Your J. B.

BRAHMS *to* CLARA.

VIENNA, *March* 19.

Instead of sending you a chronicle of the last few months
I am going to give you a piece of news. It is quite probable
that I shall be leaving for Sicily in a week (Wednesday the
27th). Professors Barbieri, Billroth and Exner are prevailing
upon me to join them on this beautiful journey. I was badly
tempted to resist them in view of your intended sojourn in
Florence. But I thought to myself it was highly improbable
that you would decide to come. But if I allow my thoughts
to dwell on all that has taken place since January, the most
pleasing and most important experience of all is to have
seen you so completely unchanged and just the same as you
always have been to me. You can picture all my other
experiences as having been as pleasant and enjoyable as
you choose.

Joachim was more affable and friendly than usual and,
owing to the enforced period of inactivity, we had a very

[1] Clara had already played it in 1840.

pleasant time together.   Just as we were going to his first
orchestra rehearsal the news flew round that the Crown Prince
was dead.   The whole orchestra had assembled, but the
rehearsal and the concert did not take place.   Unfortunately
Joachim is one of those who follows the reprehensible practice of arranging programmes that are too long and too
strenuous.

I enjoyed myself in various ways in Berlin but particularly
at the theatre.   The Joachim festival [1] was very dignified
and beautiful, but the music for the occasion was nothing
out of the way.   His Overtures to Hamlet and Heinrich
were distinctly mediocre.   On the other hand, I heard a very
interesting and beautiful sacred concert under his direction,
with three cantatas by Bach and two by Schütz.

In Hamburg I had the peculiar good fortune to enjoy a
few days of very fine weather.   The people were the same
as ever and a few were not unpleasant.   I thought Frau
Sauermann quite unchanged, she looked well and was most
agreeable.   My sister is very well and has a charming home.
I visited my step-mother and brother in Pinneberg, where
they live very quietly and happily.   If you could tell me
anything definite about your visit to Florence I should be
very glad.   Perhaps on my return journey I shall be able to
see you.

The violin sonata is already engraved and you will soon
have a printed copy.   With most affectionate greetings, Your
Joh.

BRAHMS *to* CLARA.

VIENNA, *April.*

I must let you know that I have not gone off with the rest
to Sicily.   Thus Eugenie's letter found me here, and I was
able to execute her commission in the most brilliant manner
—unfortunately, however, Richter is not producing the Ninth
Symphony in London this year.

I had been wishing that one other very special travelling
companion might have joined the distinguished trio on the
journey to Sicily.   I had hoped that Widmann of Berne
would be a member of the party.   But he is now just off to

[1] His jubilee as an artist.

Berlin, etc. So I have let the distinguished trio go alone ; for they long passionately to be rid of Vienna and their laboratories and their clinics, whereas I rejoice in the early days of spring here. Moreover, since his illness the sight of Billroth disturbs me, 'pon my soul I don't like the look of him, and when he makes an effort to appear bright and in good spirits it makes one's heart sink !

Heermann is coming soon and I understand that his wife is coming also. I hope that he has done well in the province and that the two concerts here will not be too much of a disappointment to him. Yesterday I had a telegram from Billroth in Taormina, and I could not help thinking with some irritation that I should have preferred to hear the station called out by the guard. I wonder whether you, and therefore whether we, are going to Florence. Billroth also asks in his telegram when and where we shall be in Florence. Enough for to-day. With most affectionate greetings, Yours ever, JOHANNES.

CLARA *to* BRAHMS.

NICE, *April* 23.

At last I am able to tell you that we are actually in Italy [1] and have had the pleasure of seeing a great deal of the Herzogenbergs here. . . . I am now wondering very much whether you are going to Florence. Write to me there *poste restante*. Many thanks for your last letter. I wanted to be able to tell you something definite first. That is why I did not write sooner. We found poor Herzogenberg very much altered. His leg is of course quite stiff, and so is his neck, which hampers him very much in talking as he cannot turn his head round. He says, however, that he is quite well and hopes gradually to lose the stiffness in his neck. I cannot help feeling sad at the sight of him—the poor, dear people ! I suppose you know that Woldemar is now officially installed in Herzogenberg's place. H. retains only the *Meisterschule*, but he wants to go to Berlin all the same next winter. Farewell, dear Johannes. Write soon to Your old friend CLARA.

---

[1] On the 14th of April Clara, with her two daughters, had started on her long-contemplated visit to Italy, from which she returned on May the 20th.

Brahms *to* Clara.

VIENNA, *End of April.*

If I am in no great hurry to go to Florence it is chiefly because I am hoping to see you all and the Herzogenbergs more easily in the summer, for I have taken rooms in Ischl and I suppose I may reckon with absolute certainty on being able to pay you a visit in Berchtesgaden. I should also feel very anxious to go to Florence if the Herzogenbergs were not there. I should like to be your guide and companion. But for both of these functions they are far better fitted than I.

Nevertheless, it would be a great pleasure to me to be at your side when you stand happily admiring the marble wonders of Pisa and Florence. I am particularly glad that you are in the habit of noting down what you have done every day, so that when I come to Berchtesgaden I shall be able to hear an exhaustive account of all you have seen. I don't suppose the Herzogenbergs will remain long in Florence. Were they not to go *via* Graz and Vienna to Berchtesgaden ? I should be very glad to see them in Graz. Your lady friends here had been staking too confidently on your taking Vienna on your way back. But this will hardly be possible if you have taken a tourist ticket in Chiasso. I don't believe that you will pass through Vienna ; but should the Herzogenbergs come either here or to Graz, I must implore them to let me know as early as possible. So long as I am here I can easily go to Graz and should be glad to do so. Your news about Woldemar has pleased me very much for his sake. All kind messages to the Herzogenbergs, and I hope that you will enjoy all the beauties there very much. I am constantly with you in my thoughts. Most affectionately yours, JOHANNES.

Clara *to* Brahms.

FLORENCE, *May* 5.

This time your birthday greetings are really coming from Italy. You know what they are—the best and sincerest of good wishes. I received your dear letter here. I really hardly expected that you would make your way here at once. Glad as I should have been to have you here I should also have worried a little, because you, with all your youthful strength, would never have been able to grasp how little I could do with you. I have to forgo many things, and am only able to enjoy very little, as I can neither stand nor walk for long at a time. But I have seen some magnificent sights already, although I firmly believe that one must first become accustomed to the country. What are ten days in Florence ? And unfortunately we cannot have longer, because we are unlucky enough to have a tourist ticket and must be back in Chiasso at a definite time. I was ill for three days on the Riviera which has curtailed our stay in Florence. It was extremely beautiful in Pisa. The cathedral delighted me. Inside I liked it better than the one here, but outside I prefer this one. The pine woods by the sea-shore were entrancing in the beautiful weather we had for the drive there. But I will tell you more about it all I hope soon in Obersalzberg. It is nice to know that you are at last going to pay us a visit there. The Herzogenbergs are going to " Liselei " ; they only arrived here yesterday and I shall not see them until to-morrow, when I shall give them your message at once. But if this note is to reach you in time it must be posted to-day. My brain is somewhat bewildered by all I have seen in these two short days here. Hildebrandt took us round yesterday and to-day we are waiting for him again. What has impressed me most so far has been Luca della Robbia's Madonna, the Michelangelos in the Medici Chapel and the Piazza Michelangelo, which is really magnificent, and—but I will tell you more by word of mouth soon. Ever your old friend CLARA.

BRAHMS *to* CLARA.

VIENNA, *End of June.*

I have been wanting to know for a long time how you are feeling after all your exertions in Italy and how your plans for the summer are shaping. It was always a pet wish of mine that you should see Italy, and yet I am glad not to have been with you this time. On your account I should not have been satisfied, because with your years and strength you cannot afford to merge yourself heartily into the life there. But you must certainly have formed some idea of how enjoyable travelling and sojourning in that country is when neither time nor strength need be spared. You have of course heard that they have conferred upon me the Freedom of the City of Hamburg. All that happened before, during and after the ceremony was as pleasant as the fact itself. My first thought on such occasions is of my father, and the wish that he might have been there. Fortunately he left this world contented without knowing all this. My second thought is of the letters which such an affair entails, and which consume more time and good spirits than they should. Yesterday and to-day unexpected and mysterious telegrams and cards have been pouring in from Vienna and Austria which make me scent some Austrian decoration in the air.[1] But this time I am only concerned about the letters of thanks it will entail! I expect in any case I shall have to go to a music festival at Hamburg at the beginning of September, more particularly as three short double choruses of mine are going to be produced *a capella*—*Deutsche Fest*— or *Gedenksprüche*,[2] something suitable for a national festival or commemoration, such as Sedan, etc., (with glorious scriptural texts).

But do let me hear from you some time and tell me how you found the Herzogenbergs. I was very pleased to think that you had them and Hildebrandt for company in Florence. What I could not understand, however, was your staying in Florence in that heat and then making the sudden change to Berchtesgaden. With affectionate greetings, and hoping you will find a few minutes to write, Your JOHANNES.

CLARA *to* BRAHMS.

FRANKFORT A/M., *July* 4.

I will no longer delay sending you my heartiest congratulations, but I must postpone a more detailed letter till I reach Franzensbad. Here I am so deluged with not particularly pleasant duties and correspondence that I cannot find a moment of leisure to write to you *con anima*.

Suffice it to say that we are going to Franzensbad on the 10th or 11th of this month, to Vordereck in the middle of

[1] This refers to his being made Commander of the Order of Leopold.
[2] Op. 109.

August, and to Baden-Baden in the second week of September.
But where in the world shall we see you ? The Herzogenbergs are not going to *Liselei* after all, as all their friends have
strongly advised them not to do so on account of the damp.
The three Keller sisters have taken it again. Herzogenberg
is convinced that he will be able to accept a post again in
Berlin, but I don't think the idea is a happy one. I don't
believe he will stand it and in his place and in his condition,
which is pitiful to behold, I would not again undertake any
public activity. He can walk, and does so with the greatest
energy for hours. He is massaged daily, which tires him
dreadfully, but his movements in walking are terrible and he
cannot turn his neck freely—he is in fact a broken man. He
feels he must be in Berlin on account of his compositions
which he says he must hear, and this he cannot do in Italy,
although the climate there is the one he ought to live in.
But will he in the long run be able to do so in Germany ?
We ought to make inquiries about it. But one cannot ask
him, of course. Latterly I have had no news, but have
heard that the Herzogenbergs were going to Reichenhall
where I hope to see them on my way from Franzensbad to
Vordereck.

Here everything is very quiet. Everybody is away. I
shall be glad when we too are free from all the worries of the
house. Where shall we see you ?

5th/7/89. I have kept this letter back and now avail
myself of a free half-hour to write you more. In regard to
Italy, which now already lies months behind us, let me tell
you that on looking back the place I most love to dwell upon
is Florence. Unfortunately while I was there I was so dreadfully hampered by my physical disabilities that I could not
stand more than five minutes before any picture. But Hildebrandt helped me very much in the most charming way.
He not only took us direct to the most important works of
art everywhere, but also carried a little stool about for me
wherever we went. One of the greatest pleasures I had was
getting to know his home life (there is something ideal about
it). I have brought a few beautiful Madonnas back with
me from Florence and have put them up so that I am daily
reminded of the originals. It was very silly to have gone

to the Riviera first, another time I shall go direct to Florence.
I really went to the Riviera with the idea of quickly getting
rid of a wretched cough which harassed me particularly at
the beginning and the end of the day. But it was so windy
the whole of the time that the air did not help me a bit. The
present continuous heat alone has done me good. I cannot
remember ever having experienced such a summer.

I was overjoyed at the honours that have been showered
upon you. But I do not understand about the Freedom of
the City of Hamburg. Surely you are by right a citizen of
Hamburg ? I was also pleased that the order was " conferred
on you alone." How delighted your father would have been
if he had lived to see all this ! But you are right, he had
many joys without experiencing this one—joys which no
honours can outweigh. Jansen is bothering me again with
letters. He now wishes to publish Robert's collected writings
with an introduction, but says there are so many mistakes
in the text that I suppose we must conclude that Robert
was never able to correct the proofs. I am so sick of all these
demands from biographers, including the Wieck business
for instance, that I should prefer to tell him not to worry
me with such matters. And yet on the other hand I don't
like definitely to refuse him all help as I am not certain whether
his demand is not after all justified. Would you be so good
as to read the long letter through and send it back to me
with your opinion ? It is very tedious for you, but just do
it when you are resting ; tedium is very helpful at such times.
And now let me conclude, for out of a few words this letter
has grown into a long one, although there is little in it. But
my head is so full of troubles and worries that you must be
lenient with Your ever devoted CLARA.

The children send you greetings. Eugenie is going to Bâle
and on to Mayence with Fillu. She succeeded beyond all
expectations in London and I hope that she has found a per-
manent source of livelihood there.

BRAHMS *to* CLARA.

ISCHL, *July*.

I think you might tell Herr Jansen freely and openly how
delighted you are with his industry, zeal and interest, and

that you will be agreeable to anything he may suggest,[1] in a general way, which you yourself have duly considered. You will, however, add that you are absolutely compelled once and for all definitely to decline any direct participation in his work in any way whatsoever, whether in regard to detail or general considerations. Every single question he puts to you is bound to give you more trouble than you, with your complicated life and the enormous demands that are made upon your time, can possibly put up with. In short, it is impossible, and I think you must ask him not to try to persuade you to play the smallest part in the matter. I enclose Jansen's letter. Just glance casually at it and try to form some clear conception as to how long it would take you to answer every one of his questions, to how many friends you would have to apply for information, in how many cupboards you would have to rummage, or how much you would have to leave to unreliable memory.

On the other hand, it might be possible to suggest to the good industrious fellow that, if his time and circumstances allow of it, he might come to stay at Frankfort a little while, and then you could throw open the cupboards in question for his benefit and place books and documents at his disposal, and even perhaps give him a little room to work in. I would also allow him to take certain things away, etc. This seems to me the utmost you can undertake to do and it is a good deal for him and as much as he can expect. But let me beseech you only to skim the letter full of questions from him and similar ones from other people, with the firm resolve not to give them a moment's thought.

The Herzogenbergs were here for a day. They will also remain in Reichenhall only for a day and then go for a longer period to Baden-Baden. They are not really thinking seriously about Berlin but rather of Wiesbaden. One's pleasure in the man himself is considerably reduced, if not entirely obliterated by the composer. I would like to get the better of the latter some time if I could only get him alone, but his wife is always there and one really doesn't know what to talk

[1] This refers to the Fourth Edition of Schumann's *Collected Writings about Music and Musicians*, with Appendix and Notes by F. Gustav Jansen (published by Breitkopf & Härtel, 1891).

about. On this particular occasion I heard a symphony
and a trio for cl., hautbois and horn. If I had been alone
with him I should have liked to discuss it with him quite
freely.

Incidentally, I was not a citizen of Hamburg but the son
of a burgher of that town. The distinction is a rare one,
I am number thirteen. The first were Blücher and Tetten-
born, the last Bismarck and Molkte. You might like to
read the short texts to my choruses, more particularly the
third, which ought to please you. As I find they have been
printed in a newspaper I am enclosing a cutting.

I greet you most affectionately and hope that the summer
will continue as beautiful as it has been up to the present.
When last I wrote to you the flood of congratulatory letters
had just started, but this time I may say I have really answered
them all with appropriate thanks. With affectionate greetings, Your JOHANNES.

CLARA *to* BRAHMS.

FRANZENSBAD, *Aug.* 12.

First of all my somewhat belated thanks for your kind
letter and good advice about Jansen. After a struggle I
followed it and now feel very much relieved. . . . We have
been here a month and are thinking of leaving at the end of
this week, but unfortunately not for Obersalzberg but direct
for Baden-Baden. We have left it so late this year that to
take the long journey there for a fortnight only would be
unreasonable. So we shall go on Sunday to Baden, and
if it is very warm we shall make excursions to the Schwarz-
waldberge, Plättis or Herrenalb. We want to explore a bit
for once. I don't know it—the Schwarzwald—at all. But
I cannot tell you how reluctant I am to have to give up our
usual delightful visit to Salzberg.

At present I am getting no direct news from the Herzogenbergs but shall probably meet them in Baden. Just
fancy what extraordinary people they are—not long ago
they were at *Liselei* for the first time since he fell ill and they
immediately gave a musical evening (you know that the
Keller sisters live in the house ?). But what nerves they
must have ! How their souls must have been stirred on

re-entering this "home" which was built with all their love, and which they had left with their hearts full of hope ?

Here is a whole sheet already covered, and I have not yet given you my heartiest congratulations. I had no idea that such an honour had been conferred upon you in the Freedom of the City of Hamburg. I thought the honour fell rather to Hamburg. But you may well be satisfied with the company you are in. So you are going there in the autumn ! But why aren't you conducting your choruses yourself ? I can see no reason for your not doing so. Once more you have shown good taste, particularly with the text of the last one. I am not quite sure about the first, as to whether it is quite up to date ; is it not too far removed from us ? Frau von Beckerath paid me a visit the other day. She was naturally very sad but very sympathetic with others notwithstanding. Lübke was also here for a week. He called on me once or twice and each time we had pleasant and stimulating conversation. What is going to happen this summer ? Are we going to see each other ? Or will the winter forestall us ? I almost fear it will, as I have not been to Obersalzberg where you could so easily have visited me. Please write to me about your plans, *poste restante*, Baden-Baden. Farewell, dear Johannes, Your old friend CLARA.

BRAHMS *to* CLARA.

ISCHL, *Sept.* 3.

Would you mind sending me a line to the Petersburger Hof, Hamburg. I am on my way there and would be glad to know how long you are remaining in Baden (whether you are there at all ?), where you are staying and when you will be back in Frankfort. We shall have our last concert in Hamburg precisely on the 13th. I send you my heartiest wishes [1] already and I may possibly repeat them on the 15th. That would be very nice indeed, but for the moment I am feeling very peevish at having to go to Hamburg to-morrow. I heard definitely the other day that the Herzogenbergs were going to Berlin after all in the middle of September, but I might yet meet them in Baden perhaps if I came there.

With what childish amusement I wiled away the beautiful

[1] For Clara's seventieth birthday.

summer days you will never guess. I have re-written my B major Trio and can call it Op. 108 instead of Op. 8. It will not be so wild as it was before—but whether it will be better—— ? If little Joachim and Hausmann happen to be knocking about Baden we might perhaps try it some time. I feel certain that you will have remained quietly at Baden and have enjoyed the loveliest weather there. Forgive me for not having answered your dear letter by another one— but I am peevish and can only hope that by way of exception I shall have fine weather even in Hamburg, and that I shall be able to be with you for a few days in Baden. In any case let me have a line. Affectionately yours, JOHANNES.

CLARA *to* BRAHMS.
                    BADEN-BADEN, 37 SOPHIENSTRASSE, *Sept.* 7.
I am delighted at the prospect of seeing you here, but please try to postpone your visit a day or two. As it happens the 15th will be rather inconvenient as Marie is going to Frank-fort on that day, or on the morning of the 16th, and Eugenie and I will then move to the Park Hotel to be with the Sommer-hoffs. They are coming on the 13th and will stay a long time, and I shall be with them until the 28th. So if you came on the 15th you would find us in the middle of moving and also mourning the loss of Marie which will seem to us harder than if she were going to another place—for she is going to shoulder the burden of domestic worries while we remain here amid all the delights of nature ! ! ! In any case you would no longer find the Herzogenbergs on the 15th, for they are leaving on the 14th. Possibly too Woldemar will be here, he comes on the 13th. So please try to arrange to come a few days later. I think you would find us happily settled down again on the 17th.

Unfortunately no Joachims or Hausmanns are wandering about here, and one cannot even play a sonata with either the one or the other. How then could we think of a trio ? Your news surprised us all very much—I cannot believe it yet, and I cannot help thinking you are playing a joke on us and that with your B major as Op. 108 you are present-ing us with a new trio. In any case we are very anxious to hear it. The Engelmanns, who stayed with the Herzogenbergs for a couple of days, heard of it with great interest, as you may imagine. We were all delighted with their visit. It was most enjoyable. They are such charming people.

We have already been here a fortnight and have taken private rooms, which I am loath to leave for other accommodation. But the Sommerhoffs live so far away from us (they have the house the Flemmings [1] used to live in opposite Frau Viardot's villa) that it is very inconvenient. This week Mr. Burnand is coming with his two nieces from England, so that it will be a busy week, although I shall be very pleased to see him again.

Please let me hear what you have decided to do. You have a lovely time before you, and how interesting it will be from the musical point of view—oh, if only I could hear your choruses from some dark corner! How splendidly they will fête you! So please send me a card to tell me what you decide. Always your old, literally old, friend CLARA.

CLARA *to* BRAHMS.

FRANKFORT A/M., *Nov.* 2.

How long have I not been wanting to write to you, but I had so many letters to attend to after my birthday that this is the first moment I can really say I am free of them. But now my load of gratitude for your dear visit is weighing me down.[2] But you don't mind accepting my thanks a little bit late in the day, do you? I was only sorry that owing to the bad weather you were able to enjoy the country so little, for I, alas, am such a simple creature and have so little to give—at most a piece or two on the piano. And this I did yesterday when I met with an enthusiastic reception with your Third Sonata. We (Heermann and I) played it at the Chamber Music Evening at the Museum, and once more I enjoyed it thoroughly and thought of you with a heart overflowing with gratitude. What a magnificent piece this sonata is! It made me feel how vigorously my pulse still beats to something really beautiful!

[1] Count Flemming, the Prussian ambassador.
[2] He came on the 20th of September and among other things played her his B major Trio, the *Dedenksprüche* and a few motets. See *Life*, Vol. II, p. 403.

What about your trio ? Are you going to play it to us here ? The Museum Directors, so I understand, would very much like to ask you to do so, but they dare not. They would also like you to conduct one of your own symphonies (the E minor), but apparently you were somewhat short in your refusal to do so last year ! If I knew that you would like to play your trio here I would tell the gentlemen, but of course only on condition that it was quite certain. I am longing to hear from you. Let me have a kind word soon. Your old friend CLARA.

Both the girls send greetings. Widmann has very kindly sent me his novel.[1]

BRAHMS *to* CLARA.

VIENNA, *Nov.*

It is really too lovely and delightful to think of my D minor Sonata flowing gently and dreamily beneath your fingers. As a matter of fact I laid it on my desk and in my thoughts wandered gently with you through the maze of organ-points. With you still beside me, and I know no greater pleasure than this, to sit at your side, or, as now, to walk beside you. . . .

But now I must tell you something for your worthy Museum Directors, which I will ask you to be good enough to pass on for me some time. How gladly would I play my trio there, for it would be a sign that it still pleased me a little. Unfortunately, however, it does not please me at all—not in the least, and as I have not this pleasure I must renounce the other one.

So we had better leave the Fourth Symphony also to the old fellow. In any case he will practise it with more zeal and affection than I should, and the fact that the musicians are animated by a strange conductor is only half the pleasure, the other half is taken up by the thought of the old fellow, etc.

Did you hear that the other day Wüllner (before the Faust) played Schumann's Fourth Symphony in the first version ? It pleased him very much and he is thinking of writing to Härtels about it. If the latter wished to publish it, would

[1] She had become acquainted with him through Brahms in Baden-Baden.

you have any objection ?   And in that case would you mind
if W. saw to it ?   He is a most excellent editor, as he has
often proved (for instance, in the large Bach Edition).

You ought really to hear some time how musical methods
have changed in Cologne ! Wüllner may soon be able to
let you hear my *Gedenksprüche* and other motets sung, and
very beautifully too, I am sure.   I am just engaged in getting
everything ready to send him.

At the present moment we are living under the shadow
of the phonograph and I have had the opportunity of hearing
it often and quite pleasantly. You must have read enough
about this new miracle or have had it described to you.   It
is like being in fairyland again. To-morrow evening Dr.
Fellinger will have it at his house—how agreeable it would
be if you could be sitting there with us—under certain conditions ! But farewell for the present. Best greetings to the
girls and everybody else. With love, Your JOHANNES.

1890

FRANKFORT A/M., *Jan*. 22.

DEAR JOHANNES,

I have not yet thanked you for your last kind letter at Christmas, but for a month past I have been ill with influenza and still feel so low that I can hardly leave my bed for more than a few hours. I have never experienced such a thing before and it will be a long time yet before I am quite well. . . . But I don't want to bother you with my complaints, for in the first place I have to thank you for the plaster bust which has at last been put up. If the face were not so unpleasant the expression would be quite good. . . . Just fancy, together with the bust, came Donndorf's gigantic sculpture of Joachim. But it was well meant after all. It is not, however, altogether pleasing. The intellectual expression is lacking.

You have probably heard that Borwick [1] had an extraordinary success in Berlin—collaborating with Stockhausen has, after all, been very useful to him. . . . When I was in Cologne I visited the Bendemanns. Wüllner let me hear the *Gedenksprüche* sung at a rehearsal. But writing makes me frightfully tired, and I must say farewell. May things go well with you in the New Year. Think kindly of Your old friend CLARA.

BRAHMS *to* CLARA.

VIENNA, *Feb*. 23.

DEAR CLARA,

From the enclosed letter from Hanslick, which I should

---

[1] The pianist who was Clara's favourite English pupil. In a previous letter she expresses her fears about the concert in question and says how sorry she would be if the public were disappointed owing to Stockhausen's share in the programme.—TR.

be obliged if you would kindly return to me some time, you will see that yesterday there was a rehearsal and performance of my B major Trio. I had already thrown the piece to the dogs and did not want to play it. The fact that it seemed inadequate to me and did not please me, means little. When it came to be discussed, however, no curiosity was expressed, but everybody, including even Joachim and Wüllner, for instance, started off by saying how much pleasure they had had in playing the old piece quite recently and had found it full of sentiment and romantic and heaven knows what else.

And now I am glad that I did play it after all. It was a very jolly day (for Billroth too was able to be there in the evening). I only feel sorry that I have not played it to you also, that is to say that I did not accept the Chamber Music Evening. I suppose it is too late now ? Otherwise I should feel tempted, particularly as at the beginning or the middle of March Wüllner has a choral concert at which I could hear all my new motets and when he would gladly give the trio in between.

But above all, when you send back H.'s letter I beg you to add a word to tell me that you are once more well and happy. Enough for to-day, with affectionate greetings, Your JOHANNES.

P.S. Wüllner is constantly complaining to me that you are opposed to the engraving of the parts of the old D minor Symphony. But surely there must be a misunderstanding somewhere ? Without the parts, the edition would be quite useless, and the symphony is surely much better in this version. He writes to me that the choral concert will take place on the 6th or 13th of March. I ought therefore to make up my mind. Yours, JOH.

CLARA *to* BRAHMS.

FRANKFORT, *Feb.* 27.

I did not answer your good tidings at once because I wrote to Heermann (but in such a way as to let him think that the idea about the trio in the quartet came from me). He sent my letter straight to the Museum Directors, and now I am waiting for the answer which I will of course send to you immediately.

I am highly delighted that you are now pleased with the remodelled work, and thank you for the nice letter from H. which I return herewith. You certainly have a very different set of people in Vienna from what we have here. A man like that can still show enthusiasm. But above all, let me implore you to inform me when the concert in Cologne[1] will take place. There is some difficulty about it because ours is fixed for Friday and theirs for Thursday. . . .

I have just received news of the death of another dear friend—Litzmann,[2] which has upset me very much. And so one after the other goes and the time will come—but I will not complain. For I still have my daughters, my guardian angels. Farewell, till I hear from you or see you again. Looking forward to it very much, Your old friend CLARA.

I am still struggling with the influenza.

BRAHMS *to* CLARA.

> VIENNA, *End of February.*

If it is to ring true I must write to you at once to tell you that your last letter came most opportunely and gave me much needed pleasure and comfort. I had already heard of your illness and although I am not of an anxious disposition I earnestly longed for news. But when the good tidings came it gave me a joy I had definitely expected.

There is little news to tell you from here, only just one or two things. . . . Fräulein Barbi gives her last concert to-day. If she should ever chance to be in your neighbourhood do please give yourself the pleasure of making her acquaintance and let her sing some of her beautiful Italian things to you as well as the German ones. It would be impossible to hear anything more lovely, for instance, than

Mut - ter,   Mut-ter

---

[1] In a letter written on February the 26th, 1890, which Clara had evidently not yet received, Brahms had informed her that the concert in Cologne would take place on the 13th of March.—TR.

[2] Geheimrath Professor Dr. Karl Litzmann, formerly of Kiel, but since 1885 living in retirement in Berlin. Clara's friendly relations with the Litzmanns dated from the early sixties.

I have recently come into possession of a sheet from an Album with a drawing by you. In the year 1880 you must have given somebody a very beautiful and decorative sketch of " The Bird as a Prophet." Do you remember whom you gave it to ? You cannot have many of such delightful things to give away. Shall I send the sheet back to you ? It is not so precious to me as many another thing of yours that I possess and you must often wish you had something of the kind at your disposal. . . .

I am sorry that you did not hear the other motets instead of the *Gedenksprüche*. But, in any case, the whole lot of them will reach you soon. Are you making plans for Italy again this spring ? I am reading an alarming amount of literature pointing that way. Hoping that you are once more taking your accustomed walk quite comfortably and with affectionate greetings to the whole house, Ever yours, JOHANNES.

CLARA *to* BRAHMS.

FRANKFORT, *March* 2.

Dr. Sieger has just written to me to say that he communicated with you concerning the 21st of March and urgently begged you for an immediate reply.[1] The date fits in exactly as you wish. And I therefore implore you, for my own sake as well, to answer the gentleman at once and to let me have a card at the same time. Unfortunately I am so unwell that I could not go to the Museum the day before yesterday to hear your *Parzenchor* (they performed Strauss's *Don Juan* immediately afterwards), and I had to absent myself again this morning from a concert at the School. I had invited a few people to my house yesterday and Hausmann, who is here, had promised me to play your E minor Sonata with me ; but owing to a severe cough I had to put them off the day before, for talking was too painful for me. As I could play, however, I begged Hausmann to come alone for a little while with his cello. And so yesterday we played your sonata and I have not had such unsullied bliss for a long time. He played the sonata beautifully, and I had practised it well.

---

[1] In his letter announcing that the concert at Cologne was fixed for the 13th of March Brahms had suggested that there might be a Chamber Concert at the Museum a week later.—TR.

It is really too magnificent. Sieger is sure to have written to you about the F minor Quintet. What do you think of it ? Which piece would then come first ? Forgive me for this dreadful writing. Oh, if only I could be well when you come ! I hope that by that time I shall have got over everything (the after effects of the influenza). Farewell. Your old friend CLARA.

Frau Fellinger's portrait of you is certainly delightful. I shall soon thank her for it myself.

BRAHMS *to* CLARA.

VIENNA, *March* 25.

I ought to write and let you know how my journey went off. It goes without saying and is not to be wondered at that one travels happily and comfortably when one's head is full of the most beautiful and pleasant memories [1] and when, in addition, one is heading *via* Vienna for Italy.

I have just written to Widmann to say that I reckon on meeting him on the 3rd of April at Riva on Lake Garda. We have not yet quite decided what we shall do, whether we shall be content to enjoy Lake Garda, Brescia, Bergamo and Lake d'Iseo, or whether we shall go further afield. As Widmann is sure to have paper with him I will let you know the plan of our journey some time or other—if I just add a line to say that the sky is blue, that will be all that is necessary and you will know that we are having a magnificent time.

So my prospect for the next few weeks is a very fine one, as pleasant as what I have to look back upon. What more can a man want ? . . . . I am going to lunch with the Fellingers to-day and shall start distributing your greetings. The "carefully prepared package" proved ample, and I ate the last sandwich at breakfast yesterday morning. But I have not yet felt like taking a proper plunge into the gruesome novel ! Meanwhile I have had all kinds of visits and to-day, when I give your messages, I shall add what good reason I had to enjoy seeing you again. Begin the summer well, find a nice place to spend it in, and I rejoice already

[1] Concerning Brahms' stay in Frankfort and the impression he left behind see *Life*, Vol. II, p. 405.

to think how well you will be next time I see you. With
affectionate greetings and thanks, Your JOHANNES.

CLARA *to* BRAHMS.

FRANKFORT A/M., *March* 29.

I should like to send you one more greeting before you
go away because it is impossible to find you in Italy. Your
letter pleased me very much, particularly because it confirmed
my belief that you had been happy here. I was constantly
afraid that my seriousness would oppress you and yet I could
not banish it. Since my illness I feel as if all my *joie de vivre*
had gone and I often suffer most dreadful depression. I
should like to have told you about it some time, but I was
afraid that it might get the better of me. I must write
to you about it, however, in case, if you noticed it,
you might give it some different interpretation. On the
advice of the doctor, who recommended a change of air for
me, we have been deliberating whether to go to Lake Mag-
giore. But I fear the season is still too early—the cold may
return again and in Italy there is no protection from it. So
we have decided to go to Baden-Baden on Tuesday for a
week. It is summer weather here now—if only it won't
change suddenly ! I have refused for Bonn.[1] I need not
tell you why. I do wish the festival had a different atmosphere about it (this quite between ourselves). . . . Please
tell Herr Widmann with what pleasure I read his stories,[2]
and how thoroughly uplifted I was by his humour and his
spirited descriptions, which are so true to nature and yet
so ideal. I should have written to him myself, but I always
feel a little bit shy with intellectual people. I wish you both
a thoroughly enjoyable time with a sky perpetually blue.
Farewell, dear Johannes, and give a thought occasionally
to Your devoted CLARA.

BRAHMS *to* CLARA.

VIENNA, *May* 1.

I have a sort of feeling that you will very shortly be taking
a piece of notepaper and starting " Dear Johannes." When

[1] This refers to the Beethoven festival with the Joachim quartet.
[2] *Gemütliche Geschichten* (Two Stories, 1890).

you do I should like to pray that you may be able to write of better, more pleasant and more enlivening things. But above all tell me how you are, what it was like in Baden-Baden and what your summer plans are.

My short Italian tour was as usual very beautiful. We walked in the most delightful spring weather with everything in our favour along Lakes Garda and Como, and through a whole number of delightful little towns—Bergamo, Brescia, Piacenza, Como, Parma, Cremona, Padua, Vicenza, Verona —I am mentioning the names just as they occur to me. They were familiar to both of us, and yet in every town something unexpected surprised us and we were delighted to see things we knew again. My umbrella flew into Lake Como, but throughout the whole tour we did not have a drop of rain, only an occasional shower at night. Neither did we go to an hotel, but always to extremely comfortable Italian inns, which every day and in every respect we found worthy of praise, particularly the large beds, in which one could walk in one's sleep.

I cannot tell you of all the beauties we saw. Perhaps you have received Widmann's book [1] which I sent you and have cared to read it. If so you have some idea of our travels this year. So let the envelope to your letter, my dear Clara, suffice for my birthday greeting, but inside tell me whether you were able to enjoy your walks in Baden and that you are now in excellent health.

You probably know that Maszkowski is coming to Breslau. You have probably received and are still receiving a whole series of new Herzogenbergs. How pleased one would be to feel greater pleasure at the ever-increasing bulk of these works, but it is impossible ! For however much one might over-estimate the industry, among other things—a little drop of blood ! With most affectionate greetings, Your JOHANNES.

CLARA *to* BRAHMS.

FRANKFORT A/M., *May* 6.
How glad I am to know where my thoughts can now reach you. You don't want any wishes, but they are in any case

[1] *Touristen Novellen* ?

the same every day. Nevertheless I should like at least to
tell you that all my thoughts are with you and among you
all at Fellinger's table ! If only I could be there in person !

Thank you for your dear letter. How pleased I am that
you have both once more enjoyed your Italian tour. I had
already accompanied you in spirit on your journey when
reading Dr. Müslin's Italian tour. How that book has appealed to me ! How delightfully it describes things, and how
amusing your portrait is at times ! I have not read the
other book yet ; I have had so much to read, having been
stimulated to do so by Sonnenthal's acting here, which, in
spite of the fact that I hardly understood a word he said,
I enjoyed immensely. I shall never forget his Bolingbroke
and above all his Hamlet ; they were characters that will
remain with one all one's life. I saw him six times in succession and on each occasion it was a genuine delight. I
felt really young in spirit, revelled as I used to revel in my
girlhood, but then I was unconscious and this time I was
conscious. Before and after his performances I spent the
whole time in reading the pieces he gave, and in addition
Wallenstein. And thus I have been able to read nothing
besides Dr. Müslin. Otherwise there is nothing of importance to tell you. We have had eight school concerts—that
sounds pleasant, doesn't it ? But there was much to please
one in them. If there must be so much music in the world,
ours is as good as any, one cannot wish for more, and the
orchestral performances of Scholz's orchestra class are really
enjoyable, much better than those in the Museum.

At present I have the pleasure of a visit from Friedchen,[1]
who has just taken her poor husband to Andreasberg again
and came to us by a roundabout route. . . .

The other day I played your three sonatas with the Landgrave [2] (I had long promised him to do so) and his interpretation gave me real pleasure. I have now promised him to
play the others with him some time. . . . You probably
know that the Herzogenbergs have sold their house in Berchtesgaden. I am so sorry for them, after having built it with

[1] Frau Sauermann, née Wagner, from Hamburg.
[2] This appears to have been the blind son of the Landgravine Anna
v. Hesse.—Tr.

so much love they were hardly able to enjoy it for a single year in peace. I have refused Bonn for reasons which you probably know or can guess. I am not going there either. I can no longer endure so much music the greater part of which I do not even hear. Joachim will spend a day or two with us here, so I have a pleasure in store.

Farewell, dear Johannes. Thank you for sending the books and let me hear from you soon, and in any case let me know whether you are going to Ischl. We shall do the same as usual—Franzensbad in July, Obersalzberg in August. Your affectionate old friend CLARA.

I am still suffering from the after affects of influenza.

CLARA *to* BRAHMS.
(*Postcard.*)
FRANKFORT, June 16.

I should so much like to know where you are and am addressing this haphazardly to Ischl. Unfortunately I have been stretched on my sofa for the last week, but to-day I am beginning to feel a little better. Joachim was here on the 8th (Robert's eightieth birthday) and for two days we had a lot of music. We played the Regenlieder Sonata again and I revelled in it once more—I always wish that the last movement might accompany me in my journey from here to the next world. To-night Borwick is playing your D minor Concerto under Richter in London. Oh, if only I could do it once more ! ! !

Farewell. I hope you are well and happy. Ever yours, CL. SCH.

BRAHMS *to* CLARA.
ISCHL, Second half of June.

A thousand thanks for your dear card on which there are more kind things than on many a four-page letter that I receive. It is so full of friendliness ! I did not need it to remind me and was always on the point of writing. But unfortunately I am not so much at home with the calendar as Joachim, and envy him very much for having celebrated a day of such fond memories with you. I am quietly installed in Ischl and have probably seen the finest part of the summer by now. We have had some magnificent days. Now we must be prepared for heat, rain and—the crowd. Nothing could be more pleasing, even to you, than the spring here. It is, however, no misfortune but rather a piece of luck that at this divine season of the year, all places are beautiful enough.

And now I must seriously and light-heartedly question two points in your last letter. In the first place, my vanity has been deeply wounded by your thinking that I am like Dr. Müslin and the original of his portrait. In this way one finds out quite accidentally the sort of figure one cuts in the world! No, this parody of my personality was unintentional and only grew to be like me by accident. But I do really make my appearance as the "friend from Vienna" in the last journey of the other book, though the description of me there is not so piquant. Enough for to-day. With all fond greetings, Your JOHANNES.

CLARA *to* BRAHMS.

OBERSALZBERG BEI BERCHTESGADEN, PENSION MORITZ,
Aug. 12.

How often during all these weeks have I not thought of you, but was always unable to write because, during the whole of the time, we have been busy with the most distressing correspondence about Ferdinand and his family. Besides, as I did not feel in the mood required for letter-writing I confined myself to what was absolutely necessary. But now my debt to you is lying very heavily on my conscience and I should be so glad to hear from you direct some time. I should also like you to chat to me a little about your workshop. But I suppose I may not hope for this? We have been here for ten days and literally have to steal the fine hours from the sky. We have had few pleasant days and sit from morning till night in a thick mist in our rooms. But this is very depressing and monotonous and does not exactly raise one's spirits. I shall hold out till the beginning of September, however, for the air is certainly bracing and does one good; and after Franzensbad even my physical condition improves although I am not yet quite rid of the after effects of influenza. If it had been a better summer

I should have tried to persuade you to make the acquaintance of our mountain, but as I say the weather is too bad. To-day we are again enveloped in mist. It rains incessantly and we are confined to our rooms.

N.B. The reason why I was misled by Widmann's Dr. Müslin was that he describes how fond Müslin was of children, which is such a characteristic trait in you. I admit that I could not trace your features in his other qualities and peculiarities. I have not been able to read the other book yet as I have been suffering with my eyes lately, and moreover have a number of things to read which had to be read quickly because they were lent—at present, for instance, six more numbers of the *Rundschau* from Ebner Eschenbach. As soon as I get home I shall take up Widmann. . . . I saw dear kind old Anna Franz the other day with poor Frank. The Hausmanns, who have gone to Gastein, also paid me a surprise visit. . . . You must be lenient with me, dear Johannes, I have no interesting things to tell you. So write a kind word soon to Your old friend CLARA.

BRAHMS *to* CLARA.

ISCHL, *Aug.*

The present lovely weather will induce you to stop on longer. In any case would you be so kind as to let me have a card with your address to let me know when and where you are going ? Perhaps I shall see you there or in Baden-Baden. But I don't want to start the subject of my travelling plans any more than of my workshop. Good heavens, I have never imagined that I belonged to the lucky ones who have a "workshop." And yet I will not deny that at times I have tasted of their happiness to the full. There have been travelling and workshop plans enough this year but not much will remain of them—enough of the latter perhaps for a couple of rehearsals in your room. If by this I mean perhaps a string quintet,[1] it is certainly a misfortune that my first (F major) is probably one of my finest works. You may be interested to hear that both my symphonies are appearing in arrangements for two pianos. Unfortunately I have not arranged them myself (I like writing for two pianos),

[1] G major Quintet, Op. 111.

but perhaps to your own and other people's joy they have been carefully and diligently done by Rob. Keller. They are particularly easy to play throughout, and demand little strain in the matter of octaves and tremolos. . . . You ought to see me here in the part of Dr. Müslin as a child-lover. Nowhere in the world are there more delightful people and children. I never go out but what my heart leaps with joy and I feel as if revived by a fresh drink after I have stroked the heads of one or two darling children. In Italy it is just the same, but there they don't speak such good German ! I also like the people in Baden, but not in Bavaria or Switzerland. I speak only of the people I see and meet in the streets —but who may be of greater importance to me than most of the people I get to know in houses. I have enough of seriousness at home and when I go out I love to see a smiling face. And this reminds me of your dear smiling face, and I greet you affectionately, Your JOHANNES.

CLARA *to* BRAHMS.

FRANKFORT A/M., *Nov.* 9.

I would have written to you sooner to tell you how pleased I was about the new quintet had I not hoped to be able to let you know that Joachim would play it here with his quartet in a fortnight. But now I have received a letter from him in which he says that there is so little time left before he goes away that he would hardly be able to practise the quintet, and that in addition, you had sent the score to the Herzogenbergs and that when he inquired whether you had said anything about him in the matter (i.e. that they should show it to him also) he received the answer " No." He goes on to say that he need hardly tell me what he felt at this reply. He also says that he played your first quintet recently, that it went splendidly, and that his quartet had loved it and played it with great success. He added, " You can imagine how I thought of the second at the time and with what feelings ! "

But, my dearest Johannes, how could you do such a thing ? Was not Joachim the first who ought to have had the score ? Such behaviour is quite incomprehensible, and it makes me feel so sorry for Joachim. And now his time here is so short, that apart from the matinée at the Museum on the 23rd we shall hardly have an opportunity to enjoy any music.

I have just had news that Avé, who was to celebrate his golden wedding in three weeks, is on his death-bed, which upset me very much. Borwick is at all events engaged by Richter for your D minor Concerto. Please receive him kindly. He certainly deserves it. I shall not, however, introduce him to the Streichers, for I believe he has already got into touch with Bösendorfer.

Let me also tell you that the day before yesterday I once more played Chopin's F minor Concerto in the Museum and it went very successfully. It was enthusiastically received. But it was a great effort for me. The fingers do their work well and even with ease, but the nerves no longer respond. It will probably be the last time. I have only promised to play again in a quartet. How I should love to have played your C minor Trio, but I have just read that Kwast is now playing it.

Do you know anything about Tinel [1]—his *Franziskus* is being played on the 17th. Scholz is, moreover, quite enthusiastic ! ! ! But enough for to-day, and with best thanks for your last dear letter, Your old friend CLARA.

Joachim is playing your B Flat major Quartet here—what a long time it is since I heard it ! . . .

CLARA *to* BRAHMS.

FRANKFORT A/M., *Dec.* 10.

This prolonged silence has been quite involuntary on my part and I ought to have answered your dear letter and card some time ago. But I have been overwhelmed with correspondence which has been chiefly due to Ferdinand and his family. On his behalf, or rather on that of his eldest son, we have been inquiring about a vacancy for a chemist's apprentice, and that kept us busy. Now at last we have succeeded in finding something good. Then we had to find a school for Julie. In fact it is never ending. But I will not talk about it any more. All I wanted was to give you some proof of how preoccupied I have been. Moreover, I have

---

[1] Edgar Tinel, a Belgian composer born 1854.

just packed Ilona Eibenschütz [1] off to Holland and London, and what a vast amount of correspondence that has entailed ! And now, dear Johannes, I have a request to make. I have received a letter from the Mayor of Vienna (what is his name, we cannot decipher the signature ?) which I send you with the request that you will let me know whether I can safely send him the original of Grillparzer's poem.[2] We attach the greatest value to it, and as I wish to be cautious, and know that you are also in such cases, I ask you for your advice.

We had a very nice time with Joachim. He paid us a very pleasant visit. If only we had had the new quintet ! But in regard to this you really did suspect me wrongly for once. I had not been put out about anything. I was only sorry for Joachim. If I had felt offended, I should have said so openly. I have told you over and over again that I possess too little skill and have not enough practice in the reading of such works to be able to form a clear idea of their effect, besides which I have too little time to spend day after day upon a piece as the Herzogenbergs can. I should have liked to read Hanslick's article about the quintet. Can you send me a copy ?

You are right about Tinel. That is not my music. There is too little spontaneity in it and too much refinement. They are in a great quandary here about the Director. Volkland would be glad to come here (I believe) but, much as I might wish to have him personally, I would certainly not advise him to come—the conditions are not pleasant. Now I must close and must beg you to answer me quickly concerning the enclosed and the name of the Mayor. Please return the letter. Ought I to ask for a security ? But I don't like the idea of this, for the sheet of Grillparzer MS. is priceless to me and if it were lost no sum could replace it. Farewell, my dear Johannes. I hope the New Year will bring us the quintet in your own hands. Your faithful old friend CLARA.

Everybody here sends you heartiest greetings. Old Avé is now also no more. How cruel just before his golden wedding !

[1] Concerning Ilona Eibenschütz, see *Life*, Vol. II, 409.
[2] For the Musical and Theatrical Exhibition at Vienna.

BRAHMS *to* CLARA.

VIENNA, *Dec.* 16.

I know so well the claims that are made upon you and the troubles that fall to your lot through Ferdinand and his family, and also how you are pestered with letters and all manner of things that I cannot conceive how you deal with it all and still keep going. 'Pon my soul, whenever I see your dear handwriting on an envelope I cannot help thinking of all this and feel almost relieved when I find only a dictated letter inside.

Meanwhile you have probably sent the Mayor a short note, and that is all that is necessary as far as he is concerned, if you send him your treasure. It would be useless to mention securities and things of that sort, for you must rely on him to take care of it, and he will do so. Besides, there is really no risk in the matter, and so far nothing of the sort has ever occurred in such circumstances. I sent my finest things to the Beethoven exhibition in Bonn without taking any precautions, and the Berlin Library also sent its greatest treasures—I had seen these a year previously in Bologna.

Regarding your future Musical Director I now have to write to Dr. Sieger longer letters than I have ever yet addressed to Frankfort (including those I write to you). Maszkowski is in the running, and I have now strongly recommended Julius Spengel of Hamburg. I don't know whether you know him, and if you do whether you are supporting him.

The other day Marie was inquiring about lexicons. Now it happens that Jul. Schubert's *Musik-Konversations Lexikon* [1] has just appeared in a new edition (the eleventh). In its brevity and the quality of its biographies it seems to me quite excellent, and wonderfully well bound ; it costs only six marks. Hanslick will have sent you his article himself by now. The Joachim Herzogenberg affair may have become clear to you subsequently, but in the letter in question you say to me, " But, dear Johannes, how could you do such a thing ? " etc., etc. But I am satisfied with the way the matter has been cleared up, and Joachim is now enjoying the piece very much.

I will take this opportunity of sending you my best and

[1] *Encyclopædia of Music.*

heartiest wishes for Christmas, and with the same affectionate greetings as ever, I remain Your JOHANNES.

CLARA *to* BRAHMS.

FRANKFORT, *Dec.* 22.

I really have nothing to tell you, but I should hate not to write to you for Christmas. And I also have to thank you for your prompt card and letter. . . . I have heard about the quintet from Berlin, apparently it is magnificent. Hanslick has also sent me his criticism, for which please thank him. But who wrote the other article in the *Musik Zeitung* ? I cannot guess. I have been studying the motifs of the quintet with great interest and not without some envy of those who have already heard it. But how difficult it is to imagine the harmonies belonging to them. There is, however, one movement, I know, which I shall dote on, with its soft beginning and end. Are we going to have it here now ? I very much hope so, although the production cannot be a perfect one with such unequal means as we have at our disposal. Klengel is said to be a very good choral conductor, but has he ever conducted an orchestra, I mean symphonies, etc. ? Naturally what I have heard by him has been only of the best. There is much talk here now in favour of Volkland. But I believe that what they are afraid about is that he would not always fall in with their wishes. I should be rather glad, for I have heard some fine performances under his conductorship. He is, moreover, an enthusiastic musician, not yet blasé. We are all very much excited and are really dreading a false alarm. But it must all be settled soon. To-day we have the Ninth Symphony. I could not prevail upon myself to go to the concert. The tempos in the ninth are insufferable, and then, in addition a concerto by Liszt (Menter) [1]—I can no longer endure it.

But enough for to-day. Farewell. You have all my best wishes for Christmas (things will be miserable enough at Frau Franz's, but you are probably at the Fellingers ?). With all good wishes for the New Year for you, and the finest of all good things—your quintet—for us, Your faithful old friend, CLARA.

[1] Sophie Menter was playing the Liszt Concerto at the time.—TR.

BRAHMS *to* CLARA.

VIENNA, *Dec.* 24.

How could I be better occupied on the 24th than sitting in imagination beside you at your breakfast table and talking and listening (now I must draw on my fancy) and hearing all about the kind and charming things you are preparing. Here next-door in my library there also stands a beautiful large tree which will remain concealed until this evening from my hostess's two darling boys.

We could not have finer Christmas weather. All the trees and bushes are covered with frost and snow and it is a real joy to go out for a walk in the mild air. It was just as beautiful in Pesth where I was a week ago. . . . Yesterday, by the by, I received a charming little Christmas present which I might lay beside your treasure in the Town Hall of Vienna —a composition and MS. of Grillparzer's : Heine's song, " *Du Schönes Fischermädchen.*"

Frl. Barbi has told everybody here that you made her very happy through your kindness and friendliness. But I will not detain you any longer, you will have enough to keep you busy—any new bust to put up ? Wishing you a very happy Christmas and New Year, and with affectionate greetings to all, Your JOHANNES.

1891

CLARA *to* BRAHMS.

FRANKFORT A/M., *Jan.* 29.

DEAR JOHANNES,

I have not yet thanked you for your kind New Year's wishes. Do not take it ill of me. I have so often thought of you and of this last letter. But I have had and still have so many worries that I sometimes don't know where to turn. So please accept my belated thanks, which I have been carrying about with me all this time, with a kindly smile. . . . I was over-joyed to hear how well things had gone in Pesth. Everybody heard your quintet except myself. I feel this very much and I would sing a dirge if it would do any good. We are in a bad way here. We might have got Maszkowski to come to us, but they hesitated so long that in the end he made other arrange-ments. So we are left in the lurch! He would have intro-duced fresh blood which we are badly in want of. And who knows what will happen now? I no longer have any musical treats, except now and again through my pupils. And this reminds me of Borwick whom I have at last induced to go to Vienna in spite of the fact that Richter has not answered him. Richter promised to let him play your D minor Concerto at one of his concerts, and now Borwick has not heard a word from him. You know I do not like to pester you with letters of recommendation, but I earnestly beg you to extend your pro-tection to Borwick. You already know him and you cannot help getting a little pleasure from the way he plays your con-certo. Please introduce him to Hanslick. That is so im-portant for him. And also to the Fellingers and Anna Franz. Would you be so very kind? And will you also help him with advice? You know the conditions there so well. B. knows very little about the ways of the world and that is why the advice of friends is doubly necessary to him.

Aren't we going to see you here at all ? If only the quintet were a piano quintet we should have more hope. Please let me have it from Simrock at once if it is ready—I thought I saw it announced ?

There is not much to tell you about ourselves. So far we have kept well, but everything is not as it should be, and I have a good deal of worry. Besides this, my age is weighing me down and does not allow me to face circumstances with the same old elasticity. Thank God, I can still play ! But I have hardly anything to stimulate me here. Invitations to concerts constantly pour in from outside. But that is not what I want. I ought to have congenial musical society in this place itself, but nowhere is this less possible.

The deaths of my two old friends Gade and Verhulst have greatly upset me and have given me solemn warning ! But enough, dear Johannes. Think kindly of me. Your faithful old friend CLARA.

The girls send greetings. The Sommerhoffs are going to Cannes for three or four months. If only I could !

BRAHMS *to* CLARA.

VIENNA, *Jan.* 31.

DEAR CLARA,

The next Philharmonic Concert is on the 22nd of February, and Richter told me that Herr B. was to play my D minor Concerto at it. Since I saw R. the programme has perhaps become doubtful again. But in any case Herr B. can afford to wait a little bit longer for news. If I should see Richter I shall ask him about it, and beg him to write a line to Herr B.

Why did you not turn the tables, and rather than let one Christmas evening be spoilt, celebrate it twice over ? The tree would have shone just as merrily on the 25th as on Christmas Eve.

I am sorry about my poor quintet. Your longing increases with waiting and your expectations will rise accordingly. But the piece is not prepared to face any such ordeal, so please draw in your horns. For I have always told you that the first quintet is a really beautiful piece—for heaven's sake don't expect anything better or even equal to it !

But you need not remind me to remember you. Two pieces

for four hands will reach you as soon as Simrock has them ready (you can see from the semi-quaver triplets that the movement does not go quickly).   Moreover, I am always being told of passages to which it is impossible to do justice, and the annoying answer is obviously that the right tempo makes them possible.

In case I forget, let me tell you at once, and you can let Heermann know some time that the quintet can be ordered now and will be published soon.   I forgot to answer him.   I am invited to Meiningen for the 15th of March and have accepted provisionally.   A tragedy [1] by Widmann is to be produced there on that date.   If I go I shall come on to Fr.

But I rather dread going away, because so many other things will then press themselves upon me ; Hamburg, for instance, is now on the cards.   Widmann (Hegar) and I are thinking of going to Sicily in the spring.   As to Herr Borwick, I shall be your most faithful servant, you need have no fears.   I shall let him see and know everything that can be of the slightest possible use to him.   With all good wishes and affectionate greetings to you and yours, Your Joh.

CLARA *to* BRAHMS.

Feb. 3.

A thousand thanks for your letter.   I only wish to tell you not to worry yourself too much over B.   Just let him play you something from time to time and make one of your shrewd criticisms occasionally—that will help him very much.   Betty Oser has given him a number of letters.   If he presents them he will be sure to make friends.   Would a letter to Lewinsky be useful to him ?—I mean in connection with the *Burg Theater.* I addressed my letter to him (Borwick) to the Hotel *König von Hungarn.*   I hope he will get it all right.   Your old friend CLARA.

BRAHMS *to* CLARA.

VIENNA, *Feb.*

. . . You will already have heard enough from your lady friends here about your charming young Englishman, so I need make no attempt to add further comments.   Nor could I do

[1] *Œnone.*

so if I tried, for I see him so seldom. He immediately made
tremendous headway with the ladies in question, but I go out
very little and can hardly lure him into a tavern with me.   You
will hear a lot of good about him and his playing, and very
rightly too.   If his success with the general public should not
prove to be in keeping with this gratifying prelude, you must
not take it too much to heart.   May I offer you my humble
opinion on the matter and beg you not to take it too seriously
or to misunderstand it ?   The Viennese are better and more
intelligent listeners than the people of Frankfort, and I believe
that like myself they will think that Herr B. is precisely at
that stage at which his excellent execution does credit to and
reflects the supreme qualities of his teacher, but for the time
being does not express the man himself nor his spirit nor his
will.   You know much better than I do the sort of young man
he is and are better able to judge how he will develop.   In the
case of Frl. Soldat, whose temperament was most energetic
and lively, I had a striking example of how for a while she was
merely the very perfect pupil of Joachim, whilst before and
afterwards she was exquisitely herself.   But please regard this
as in every respect irresponsible and unjustifiable chatter.

It is with the utmost reluctance that I undergo any fresh
experience.   At the present moment I am lending my head to
a sculptor and to an engraver at the same time.   I thought I
should be rid of them when I told them that I could not sit
more than once.   But it was no good.   They came to an
agreement and now etch and mould together.

Do not let yourself be seduced into reading Hebbel's Correspondence.   You would never get far enough to enjoy anything
beautiful and important because you would come across so
much that would bore and displease you.

But let me have a word some time about your holiday trip.
With most affectionate greetings, JOHANNES.

CLARA *to* BRAHMS.

FRANKFORT A/M., *Feb.* 21.

I cannot wait until I have heard the quintet in its complete
form.   I must tell you now at once, after having learnt it in its
arrangement for four hands, how very much it pleases me.   I
cannot yet form a very good idea of the effect of the first and

last movements, but even on the piano I can enjoy parts of it very much, particularly the development in the first movement. In the last movement I have not yet been able properly to interpret the finale with the Hungarian rhythm, but I can well imagine its inspiriting effect when played by a quartet of first-rate musicians. The second and third movements are fresh pearls in the chain with which you have endowed the musical world. How serious and melancholy is the beginning (I feel as if I knew it already ; can I have seen it among some early notes of yours ?). How wonderfully it flows along ! And then there is the charming Scherzo which is so soothing. How glad I am that we are to hear it on the 6th of March ! If only we had a superior quartet with better matched players. Koning's violin is no longer beautiful (he doesn't practise any more) and Welker's viola is too harsh.

Shall we see you here then, dear Johannes ? Have you accepted for Meiningen ? I heard from the Heermanns that you were coming, but I should prefer to hear it from yourself. So to-day Borwick has had his rehearsal ! I do hope things will go well with him to-morrow. I should be so sorry if he does not have the success which his ability really deserves. He wrote me a most desperate letter saying that he had come a cropper with Bach the other day at Frau Franz's. It will be a lesson to him not to start with Bach in such company (anyhow not such a long work). But enough for to-day. The girls and I thank you for the quintet, and I for your friendliness towards Borwick. Let us hear soon when we may expect you. With affectionate greetings, Your old friend CLARA.

CLARA *to* BRAHMS.

FRANKFORT A/M., *Feb.* 23.

. . . I was deeply moved by what you told me about Borwick as it is exactly the same as I said to his father at the very beginning, and have constantly repeated to my children quite recently. . . . Thank you for having given me your opinion so frankly. . . . Please thank Frau Franz for her kind letter (after the rehearsal). I am too busy to write to her now. Now let me hear from you soon, dear Johannes, and with heartiest greetings, I am Your old friend CLARA.

24th. I was just going to take your letter to the post when your dear card came.[1] You can imagine how this delighted us, particularly after I had been thinking so much about Borwick. So we may after all perhaps have been wrong with our fears. But Borwick always played your things with the utmost warmth, and this time your presence in the hall must certainly have inspired him. I am full of new and joyful hopes for him. Thank you, thank you for having written to me so soon. Otherwise I should have heard from nobody. Nobody can give me such pleasure as you, dear Johannes. Farewell, once more.

CLARA *to* BRAHMS.

FRANKFORT A/M., *March* 4.

It has been lying heavily on my conscience that I wrote to you a little while ago to say that I was not yet quite at home with the first and last movements of your quintet. Now I am thoroughly, and I am highly delighted with both. The first movement lays a soft caressing arm about one with its first and second theme, and is followed by the wonderful development which in your work is always a fresh creation. And then the last, how original and delicate it is, with the Hungarian Gipsy rhythm as its principal motif ! Finally the conclusion, which is just the sort of magnificent confusion that one hears in a dream after a Zigeuner evening in Pesth.

We shall certainly hear it here in the last of the series of quartets, but the manner in which it will be played, with two such instruments, is questionable. I should so love to play the third movement as a piano solo.

What I wanted to ask was, what is happening about your coming here ? We are thinking very seriously of the Italian Lakes, but certainly not before April. I must now close, and hope to be able to discuss many things with you soon. Fare-

---

[1] In this card Brahms says : " I am writing to you after a concert to tell you with very great pleasure that Borwick played quite excellently, with the most perfect freedom, warmth, energy and passion, in short everything that one could desire. I of course thought as well of all the beauty for which he has to thank his teacher ! ! ! Really one could not have wished for anything better or more beautiful, and you may readily believe everything that your lady friends will tell you about it." See *Life,* Vol. II, pp. 409–410.

well, my dear Johannes, and think kindly of Your old friend
CLARA.

Poor Frau Herzogenberg is not at all well. She has been in
bed now for over six weeks and is not allowed to do anything.

BRAHMS *to* CLARA.

MEININGEN, *March* 15.

Your letter was a wonderful and lovely surprise ! [1] That
you should have played my *Haydn Variations* and that they
should have pleased to the point of an encore and, above all,
that they should have stirred your heart so much—all this I
had to read over and over again with joy. I have always had
a weakness for that piece and I think of it with more pleasure
and satisfaction than of many another. But now, listen !
Once and for all, you have the most cordial standing invitation
to come here whenever you like and for as long as you like. [2]
In fact I was expected to telegraph to you *in extenso* to ask you
to do so at once. But unfortunately I thought it would be so
impracticable for you and Frl. Marie that I did not make the
attempt. But if I was wrong and you can possibly come at
once, just telegraph to me and I will wait here for you. You
might manage to be here on Thursday, or Sunday, or whenever
you like.

You need fear no inconveniences of any kind (not even
regarding clothes) and you can allow yourself to be driven
about and carried about (even up the castle stairs) if you like.
I have often enough told you about the benevolent kindness
and considerate hospitality of this place. Perhaps you will
decide to come next week. If I should not have the incredible
surprise of hearing of your sudden arrival, I propose to leave
on Friday for Frankfort, and could therefore be present at the
rehearsal early on Saturday.

On the first morning of my arrival here and when I was
quite alone I allowed myself the pleasure of a rehearsal. When

---

[1] On the 13th Clara had written saying that she had played Brahms'
Haydn Variations with Kwast, and that the piece had raised a storm
of enthusiasm.—TR.

[2] This was in response to Clara's own suggestion. In a previous
letter she had expressed the wish that the Duke of Meiningen might
invite her to the castle.—TR.

the family is here it is always Brahms and again Brahms.   But
I got the orchestra to play me a concerto by Mozart for four
wind instruments, and a concerto by Bach for three violins,
three violas and three violoncellos.   In the theatre this evening they are giving Widmann's Greek tragedy *Œnone* (for the
very first time).   He is also here as a guest of the Duke, and we
have already had great fun with the rehearsals.   There will be
a play on Thursday and that is why I am thinking of only leaving early on Friday.   Let me tell you, quite between ourselves
of course, that I am not the least bit anxious to hear my quintet
in Frankfort.   But this goes without saying.   If, therefore,
you should feel any temptation you have only yourself to consider in the matter.   But—well I like reading fairy tales, but
to believe or to hope anything so fantastic is beyond me !   I
still think with the greatest joy of your letter and of your love
for the *Haydn Variations*, and look forward most heartily to
our next meeting.   Affectionately yours, JOHANNES.

CLARA *to* BRAHMS.
(*Letter Card.*)

FRANKFORT, *March* 16.

It was only a thoughtless suggestion of mine, for such a journey requires a good deal of preparation.   What a lot I should
have to think out and arrange.   It was silly of me, and I have
only succeeded in involving you in a lot of correspondence !—
Unfortunately the quintet will not be produced for another
three weeks, but I hope that you will practise it with the gentlemen at once.   All further news on Friday when the trio in
Myliusstrasse are joyfully expecting you.

BRAHMS *to* CLARA.

MEININGEN, *March* 17.

As I wish to tell you definitely that on Friday (about nine
o'clock) I shall travel *via* Eisenach and expect to reach Frankfort about four, I take this opportunity of thanking you for
your friendly letter—which I certainly did not hope would be
any friendlier, that is to say more favourable.   I did not hold
out any hopes to the family, but your grand piano was nevertheless tuned in case you came, and the suite destined for you
was heated so that you might find everything warm and com-

fortable. If you had come here this week you would have heard, in addition to my symphonies and the *Haydn Variations*, for instance, the very fine F minor Concerto for the clarinet.[1] It is impossible to play the clarinet better than Herr Mühlfeld does here. Händel's *Feuer-* and *Wasser-Musik*—for the moment I cannot think what was given yesterday, and what will be given to-morrow.

Dr. Widmann thanks you very much indeed for your kind message. Be sure to say nothing to —— about my arrival on Friday afternoon.[2]

With affectionate greetings, Your JOHANNES.

BRAHMS *to* CLARA.

VIENNA, *April.*

Before my epistolatory zeal had enabled me to thank you for having entertained me so long, a fresh reason for thanking you has arisen. Frl. Geisler sent me the tobacco and I think it very kind of Frl. Marie to have thought of this, my weakness, and I thank her heartily. Otherwise I have no new adventure to relate. But unfortunately this is not the case with regard to Widmann. In Nuremberg (while climbing the stairs of an underground wine restaurant) he broke the fibula of his left leg and had first to lay up in the hotel and must now stay at home for weeks. The only amusing feature about it is that for the first time on this journey he had had the idea of insuring himself heavily against accidents. So he will at least recover all expenses.

As I say, nothing has happened to me ; everything is just the same here and my journey was very comfortable, as hardly anybody travels on Good Friday. Frau Speyer had the idea of giving me a little box of dates, but she probably never

---

[1] By Weber.

[2] This visit, which lasted from March 20th to the 27th, was ill-fated. On the very first day, as the result of a conversation about Borwick and his reception at the hands of the Vienna Press, Clara became so much excited, and, finally, depressed, that even the apparently peaceful days that followed failed to restore her serenity—not to mention the open light-heartedness necessary to enjoy friendly companionship. " The last eight days have been like a nightmare," she writes in her diary after Brahms had left. " To me it was a release, but a melancholy one." See *Life,* Vol. II, pp. 410, 411.

thought how much I should enjoy them. Armed with these
luxuries and my imagination pleasantly occupied, I don't
think I have ever breakfasted so well as I did at dawn that
day.

It often strikes me that your weather is not so kind as ours
here and that you probably still have to stay indoors. So I
hope you will at least have fine weather for Lake Como in May.
Heartiest greetings to all, and I trust that the third of your
trio [1] will not have to go too far across the sea, only to Cyprus
or Ceylon. With most affectionate greetings, Your JOHANNES.

BRAHMS *to* CLARA.

ISCHL, *May.*

I took this away with me yesterday to send to you.[2] And
just as the blue waters of Lake Wolfgang flow in front of the
delightful house so may my words flow smoothly along. Billroth has quite recovered, and has now got rid of his cough and
hoarseness.[3] In any case he will go back to Vienna this week
and only come back for a longer stay later on. . . .

I was, of course, very much interested to hear that Eugenie
had been able to write from Malta. All unwillingly I had
imagined that the letters from Palermo and Syracuse were
hocus-pocus and that she was on her way to India with her
friend who refused to part with her. If, however, the parting
and the return journey are really true, I hope that Palermo
and Sicily were not disposed of in one letter and that she has
seen a good many wonderful things between these stages. I
am really immensely interested and I should be extremely glad
if you could find time either to dictate or write a letter to let
me know where and for how long she was able to revel. Good
God, when I think that you might have walked in that paradise
like one of us—I would gladly have missed it all and been
content with the description of it from your lips and the glory
of it in your face ! I don't feel as if I could speak about any-

[1] Eugenie Schumann.

[2] A sheet of paper with a picture of Billroth's house on it (St. Gilgen,
near Ischl).

[3] In a previous letter from Clara, which was of no particular interest,
she expressed anxiety about Billroth of whom she had read disquieting
reports.—TR.

thing else, for to say that everything is beautiful here seems out of keeping.

And now what else ? I don't suppose any glory came into your face through Herzogenberg's Requiem. I can't think what to say to him about this hopeless piece. And yet, on the other hand, I certainly cannot praise his string trios and his octets, or show any pleasure in them. What can you find to say about them ? And what do you tell them ?—But let us rather go for a walk, you in Oos and I in Ischl, and let us think of Palermo ! With affectionate greetings to you and everybody, Your JOHANNES.

CLARA *to* BRAHMS.

FRANKFORT A/M., *June* 7.

I was just going to thank you for your last letter from Ischl, when we received news of the death of our poor Ferdinand. You can imagine how deeply distressed I am ! But we ought really to regard it as a happy release, for the doctors declared that his constitution had been so much undermined by his constant use of narcotics that, had he lived longer, his life would have been even more miserable than it had been before. What grieves me most, however, is that not one of us was with him, as we only heard of the danger when it was too late. Marie has gone to the funeral at Gera to-day, and to my intense relief Louis has gone with her. What a wretched life the poor fellow had led for the last ten years ! . . . Thus one brings up one's children with love and care only to bury them ! It really is too sad !

We met Eugenie here all right and found her highly delighted with her journey about which she has lots of interesting things to tell us. Unfortunately, she had a week's illness in Malta, probably a severe attack of influenza. She went to Malta, Sicily (Syracuse, Palermo, Taormina), and was away altogether for five weeks. I was very glad she undertook the journey because what she went through in London was really terrible. She stayed with the Burnands, and one morning a week after her arrival, Mr. Burnand went out and even cracked a joke with her at the door, and then, two hours later, was brought back to the house and died the same night. Really, what one has to go through is terrible ! What with losses and other

things, our poor bodies hardly have enough resistance left to
go on.

I derived little benefit from Baden. The weather was too
cold, and we had to have fires almost the whole time. But I
shall go to Franzensbad as usual in July and then to Obersalzberg. You seem to write very desperately about Herzogenberg's Requiem. I know nothing about it ; he did not send
it to me and unfortunately I can only feel relieved. Farewell,
and have a nice peaceful time in beautiful Ischl. With affectionate greetings, Your sorrowful CLARA.

BRAHMS *to* CLARA.

ISCHL, *June.*

Your life is one of rare beauty and richness, but you know
the sadder side of existence as few others do. Of how many
people have I not already calmly taken leave, but your parting
with Ferdinand and your English friend had a double sting.
The fact that Eugenie was present at the latter's death makes
me feel as if the tragedy had been brought home to my own
door. If only the summer could bring you all manner of joy
and above all improve your health ! For that is not only
necessary in order to resist misfortune, but also in order to
enjoy and take pleasure in the good that comes our way.

I suppose that the *Berliner Musik Zeitung* of May the 30th,
with the autograph letter of Robert Schumann,[1] has been sent
to you. If not I shall send it to you some time. The letter is
to Jul. Stern and is wholly charming and beautiful, as for instance, when Schumann says (he evidently felt offended about
something), "So we will let the grass grow over it, or better
still the lovely flowers." As for myself, I have only good news.
It is wonderfully beautiful and pleasant here, and, as I have
often said before, I am made most happy by the charming
people about me. Of the many and sundry musical fancies
that flit through my brain not much will survive, though a
little may. And if, for instance, in a week or so six solo quartets,[2] including one piano part, should lie in a fair copy before
me I shall be tempted to send them to you, as I believe they
might give you pleasure. . . .

[1] Dated 13th of February, 1851.
[2] Op. 112.

With most affectionate greetings and best wishes for the summer, Your JOHANNES.

CLARA *to* BRAHMS.

FRANZENSBAD, *July* 28.

How often have I not been on the point of writing to you, but I have been so constantly ailing that I have hardly been able to discharge the most necessary duties. And even to-day, owing to a severe attack of lumbago, I am again feeling very miserable. Nevertheless I should not like to leave here with my debt to you on my conscience. My last severe trial and everything connected with it, has really meant more to me than I at first thought it would. Thank God, we found in Gera a very faithful friend of Ferdinand's,[1] who throughout the whole time did all he could to help Antonia. Now, of course, the whole of the responsibility for the children rests upon us. . . .

I too have now received Herzogenberg's Requiem, but have not been able to get to know it here—I am rather frightened of it, and should so much like to be able to tell him what he would like to hear. I should be very pleased if you could send me the letter you mention from Robert to Stern, and I need hardly say how glad I should be to receive the solo quartets—I hope you will not resist the temptation to send them. In Obersalzberg I have a piano at my disposal occasionally and could get to know them well there, so far as this is possible on a piano. . . . If only I felt better ! I hardly have the courage to settle what I shall do an hour ahead—it is very hard for me. I have certainly learnt how to fight in my long life, but hitherto I have had the health for it. But now this is so much impaired that I feel extremely old and have no energy left. But enough of this ! Write soon to my address in Obersalzberg, near Berchtesgaden, and delight Your old friend CLARA.

Marie greets you. I have a real guardian angel at my side in her. P.S. I have not told you yet how deeply I was distressed by Mr. Burnand's death. But this surely goes without saying, for I have lost my " home " in England. A few days ago dear old Frau Wagner died in Hamburg and poor Princess Wittgenstein after a serious illness in Düsseldorf. Every day our world grows emptier.

[1] Dr. Budy, of Gera.

BRAHMS *to* CLARA.

ISCHL, *July.*

Let me reply at once, however briefly, to your dear letter. I hear from the people at Meiningen that you are expected there on the 1st and that they would like to invite themselves to the Vosses on that day in order to meet you.[1]

I would gladly think about coming to B. if everything and everybody I wanted to see and must see were not such miles apart. But I am afraid I should only be continually harassed, and nowadays I really only feel happy when I'm left in peace.

" Every day our world grows emptier ! " Yes, dear Clara, that is true—and not true. If I liked to enlarge upon this, I can imagine only too well what your criticism would be. But so it is, and so it will remain, and I shall not attempt to make the thought a more cheerful one for you—that life will do often enough itself, and you will realize it with gratitude and joy.

So old Frau Wagner is dead ! That is the second time as far as I am concerned, for I thought she was dead long ago. . . . After dinner at the Vosses I shall not need to remind you that I have enriched life with another crop of summer fruit [2] (which incidentally includes quite a pleasant collection of canons for women's voices). Baroness Heldburg will have told you of a trio for pianoforte, violin and clarinet, and of a quintet for a string quartet and clarinet. If only for the pleasure of hearing these I am looking forward to Meiningen. You have never heard such a clarinet player as they have there in Mühlfeldt. He is absolutely the best I know. At all events this art has, for various reasons, deteriorated very much. The clarinet players in Vienna and many other places are quite fairly good in orchestra, but solo they give one no real pleasure.

So that is why I am looking forward to Meiningen. . . . I cannot believe that you are coming, in spite of your good intentions and in spite of theatre, orchestra, trio and quintet. It is a pity that owing to the need of so much transposition you cannot read the pieces. For there are some that you would certainly want to repeat at once ! ? (I am thinking of a very soft adagio.)

I am still hoping to get the Schumann letter, but I gave my

[1] See *Life*, Vol. II, p. 412.   [2] Op. 113, 114, 115.

copy of the newspaper away. To-morrow Wendt arrives—
greet Frl. Wendt for me if she is there—and many others who,
let us hope, will add to the pleasure and attractions of the visit
for you. With most affectionate greetings, Your JOH.

CLARA *to* BRAHMS.
BERCHTESGADEN, PENSION MORITZ, *Aug.* 15.

At last I have succeeded in snatching a quiet hour at the
piano (only a very mediocre upright piano, it is true) and have
revelled, albeit imperfectly, in the beauty of your songs.[1]
Once again they are the embodiment of all one could wish, and
full of interest. Any singer might be proud of his voice in
singing them, for he is everywhere so skilfully considered and,
in spite of all their thoughtfulness, they are full of charm. I
am particularly fond of the two first, the second, notwithstanding its 5/4 time which lends such mystic feeling to the
whole. Of the *Zigeunerlieder*, the first is the one I like least.
In the second I had to accustom myself to the ninth bar, but I
like it, nevertheless, as well as the two others. If only we could
hear them soon ! Directly they are published I will get hold
of Stockhausen and see that he practises them at once. But
that he will do without my having to tell him.

So let me thank you most heartily for your parcel, which I
send back to you to-day with the two letters which have interested me very much. I have already received an invitation
from the Duke and his wife whom it was a great pleasure for
me to meet at last. Never have I felt so free and easy with
people in high places as with them. Oh, if only I could hear
your new pieces in Meiningen ! But in that case I should have
to feel better than I do at present !—I don't seem to have the
courage for the smallest undertaking, but am continually
racked with pain now in one place and now in another. I cannot discover the cause of it. To my great regret I cannot even
walk, for at the end of fifteen or twenty minutes I get the most
excruciating pains. They tell me it is the effect of the baths
in Franzensbad—but I don't believe it, for they started some
time before that. But enough of this ! Nobody can help me.
If only I did not make life so hard for poor Marie who hardly
lets a moment go by without showing me some tender solici-

[1] Op. 112.

tude.   How lucky I am to have my daughters !   But I pray
God I may not be too great a burden to them !—I am very
glad to read that the Duke of Meiningen has commissioned
Hildebrandt to make him a statue.   How pleased Hildebrandt
will be !   When we were in Munich we were delighted to see his
rough model (life size) of the fountain which will be one of the
ornaments of Munich.   Hildebrandt is so enthusiastic over his
work that it is a real pleasure to watch him. . . .   Frau Herzogenberg is much better.   How glad I am !   Her doctor, who
is here now, declared that she was so bad for a while that she
was at death's door.   I am not sure that the unbridled ambition of this good lady does not do her a lot of harm by keeping
her in a constant state of agitation.

And now farewell !   Once more hearty thanks, and let us
hear from you soon.   Your old friend CLARA.

BRAHMS *to* CLARA.

ISCHL, *Second half of August.*

Everything in your letter pleased me immensely—your kind
eulogy of the quartet, and particularly that the Meiningen
people were so sympathetic to you ; for I am convinced that
when you have spent more time with them and been an inmate
of the castle your favourable impression will only be confirmed.
When you are there you can make yourself quite at home in
every way.   You can, if you like, have your meals sent up to
your room at midday or in the evening, and you can settle this
at the last moment.   Carriages are, of course, to be had whenever you like, and in the castle itself you can be carried about.
(The family lives on the second floor.   But you, like me, will be
on the ground floor.)   The suites we shall occupy are not only
exceedingly beautiful and luxurious but also as comfortable as
you can possibly imagine.   Particularly pleasant is the lavish
supply of candles and lamps and the outlook on the park, etc.
But though I have little hope you will give me this joy I should
like to know all the same when it would be most convenient
for you to go.

In case Joachim should come and would care to do so (when
his collaboration in a concert might be arranged), I would also
have Hausmann invited.   Failing this, I think we might ask
Heermann and Becker.   To listen to the clarinet player would

mark a red-letter day in your life—a *gaudium*. You would revel, and I hope that my music would not interfere with your enjoyment !

As the weather is fine to-day Herr Wendt will have started off and will probably arrive in Berchtesgaden with this letter. I was very glad to learn that Frau Herzogenberg is better. I had had no news of them, even indirectly, for a long time, and I am growing accustomed to not hearing from them. Yes, ambition ! It looks as though the same thing were happening with them as has already happened with X——. In both cases intercourse has become impossible owing to their otherwise quite amiable wives. Both women grow more fanatical about their husbands' work every day, and yet, even in more favourable circumstances, one finds it impossible to discuss an artist's work with him, and perhaps to criticize it, if his wife is listening, not to mention arguing, with one. Alone with the men, I could come to some conclusion, and then how happy I should be to enjoy the company of the ladies afterwards !

Now with heartiest greetings to Marie, the Vosses, Frau Franz, Frl. Wendt and everybody else, Your JOHANNES.

CLARA *to* BRAHMS.

FRANKFORT A/M., *Sept.*

(*Dictated.*)

Unfortunately I do not feel well enough to write to you myself, but I must tell you something that is worrying me, and it is most important for me to have your answer as soon as possible. You know that in Mozart's D minor Concerto I have always played my own cadenzas, and in working them out you allowed me at one time to make use of certain features of a cadenza first employed by you. For some years now I have frequently been approached with the idea of publishing these cadenzas and, as I no longer play in public, I decided to do so this summer. The cadenzas have become so much part of myself that, with the exception of one very fine passage (which I had thought of marking with J. B.) I had really forgotten that I had borrowed very much more from you. But to-day when I received the second proofs from Rieter I fortunately thought of looking up your old cadenza, and then to my horror I saw to what extent I had been parading in borrowed plumes.[1] I am now in a most appalling dilemma as regards Rieter, and I can only see two alternatives—either I must withdraw my cadenzas, on the understanding, of course, that the matter remains between ourselves, or else you must allow me to add to the title " Founded on a cadenza by Johannes Brahms." If you agree to the second alternative, will you be so kind as to tell me the proper form of acknowledgment. It is terrible that such a thing should happen to anybody as conscientious as I am.

Unfortunately I am feeling so ill that I cannot start my teaching and am almost incapable of doing anything. For the last three weeks I have been suffering so badly night and day from noises in my ears that I often feel quite desperate. The doctors declare that it is all nerves and comfort me with the assurance that it will go away. My hope that they are right has been confirmed by the fact that for short periods at a time it has entirely disappeared. Begging you to let me have an answer as soon as possible, with affectionate greetings, Your old friend CLARA.

BRAHMS *to* CLARA.

VIENNA, *Oct.* 2.

Please let me implore you to let the cadenzas go out into the world in your own name without further ado. Even the minutest of J. B.s would only look strange. It really is not worth while, and I could show you many a recent work in which there is much more of me than a whole cadenza. Besides, if you did that I ought by rights to put against my best melodies " Really by Clara Schumann," for with only myself to inspire me nothing profound or beautiful can possibly occur to me ! I owe you more melodies than all the passages and so forth you could possibly take from me.

In this connection I cannot help thinking what a pity it is that I cannot hope that you will hear your newest adagios in Meiningen. I honestly believe that the trio and quintet would not spoil your enjoyment of other things there, and simply to play them to yourself at a piano might be a doubtful pleasure to you.

[1] As a matter of fact the truth is somewhat different. See *Life*, Vol. II, pp. 412–413.

But with regard to the cadenzas, you must promise to set your mind at rest at once, won't you ? With affectionate greetings to you and yours, JOHANNES.

(In Vienna since yesterday.)

CLARA *to* BRAHMS.

FRANKFORT A/M., *Oct.* 5.

So I am to allow all scruples to drop !—after permission so graciously given I cannot do otherwise. But I only wish a quarter of what you say about me were true. Unfortunately I am still very unwell and can do nothing. Scholz is now taking my lessons for me. He has been most friendly in the sympathy he has shown me and is constantly comforting me. Oh, if only my poor daughters did not have such an anxious time on my account !—they look after me with angelic patience and are my sole comfort. But I don't wish to write a letter full of complaints, in fact, I ought not to write at all. But I felt I must answer your kind letter at once. Farewell. After all, I shall only be able to go to Meiningen in spirit. As ever, Your CLARA.

BRAHMS *to* CLARA.
(*Postcard.*)

Oct. 5.

I promised to do so, and consequently inform you forthwith that Joachim has just suggested the 23rd and 24th of November for Meiningen. I sent them the message at once, and this will probably be fixed. I shall not speak, seek or sigh any more, but remain, with most affectionate greetings, Your JOH.

BRAHMS *to* CLARA.

VIENNA, *Oct.* 10.

I am pained and grieved to hear that the publication of the symphony should have come as such a surprise to you.[1] But I

---

[1] In October Clara had seen in the *Signal* that Wüllner was about to publish as a Schumann relic the original version of the fourth Symphony, which he had received from Brahms, and had consequently written at once to Brahms to express her (justifiable) indignation over the matter. Unfortunately this letter, to which Brahms now refers, cannot be found. The description of this unhappy conflict which, as the following letters show, threatened to destroy a friendship of almost

am relieved to find that you speak only of the business side of the matter. So let me tell you at once that it is a stroke of business for nobody, it could not even have been a good one for yourself. You would only have been able to demand very very little if Härtels had undertaken the matter. Whether Wüllner will get a fee (a small one in any case) for the trouble he has taken, I do not know. All I do know is that I have had a heavy bill for copying ; but I am much looking forward to the beautiful double scores (in which the two versions are printed on opposite pages)—and shall probably have to buy a copy myself if I want one. I have long been of the fixed opinion that the work must appear in this form ; and you also were aware of this.[1]—At all events you never said no, of this I am certain. But whether I can find proof of this, and whether it was written or spoken, I do not know. If I have not written or spoken to you about it more often recently, it is simply because unfortunately I could not take it for granted that my advice and tastes in this matter would have any weight with you, or meet with your approval. That is how the matter stands. I don't wish to advance any proofs or, above all, to mention any names. But how pleased I should have been to let you make a thorough examination of that wonderful double score if from the outset you had not looked so dubious. It was only when Müller pronounced judgment that you calmed down and were satisfied that the matter had been settled for you. I do not wish to enlarge now upon my reasons for liking and admiring this first version and for considering its publication necessary. But I am in no doubt whatever that you will ultimately agree with me about it, if only tacitly.

I hope your annoyance is only connected with the business side of the matter. The fact that I did not take your interests into consideration, you will surely easily forgive, when you realize that you could have got very little out of it anyhow.

For the moment I cannot think of anything more to say. So hoping that you are feeling better, and with most affectionate greetings, I am, Yours ever, JOHANNES.

forty years' standing, is seriously marred in Kalbeck's Biography owing to the author's hostility to Clara, and gives quite a false impression.

[1] Brahms is right here. Cp. the letters to Clara of April and June, 1888, and of November, 1889.

CLARA *to* BRAHMS.

FRANKFORT, *Oct.* 13.

I must have given you quite a wrong impression if my letter led you to suppose that it was only the business side of the matter that had caused me annoyance. This is very far from being the case. When I saw the announcement my first thought was of the injustice I had suffered. Although I had given the manuscript away, and thus perhaps lost any legal interest in it, I had at least the right to expect that any person with proper feeling would not have embarked on an undertaking of this kind without having obtained my express consent. Even if in the course of conversation I may once have remarked that I should have no objection to the publication of the work, this could not by any manner of means have been construed as a permission to publish it, and how Wüllner, of all people, with whom I have less in common than with any other musician, should have been entrusted with it, is utterly incomprehensible to me. It would have been quite another matter if you, who were nearer and dearer to the composer than anyone else, had published it. About all your other reproaches I will say nothing. We should never agree whatever we might say.

In conclusion it goes without saying that if my objections to Wüllner are likely to give rise to any unpleasantness for you, I will let the matter drop, the richer, it is true, by a sad experience.

Kindest greetings from Your CLARA.

BRAHMS *to* CLARA.

VIENNA, *Oct.* 16.

I alone am responsible for the publication of the Symphony and the only person who has given instructions for its issue and is answerable for it.

I could not put my name to it, first because I have no orchestra at my disposal with which to make the necessary experiments and aural tests, and secondly—because I am sorry to say I know by experience that I am not a good editor. I have often tried my hand at it, and brought love and enthusiasm to bear, but it is impossible for me to give myself a testimonial for such work and I have to confess that others are far better fitted for the task. In these circumstances I could not for the moment think of anyone better than Wüllner, whom I regard as one of our soundest and most cultured musicians, who has an excellent orchestra at his disposal, who took the greatest interest in the work, and who finally has proved himself to be a first-rate editor (e.g. in some of the hardest volumes of the Bach edition).—All this may sound too arrogant to you, as in your letter you seem to regard W. and myself not as two upright men and musicians, who are in your opinion perhaps misguided, though in their own they are carrying out a sacred and holy task with love and zeal—but as in every respect the opposite.

I don't know of anything more I can say in reply to your letter. As to what can be read between the lines—the whole spirit pervading it, I should not like to enter into that. I have felt and suspected it for a long time, but never feared that I should have it brought home to me so plainly. I have thought about it a good deal but have always come to the same conclusion as I have to-day, that it is hopeless to try to fight against it. But for an honourable man your letter of to-day is too hard and forbids my saying more. Always with the same respect, Your devoted J. B.

BRAHMS *to* CLARA.

VIENNA, *Dec.* 22.

The coming festival always seems to me a time when our lords and masters hold universal audience, when those, who might otherwise doubt their right to do so, may dare to draw nigh. So in company with many others let me tell you how much I am thinking of you, and above all hoping that through your complete restoration to health these days may indeed become a festival. During the last few weeks nobody has been more in my thoughts than you. Why this should be so, I hope others have told you.

I could not very well have talked to you about it, neither would you have been in the mood to listen. Of your interest in my music and sympathy with it I feel I can always rest assured. But the artist cannot and should not be separated from the man. And in me it happens that the artist is not so arrogant and sensitive as the man, and the latter has but small

consolation if the work of the former is not allowed to expiate
his sins.   But to-day I am thinking not of myself and still less
of my music, but am only hoping with the most heartfelt sin-
cerity that everything will go ever better and better with you.

I should also like to tell you that I went to Hamburg to see
my sister, who has been lying ill for months.   I expect to go
there again in the course of the winter.   As ever, Your wholly
devoted J. B.

CLARA *to* BRAHMS.

FRANKFORT A/M., *Dec.* 30.

Let me thank you for your dear letter which gave me so
much pleasure on Christmas morning.   I had of course followed
your footsteps with the same old sympathy, first to Meiningen
and then to Berlin, and how deeply pained I was that I could
not hear any of your glorious pieces !   How wonderful these
new works must be,[1] particularly the quintet.   What a lot I
have to forgo.   For five months I have not heard a note of
music (the last time was when I heard your vocal quartets
which you sent to me at Obersalzberg), and yet I feel no better,
and cannot occupy myself much even with other things, either
writing or reading.   How hard it all is !   I am extremely sorry
to hear that your sister is seriously ill.   I hope she is being
well looked after.   When you write to her please tell her how
much I sympathize.   I cannot write any more.   I have to limit
myself to the minimum, so can only add my heartiest wishes
for your happiness in the New Year.   And these wishes are for
the man as well as for the artist, of that you may rest assured.
Ever your devoted CLARA.

[1] The Clarinet Trio, Op. 114, and the Clarinet Quintet, Op. 115.

1892

Brahms *to* Clara.
(*Postcard.*)

VIENNA, *Jan*. 4.

A thousand thanks for your letter which made me so happy. It is with twofold pleasure that I send you a small further instalment, assuming that it will not be regarded with less favour than the first.[1] I have not seen the appendix to the complete edition either, but thanks to it my investigations have become unnecessary.

I shall be delighted to let you have the three pianoforte pieces, if they will give you the slightest pleasure. I am curious to see whether the three things I am sending you to-day will do likewise. Your devoted J. B.

Clara *to* Brahms.

FRANKFORT A/M., *May* 7.

DEAR JOHANNES,

I am not allowed to write much [2] but I feel I must send you my warmest greetings for your birthday with my own hand. Yesterday I was so unwell that I could not write, so this will reach you a little late. May you enjoy good health and once more this year be able to give further glorious gifts to mankind. Oh, how hard it is for me.—I could not get to know anything because everything I hear sounds all wrong.

---

[1] This can only refer to Op. 116 and 117. Unfortunately Clara's letter, to which Brahms alludes, and which from the psychological point of view would have been of the highest interest, must be regarded as lost.

[2] On the 1st of February Clara had had a severe attack of inflammation of the lungs, and owing to the after effects of her illness and the troubles connected with the resignation of her post at the Conservatoire, which she had sent in from her sick-bed, she had a good deal to worry her at the beginning of the year. See *Life*, Vol. II, p. 416.

To-morrow we are going to Locarno, where Eugenie has been staying for the last month.[1]   Marie will take me as far as Bâle ; from there Frau Vonder Mühll will accompany me. On account of the School Marie will have to be back by the middle of June. What will happen then—where ? whither ?—God alone knows !

May this day and all that follow bring you happiness !   Your old friend CLARA.

BRAHMS *to* CLARA.

VIENNA, *May.*

DEAR CLARA,

I cannot thank you heartily enough for the letter which came on the 8th.   It was a unique aftermath of my birthday, so unique that for to-day I must beg you to be content to take my simple thanks for it.   It means more to me than to you because I have so little that means anything.

But I do not feel justified in detaining you with this subject. To-day I could not do so even on my own account, for what I wish to do first and foremost is to thank you for having pierced the greyness of my day with a ray of sunlight.   So turning gladly away from myself and my affairs, let me have the pleasure of giving you news about your friends here and discussing other things that concern you.

In case you do not know it already the most important thing to tell you is that R. Pohl no longer has the *Manfred* in his possession.   It is on show at the exhibition here as the property of Fürstner the Berlin publisher.   This is a pity because I had offered a high price for it and had hoped to secure it.   In any case you will be pleased to hear that both Pohl and Fürstner have solemnly undertaken not to allow the manuscript to be broken up or sold to England or America, but it will be sent to Berlin to take its place among the other Schumann relics.

I cannot realize that you and your daughters have left the School.   Surely you will retain some exceptional honorary position there.   I should think that Frl. Marie will miss the customary matutiral noise more than Eugenie—I don't know whom I may have insulted by this.   The Landgrave has had a

---

[1] She was also suffering from the effects of a severe illness which she had had in March.

glorious time here and in Pesth and is now going to try to meet you and tell you all about it.   Frau Franz has gone with her daughter to Rome and I am sure would be glad to meet you on the return journey.   You probably already know how flourishing the Fellingers are and how extraordinarily and magnificently their factory, their business and their circumstances have changed.   I cannot give you more explicit details as I do not understand the matter and have no memory for figures and such things, but it would really be worth your while to ask Frau F. to give you a full account of her factory and her activities.

In spite of all my protestations they have installed electric light in my rooms.   She is also in very much better health and is on the point of going off to Misdroy.   You too are going into a beautiful country and I heartily hope towards ever greater joys.   Your J. B.

BRAHMS *to* CLARA.

ISCHL, *June.*

I like to think of you as enjoying the most wonderful summer peace and therefore hesitate to tell you something which, though it is really something we ought to feel relieved about, is nevertheless a message of sorrow.   After prolonged and severe suffering my sister has been ultimately released by death.[1] You were always so friendly to her that I feel I must tell you about it.   She lay desperately ill the whole winter, but she clung so hard to life that she certainly never gave up hope until the end.   We who were watching could not help wishing for the end long ago, for in her case it was only a release.

I visited her during the winter and wrote to her on the very day before her death that I was thinking of going there again in the course of the next few days.   Of course everything that could possibly be done for her was done, and I am deeply indebted to a Hamburg cousin and to Böies in Altona for the devoted way in which they seconded all my efforts.

I do hope this bit of news will be the saddest that will come to you this summer, which I heartily hope will be as beneficial and as pleasant to you as possible.   Your JOHANNES.

---

[1] On the 11th of June.

CLARA *to* BRAHMS.

INTERLAKEN, PENSION OBER, *June* 20.

How sorry I was to receive your sad news ! So you have now buried your dear sister. How sad it was to have to regard her death as a release from such severe suffering ! What a number of pleasant experiences are recalled to my mind by the thought of her. Thus one after the other of our loved ones goes and the wilderness about our hearts increases. I dearly loved Elise and was she not, after all, your sister ! The loss must indeed be a hard blow to you, but you have the great comfort of knowing that you made her life easy and sunny both through your brotherly help and your art.

I am now in Interlaken with Marie. I left Eugenie in Locarno with the friend who was with her in Malta. She has been very ill and has given us great anxiety. She is better now but still remains very delicate. I had to leave her [1] as I could not recover my own strength in the midst of all the commotions which her fluctuating condition entails. I need peace and so does Eugenie. We got on each other's nerves and that made things impossible. I shall remain here with Marie [2] until the weather gets warmer and then we shall go to the Brünig. The doctor says that the altitude of 2,000 feet here is high enough for me.

The *Manfred* business is very vexing. But if it ultimately joins the other works I shall be satisfied. . . . Please tell Ilona [3] that I thank her for her little note, but that owing to neuralgia in my arm I am forbidden to write, and Marie can hardly deal with all that is necessary.

Marie wishes me to send you her deepest sympathy—now Hamburg no longer shelters anyone dear to you. Farewell, and with all good wishes, Your CLARA.

BRAHMS *to* CLARA.

ISCHL, *June* 23.

It is extraordinarily pleasant to know where the person is of whom one delights to think and perchance to be acquainted

---

[1] Clara had left Locarno on the 28th of May and, after a stay of a week in Bâle, with the Vonder Mühlls, went to Interlaken.

[2] Concerning the stay in Interlaken see *Life*, Vol. II, p. 416.

[3] Ilona Eibenschütz.

with the beautiful spot as well.   It was a great joy to me when
I read Interlaken in your letter, and my face immediately
lighted up as if I myself were there and saw you before me.

Whenever I have been there in the summer I have never
noticed the altitude of 2,000 feet, and believe, on the contrary,
that the severe heat will drive you away soon enough and
make you go in search of one of the many beautiful heights in
the neighbourhood.   What a blessing it is that Marie at least
keeps well and can remain with you !   I thank you both for
your kind sympathy.   So I am the last of our branch of the
family !   Nevertheless, I am glad to say my step-mother is
still alive and is living very happily with her son, a clockmaker,
in Pinneberg in Holstein, close to Hamburg, so that when I
go there I can see her in her comfortable home.   I look around
among the neighbouring heights, Abendberg, Beatenberg,
Brünig—my favourite mountain.   The choice will not fall on
Mürren.   There is a railway going up it now—but I hope you
won't risk the journey.   In any case I trust that the height
you choose will treat you well and kindly so that you may leave
it the happier and the stronger.   With hearty greetings to you
and Frl. Marie, Your JOHANNES.

BRAHMS *to* CLARA.

VIENNA, *Sept.* 13.

Please allow a poor pariah to tell you to-day that he always
thinks of you with the same respect, and out of the fullness of
his heart wishes you, whom he holds dearer than anything on
earth, all that is good, desirable and beautiful.   Alas, to you
more than to any other I am a pariah ; this has, for a long
time, been my painful conviction, but I never expected it to be
so harshly expressed.   You know very well that I cannot
accept the ostensible cause, the printing of the Symphony, as
the real cause.   Years ago I had a profound feeling that this
was so, though I said nothing about it, at the time when the
Schumann pianoforte pieces, which I was the first to publish,
were not included in the Complete Edition.   All I could think
of on both occasions was that you did not like to see my name
associated with them.   With the best will in the world I can
neither discover nor acknowledge any other reason.

In my dealings with my friends I am aware of only one fault

—my lack of tact. For years now you have been kind enough to treat this leniently. If only you could have done so for a few years more !

After forty years of faithful service (or whatever you care to call my relationship to you) it is very hard to be merely " another unhappy experience." But after all, this can be borne. I am accustomed to loneliness and will need to be with the prospect of this great blank before me. But let me repeat to you to-day that you and your husband constitute the most beautiful experience of my life, and represent all that is richest and most noble in it.

I feel owing to my peculiar ways—not anything else—I may have deserved the great pain of seeing you turn away from me, but loving and reverent thoughts of you and him will always shine warmly and brightly in the heart of Your devoted J. B.

CLARA *to* BRAHMS.

FRANKFORT A/M., *Sept.* 27.

Your good wishes reached me in Interlaken just as we were about to leave. Meanwhile we have been travelling about a little and have only just settled down here with the peace and quiet necessary for answering your momentous letter. It made me very sad. But I am glad that you have spoken out so frankly, for I can now do the same. You reproach me with having shown you too little consideration in connection with the Schumann Edition. But I cannot for the life of me remember why the pieces did not appear in this way and have always cherished the belief that everything I did in regard to the Edition was in accordance with your advice. If, however, I offended you, you should have told me at once quite openly and not have given free rein to the base suspicion that I did not like to see your name connected with Robert's. Such a thought could only have occurred to you in an evil hour, and, after so many years of artistic association, it is utterly incomprehensible to me how you could suspect me of such a thing. Surely it is quite out of keeping with my attitude of reverence towards you all these years, and also with what you say to me at the end of your letter. If your suspicion were well founded surely I could not be reckoned among the most pleasant recollections of your life ? You are certainly right in saying that personal intercourse with you is often difficult, and yet my friendship for you has always helped me to rise superior to your vagaries. Unfortunately, on the occasion of your last visit, I was unable to rid my heart of the bitterest feeling that it harboured against you.

. . . But enough of this ! Nothing makes me more miserable than these disputes and explanations. Am I not the most peaceable person on earth ? So, my dear Johannes, let us strike a more friendly note, for which your beautiful pianoforte pieces, about which Ilona has just written to me, afford the best opportunity if you will only take it. Greeting you with the same old affection, I am, Your CLARA.

BRAHMS *to* CLARA.
Beginning of October.

From the bottom of my heart I thank you for your kind and comforting reply to my letter. The subject of our altercation, which seems to have upset you so much, I do not even remember, but I infinitely regret not having kept sharper guard over my tongue. With regard to the Schumann Edition I cannot remember whether it was you or I who wrote ambiguously.

I mentioned the G minor Presto, the F minor Scherzo and possibly, too, some of the posthumous studies which were published by Rieter. You " do not remember why the pieces were not published as I wanted them to be "—but what I would point out is precisely that they were never included at all in the Complete Edition. And that is what I cannot understand, for the pieces are unquestionably among Schumann's finest works (admittedly numerous). I am delighted that you have so thoroughly enjoyed the summer and that you like Interlaken enough to return there next year. I feel sure you will be able to have many a pleasant time there. A fairly large place of that kind has its peculiar advantages.

As you wish to have them I am sending you a volume of pianoforte pieces. On Monday I go to Berlin. When I return (in about a week) I shall have a few more copied out for you and shall send them to you. You can let me have the whole lot back at your convenience. I do not need to ask you not to let them leave your hands nor, alas, not to let them tire you but only be a pleasure to you.   In the short C minor piece you will probably do well to take the six-eight time as it is given in brackets at the up-beat.   Of course the particular charm which every difficulty has, thus gets lost, and in this case the strong and supple bending of hands—of large hands !

But the pieces are not worth so much talk.   Lay them aside and turn perhaps to the Rhapsodies if you are good enough to wish to remember the music of Your heartily devoted JOHANNES.

CLARA *to* BRAHMS.

FRANKFORT A/M., *Oct.* 13.

First of all, many thanks for the wonderfully original pianoforte pieces, all of which I now know very well.   I can only give a quarter of an hour to them at a time when the humming in my ears dies down a little.   Then I try modulations first of all in higher octaves several times until I get the right sound.   I am particularly enchanted with the A minor Intermezzo, then the intermezzos in E minor and E major and the last of all—in short with all, each one in its way.   I like the deeply passionate as much as the dreamy ones, in which such exquisite effects of sound are conjured out of the piano.   But I should never like to hear the E minor with the single notes only, because it is just the position of the hands, one on the top of the other, that has a peculiar charm and sounds quite different.

One literally rocks oneself to sleep by it.   May I keep the pieces for a little while, and then may I show them to Joachim when he comes next week ?   Perhaps I might play a few to him ?

Now may I ask you once more to tell me plainly what it was about the publication of the pieces from Robert's posthumous works that offended you ?   What I thought was that they had not appeared at all in the complete edition and wrote at once to Härtels that they were to have them printed as an appendix.   Whereupon to my astonishment he sent me a printed copy of them.   What was I to think ?   I have never corresponded with Härtels about these pieces but merely looked through what he sent me and thought no more about it.   Please enlighten me.   I hate all this uncertainty.   If I have done wrong you must ascribe it to my absent-mindedness. Farewell for to-day ; with affectionate greetings, Your CLARA.

CLARA *to* BRAHMS.

FRANKFORT A/M., *Nov.* 6.

. . . There is a great deal of excitement here about Dessoff's successor.[1] A few days ago Alois Schmitt arrived here, I fancy in order to apply for the post, though he said nothing about it. Scholz is taking charge of the next concert at the theatre and I should think will also do the others if a temporary conductor is not appointed. . . . Finally, let me tell you how full of enthusiasm I am for your three last pieces. The first and third I am constantly playing. How wonderful they are, each in its own way ! In the third, which has such a national character (is it Scotch ?) I can forget myself completely. How heavenly the final bars are ! But there is also the first, the Intermezzo in B minor, with the *non troppo presto*, where I allow my fingers to let themselves go. Then the Capriccio in G minor with the March, and lastly the Notturno. I also play these with passion, and must thank you once more for them. They brighten an otherwise dreary musical existence, for I can only enjoy music at the piano now ; I cannot endure either an orchestra or quartet music, for I feel as if each musician were playing something different.

And now in conclusion just one more affectionate greeting from Your CLARA.

CLARA *to* BRAHMS.

FRANKFORT A/M., *Nov.* 16.

. . . I worked at the second of your pieces, the B Flat minor, with great pleasure to-day. How fortunate it is that as far as the D minor these pieces are not too much for me. I shall soon be able to manage the subtleties. Just fancy

---

[1] In a letter dated 28th of October, 1892, Clara had informed Brahms that Dessoff was dead and had declared that his end was all the more astonishing because he had told everyone recently that he had never felt so well. Replying to this letter Brahms said : " You have had a great loss in Dessoff ; that I know, because we felt it when we left here. It was impossible for anybody to take his place. He was an excellent man and as a musician was exceptionally sensitive and scholarly."—TR.

in the D minor piece my ears play me the trick of always making the whole of one passage sound wrong !

They are seriously considering the appointment of Mottl as successor to Dessoff here. What a miserable prospect ! So we shall soon have no more Mozart and Beethoven. With most affectionate greetings for to-day, Your old friend CLARA.

Joachim is coming on Sunday with his quartet. If only I could hear it ! But I shall be glad to see him.

CLARA *to* BRAHMS.

> FRANKFORT A/M., *Nov.* 21.

. . . Joachim left to-day, but he is coming back on Thursday for a day. Yesterday he had his quartet here—I heard two things—it was a trying ordeal for me, for I only heard snatches. Joachim seemed very much depressed. . . . Your old friend CLARA.

Have you heard nothing from the Meiningen people ?

BRAHMS *to* CLARA.

> VIENNA, *Nov.* 25.

. . . The Meiningen people are not as well as they might be. After making a thorough examination of both of them the doctor has advised them to go south (Cannes) at the New Year. But they are really too kind. Widmann of Berne wanted to try a new play there in January, and now in spite of everything they have invited him and his wife (as well as myself) to stay at the castle, and to rehearse and do anything he likes in the theatre. I shall probably go if only to be with the dear man himself. Joachim probably has good reasons for being depressed—but—but I shall leave the last page empty, otherwise our faces might grow too long. With most affectionate greetings, Your very devoted JOH.

CLARA *to* BRAHMS.

> FRANKFORT A/M., *Nov.* 29.

. . . I have been pondering over what you said about Joachim. I only saw him alone here for half an hour and found him so gloomy, haggard and wizened that I could not get over it for a long time. I tried to talk to him about his children but he insisted on changing the subject, which hurt

me. For who could take a deeper interest in them ? . . .
How delightful the Meiningen people are ! I was secretly
cherishing the hope that I might possibly see them there this
winter—I have such pleasant recollections of them in Berchtesgaden. All my good wishes for both of them !

Farewell for to-day. I have just heard that Schmitt from
Schwerin is coming here. Ever your faithful old friend CLARA.

BRAHMS *to* CLARA.

VIENNA, *Dec.* 23.

It is a long time since I celebrated my last Christmas with
you, but I have not had such a pleasant one since, and the
best part of this one will be the recollection of how on that
evening the brightly lighted tree shone forth and all eyes
young and old reflected its glory. May this year's festival
be like it ! . . .

The Variations are remarkable and irresistibly charming.[1]
The other day on coming home from a general rehearsal I
again sat down at my piano and without any particular object
in my mind played them over to myself quite naturally and
with profound emotion. I felt as though I were walking,
on a beautiful soft spring morning, in a grove of alders, birches
and lovely flowers, with a babbling brook at my feet. One
never gets tired of the mild still air, the delicate azure, the
tender greens ; there is nothing to remind one of the hurly-
burly, and one feels no wish for darkling woods, for rugged
rocks and waterfalls amid all this beautiful monotony. If
one examined the music alone with the eyes of a Philistine,
one might notice, perhaps with misgiving, how the theme
ends four times on the same tone, and one might be inclined
to regard the soft sweet harmonies as sickly and flabby, and
dread hearing them repeated too often in the Variations. Vain
fears ! One plunges into them again and enjoys the delightful music just like the gentle refreshing breezes and landscape
of spring. But good God, if every letter writer were to remain
so long over one letter to-day, what time would there be left

---

[1] This refers to Robert Schumann's work, about the publication of
which and other matters connected with the complete edition of his
works there had been much correspondence between Brahms and
Clara which seemed too technical to be of interest to the reader.—TR.

for work on the Christmas tree ?   I am now going to start on
it myself and will think of you as I am doing so.   With most
affectionate greetings, JOHANNES.

CLARA *to* BRAHMS.

FRANKFORT A/M., *Dec.* 30.

That was a charming Christmas letter of yours, and I would
so much have liked to tell you at once how much I enjoyed
it.   But at the present moment I am overwhelmed with work
and have too little strength for it.   Your musings over the
Variations filled me with a sense of well-being.   You have
expressed so exquisitely what I have so often felt about them.
Many a time and oft have I too reflected upon that beautiful
monotony which, in the Variations, play so refreshingly upon
one's heart-strings.   Let us have them printed in their original
form.   I am looking forward very much to seeing them in
this shape, and it is quite enough for me that you are in favour
of it.

We spent Christmas Eve quietly at home and our finest
gift was the presence of Eugenie well and happy in our midst.
You were probably at the Fellingers ?

There is one request I should like to make to-day.   A certain Mr. Shakespeare and his wife from London, both charming people and musical to the core, are going to Vienna, and
their greatest wish is to meet you.   He is the first teacher of
singing in London ; he is also a pianist ; and his daughter,
who is singularly gifted too, has been Marie's pupil for some
time.   I cannot refuse them their wish and comfort myself
with the thought that you will not take long to recognize in
them two of your most ardent admirers.   They are only
going to stay three or four days.   I should also like to introduce them to Anna Franz so that they might see a little home
life in Vienna.

I have many letters of thanks to write, so must close.   We
all send you our good wishes for the New Year—but here I
can say no more, for out of the fullness of the heart the mouth
is sometimes dumb.   Ever your faithful CLARA.

1893

Brahms *to* Clara.

VIENNA, *Jan*. 23.

DEAR CLARA,

In a few days' time I shall be going to Meiningen and propose to seize the opportunity to go to Hamburg, where there are many things to settle and put in order after the death of my sister and my cousin. The principal object of this winter journey is really that I should like to be in Frankfort on the 31st in order to see you again at last. What is seriously exercising my mind, however, is whether you feel inclined to put up with any kind of disturbance, although I am thinking of sparing you as much as possible by going to an hotel. In fact I am hesitating and wondering what to do. Now it would be extremely kind of you if you would drop me a line at Meiningen (to the castle) to tell me quite frankly and openly whether you would like me to come and what arrangement would suit you best. I shall probably have another little concert on Monday the 30th in M. and, on Tuesday the 31st, according to how you decide, I shall get into the train either a very happy or a very miserable man. Once more let me implore you not to hesitate to tell me exactly what is most convenient and agreeable to you. With most affectionate greetings, Your J. B.

Clara *to* Brahms.

FRANKFORT A/M., *Jan*. 25.

DEAR JOHANNES,

I shall await you with mingled feelings of joy and sorrow —sorrow, because, though you will find me better than I was last year, I am nevertheless not as robust and vigorous as I once was. What often upsets me most of all in my present extremely depressed condition is the continual humming in

my head. Nevertheless it would grieve me very much if
you stayed at an hotel and I most heartily beg you to put
up with us as you have before. Besides, I am quite well
enough to be able to receive visitors, and so you need have
no qualms.

I am spending much time at present playing your quintet
for four hands, and as often as I do so my desire to hear this
heavenly work with Mühlfeld and his clarinet increases. I
know it so accurately now that I should be able to hear a
good deal—I mean correctly. Marie plays it with me and
revels in it also. All further news then when we meet. But
I reckon on your sending me a postcard. You will not find
Eugenie here, and she will be very sorry. The place will be
even quieter for you than it usually is. With most affectionate
greetings from both of us, Your old friend CLARA.

BRAHMS *to* CLARA.

MEININGEN, *Jan.* 28.

Delighted by your dear letter, let me tell you quite briefly
that, as I wrote to you before, I expect to reach you on Tuesday evening. I shall leave here about half-past two, and will
arrive about nine o'clock. You will be able to find more
precise details from a time-table—I haven't got one.

We are living here in the midst of rehearsals of a very interesting play [1] by Widmann, which requires very special staging,
and the first performance of which will be extremely difficult
in every way. If you were with us you would take a delight
in the beautiful and poetical scenery, transformations and all
the more important things connected with them. Then on
Monday you could hear the quintet by Mühlfeld, and on Tuesday afternoon contented and happy get into the train for
Frankfort as hopes to do Your ever affectionate JOHANNES.

BRAHMS *to* CLARA.

VIENNA, *Feb.* 22.

Having reached home at last, I must tell you with what
joy I look back upon my days in Frankfort. I undertook
the journey with that visit as my sole object, and how glad
I am now that I did so. But you know all this as well as I

---

[1] His comedy, *Jenseits von Gut und Böse.*

do and must certainly realize how grateful I am for the delightful time which did me so much good.

How the gods deal with us mortals will remain for ever a
gruesome mystery. But that they should plague you with
hideous music is surely too absurd ! " Of other sins you are
innocent," and as far as both the gods and our glorious art
are concerned you have not deserved this treatment. How
many in these days would not find pleasure in what to you is
insufferable agony. Our great Bruckner would be only too
delighted to have your odious hummings in his ears. We
should then get them on Sundays in the form of symphonies,
and Heyse and Levi would write appreciative criticisms about
them !

Now let me describe quite briefly how I ended my journey
in Hamburg and Berlin, for it was quite as successful there
as was its beginning in Meiningen. I spent an extremely
happy time with Friedchen, about which she must already
have written to you. Everything was very pleasant too in
all other respects, not excepting even the incredibly vile
weather ; for any particular love of my native city, and hence
any home-sickness that I might have felt, was completely
washed away by the genuine Hamburg weather which was
my lot.

In Berlin I saw many of our common friends, Bargiel, Herzogenberg, Fr. Soldat, etc. Johannes Joachim was sitting for
his Doctor's examination at the time. . . .

And now with reiterated thanks to you and Marie and
begging you to remember me very kindly to the Sommerhoffs
on Sunday, wholly yours, JOHANNES.

CLARA *to* BRAHMS.

FRANKFORT A/M., *Feb.* 25.

I was extremely delighted to hear your good news and
doubly so because I, as you say, was the object of your journey.
I was particularly glad to hear that you were happy with us,
although I could not help constantly deploring the fact that
we had nothing except ourselves to offer you, which was little
indeed !

Friedchen wrote me a very happy letter about your visit.
How glad I am that she had the twofold pleasure which you

gave her.   The way she manages with her weak frame to rise
superior to all her troubles, fills me with admiration. . . .
There has been much excitement here of late, but I have only
been told about it.   Everybody has gone quite mad about
Rubinstein.   They received his compositions with acclama-
tion, in the hope presumably that he would play to them himself ; and he ultimately did so, but only after the matinée.
Marie said that much of what he played was enchanting, but
that other things were so unrestrained and wild that it seemed
as if a hurricane had broken loose in the hall.   As I do not
attend concerts now I did not see him, but Marie thought he
looked terribly wan and haggard.   By all accounts he seems
to be entirely absorbed in his own compositions.   He grumbled
at the theatre for not producing his operas.   But they were
tried, and the only time there was any audience was when he
conducted himself ; afterwards they played to empty houses.
He spoke very openly about all this.   Among other things he
said when somebody observed that Kogel [1] imitated Bülow
that he did not know which was the greater donkey, Bülow
or Kogel.

A whole crowd of people left here for Bonn last week to
attend the Beethoven evening which he was giving for the
B. House.   He played four sonatas and threw in another—
five in all therefore.   I cannot help thinking that such a heavy
bill of fare is inartistic.   One puts one's whole soul into one
sonata, can one put it into five ?   But this is perhaps pedantic.
Evidently I belong to a bygone age.   Thank God, there is
someone left to whom right-minded people can still fasten
themselves as to a sheet-anchor, and that is you.   And when
I think of it my heart warms with gratitude that it should
be so. . . .

Last week I was able to pay a few visits (early in the day,
of course), and I was none the worse for it.   Everybody greeted
me so heartily that it was as if I had risen from the dead.
But what a gossiping letter this is ; I must end it quickly.
With most affectionate greetings from us both, and hoping we
may soon hear from you, Your old friend CLARA.

[1] Director of the Museum Concerts.

CLARA *to* BRAHMS.

FRANKFORT A/M., *March* 18.

I am not really feeling well, but I must write you a line after having at last heard your exquisite quintet.[1] What a magnificent thing it is and how it moves one! How the subtle fusion of the instruments with the soft and insistent wail of the clarinet above them lays hold of one! The adagio is most affecting, and how wonderfully interesting is the middle movement. But words are inadequate to express what I feel! And the man plays so wonderfully, he might have been specially created for your works. I marvelled at his profound simplicity and the subtlety of his understanding. I cannot tell you how much I enjoyed it. But just imagine how unlucky I was—I did not hear the second rehearsal, I had caught such a violent chill in Heermann's cold room that on the following morning I had to remain in bed. That was really hard lines! But I will not complain. The joy that I had survives in my heart and for that I am grateful.

A few days ago Dr. Rottenberg conducted in the theatre here, and among other things played your Haydn Variations, and all the musicians are very much taken with him. He will probably take Dessoff's place. Clara Wittgenstein told me that you know him very well. So we can look forward to his coming. There have been great discussions at the *Cäcilien Verein* and Kogel was defeated. Rudorff would like to have the post, but I am afraid his hopes are vain. With most affectionate greetings, Your old friend CLARA.

BRAHMS *to* CLARA.

VIENNA, *March* 20 ?

That's the way to enjoy a concert! It took place in Frankfort, while I sat calmly in Vienna. But have you not written me a delightful letter about the rehearsal and how you enjoyed the quintet. I have long wished that you might hear this piece played by Mühlfeld. I knew how sympathetic the man would be to you and how he would win your heart as an artist. What a shame that Heermann's cold room robbed you of the joy of hearing him more often. Possibly he might have come to you and you might have had some music together. . . .

[1] See *Life*, Vol. II, p. 422.

I am planning, or rather, Widmann, Hegar and Freund are
planning a trip to Sicily, but I don't think anything will come
of it, and I am thinking instead of one to northern Italy and
of a certain beautiful lake where I shall meet dear and charming friends. . . .

Thank you again most heartily for your letter. It gave
me untold joy. Affectionately yours, JOHANNES.

CLARA *to* BRAHMS.

FRANKFORT A/M., *May* 5.

Whither can my thoughts fly to you to-day ? You do not
even allow your oldest friend to know where you are, and I
must scatter my wishes to the four winds. I can only hope
that you are dreaming the day away or celebrating it merrily
amid the glories of nature. Your beloved travelling companions will surely see to that ! (probably H. Widmann and
Hegar ?) Thus you have attained to a dignified age which
the world should certainly be thankful for, though you are
perhaps less so. I wish you many more years of the health
and strength you have always enjoyed, so that you may rejoice
our hearts with fresh creations of your genius.

We returned safely a few days ago, having spent a very
pleasant time in Pallanza,[1] particularly on the lake. As the
roads were very dusty, to take the boat was our only means
of making pleasant excursions, and thus our fear of the water
gradually disappeared. We were enchanted with the wonderful vegetation which often transported us into dreamland.
We were lucky enough to make pleasant acquaintances in
Dr. Scharrenbroich and his wife who, thanks to the Doctor's
great enthusiasm for music and to his kind interest in my
health, soon grew to be friends, so that our parting from them
was quite a wrench. He strongly urged us to take more pains
about my health, and slightly modified our plans for the summer by advising me to spend the whole of July in Schlangenbad, because I suffer from my nerves, and only to go to Switzerland in August and September and to choose Interlaken
again. I played him your pianoforte pieces once, whereupon
he said that anybody who was capable of feeling and playing with so much life ought to be able to increase her general

[1] From the 5th to the 25th of April.

efficiency a great deal, and all his advice was directed to that end.

I am writing all this because our minds have been full of it for a long while. Besides, I hate always having to be moaning and groaning. Heartiest thanks for your last dear letter. I wonder whether you are going to Ischl now. In any case I am sending my letter to Vienna, whither you will be sure to return some time. Please, dear Johannes, let us hear from you soon, so that I may know where to find you again. Marie sends her most affectionate wishes, and I am always, Your faithful old friend CLARA.

P.S. People believe that Trautmann, who is very young and very gifted, will get the post at the *Cäcilien Verein*—he is certainly still only a beginner. I have been pestered with all kinds of solicitations about this post. People think I have so much influence, when, as a matter of fact, I have no voice in the matter at all. I should have been glad to have Rudorff.

BRAHMS *to* CLARA.

VIENNA, *May* 10.

It was a tremendous joy to me when I returned home to find good news from you. I should have liked to write to you too and tell you all about the beautiful and happy experiences which I had in such abundance. But it is difficult to find time to write in Italy, besides which I really try to avoid doing so, for one can read such beautiful letters about Italy in print. But after all I have landed here in the midst of a most awful turmoil, and am trying to find a short cut out of it by means of letters, telegrams, etc. But when the Mayor, the City and the University join in a chorus of congratulations, one must take off one's hat and thank them. The *Gesellschaft der Musikfreunde* has had a very fine gold medal struck, which I am sure would please you. Fortunately my sixty years come very little into my reckoning, but then I always was bad at arithmetic. On our travels I was certainly the most vigorous and had the greatest staying power. I was always the last to bed and the first to rise, although my three travelling companions are much younger men—Widmann, Hegar and Robert Freund, a most delightful and cultivated young fellow from Pesth who is a pianoforte professor in Zurich.

Our trip was in every respect a perfect one.   The weather was continuously fine, just like the country and its people. One travels through the whole of Italy as though it were a most beautiful garden, and to my mind it often rises to the heights of a paradise.   At such times one gets out and looks more closely at everything.   This is what we did, among other places, in Naples, Palermo, Girgenti, Syracuse, Taormina and again in Naples and Venice (Freund and I) on our way back.

Unfortunately, however, so as not to miss the human touch, I lost all my money at the very beginning of the journey.   I cheerfully concluded that it was merely a sacrifice to the gods, and hoped that it might suffice them.   But as luck would have it, they demanded more.   On the return journey from Messina to Naples Widmann had a serious mishap in the stowage room of the steamer.   It was a terrible moment and he had a hairbreadth escape (this was literally so because for an instant his foot was caught in the link of a chain).   We expected to see him smashed to atoms, and hurled into the abyss so that we should only have been able to bring his dead body back to his wife.   So we felt relieved that he only had a broken leg.

He will get over it in six weeks.   But how nervous it will make him about travelling in the future, and his wife even more so.   But I must turn my attention to other letters and will merely add, therefore, that the last volume is now printed and ready.   As soon as I have corrected it I will return the MSS. to you, but I liked to have them by me.   I am tempted to send you the short preface.   If I don't do so, let me tell you at once that it is because it consists only of necessary formal matter and that I have been to great pains to refrain from enthusiastic comment (about you too) in its composition ;   for I do not think this is the proper place for such expressions of opinion.

The little Eibenschütz was here yesterday.   Young Rottenberg is a nice refined fellow, a very good musician and a most gifted conductor. . . .   And now with my most hearty greetings, I hope you will put up with this gossiping letter as kindly as you do with the whole of Your loving JOHANNES.

BRAHMS *to* CLARA.
(*Postcard.*)

May 23.

You remember about the medal which the *Gesellschaft der Musikfreunde* struck in my honour ? I now hear that the Directors are going to have a limited number of replicas made for my very special friends, among whom you will be the first. I am telling you this, because although, as a rule, such gifts are accepted off-handedly without acknowledgment, I should like the Directors to have the pleasure of receiving a note of thanks from you. For this purpose I am quite ready to take your replica in exchange for my gold one—that will be a very different matter. Forgive me for this. It seemed to me so necessary. With most affectionate greetings, Your JOH.

CLARA *to* BRAHMS.
(*Postcard.*)

May 26.

For God's sake don't send me the gold medal. I should like to gloat over the medal every day, but if I had the gold one I should have to put it away in my safe among my other gold treasures. So please give up this sublime and generous idea ! I am much looking forward to receiving the replica which the Directors intend to send me and I shall not be slow to thank them. The MSS. have arrived. Don't you want any of them ? Affectionately yours, C. SCH.

CLARA *to* BRAHMS.

FRANKFORT, *May* 24.

First of all many thanks for your dear letter which gave me so much pleasure, and also for the beautiful portrait which, together with the charming illustrations, delighted me. I think the Hanfstängel one more intellectual in expression, but I found even the other—particularly at a distance—a striking likeness. The fact that it was you who had it sent to me makes my joy all the greater. So once more, heartiest thanks. I am enclosing a little note for Herr Michalek which please forward to him as he has not sent me his address.

How magnificent your journey must have been and in such pleasant company. But I was greatly shocked to hear of

Widmann's mishap, and I have been busy wondering whether anybody remained behind with him. He is probably still lying in Naples. How dreadful ! I should have been so glad to send him a word or two of sympathy, but where ? I know no address, not even the one in Berne. When you write to him please say a word or two from me. How on earth did he get into the stowage room ? Surely nobody goes down there ? Your loss of money was also annoying, but philosophy is a great help on such occasions.

We have got into the old groove again here and I am glad, because a life of wandering does not suit me at all. We spent Whitsun at Schlangenbad in order to find rooms there for July. It is an enchanting spot and one can get into the woods easily anywhere, which is one of my chief reasons for going. Eugenie will join us there, and in August we shall probably go to Interlaken again. I suppose you are already preparing for Ischl. What a pity that it is so relaxing there. It certainly cannot be the right place for Ilona [Eibenschütz] either. I have not received the last Volume yet. Please do not hurry about sending back the MS. and if you should care to keep one or two things to add to your collection of autographs I should be delighted to let you do so.

The musical festivals are now over and I am glad ; for during the period of the Bonn festival more particularly I could not help feeling depressed that I could no longer be where after all I really belong. At any time it would certainly have been rather much for me. There was very little attraction in the Düsseldorf festival, and all the commotion connected with it has nauseated me for a long time. If I have deciphered the name of the artist wrongly please send me back my little note. I don't like to write anybody's name (particularly when he has one like that—I mean a peculiar sort of name) incorrectly.

And now, with affectionate greetings, Your faithful friend CLARA.

BRAHMS *to* CLARA.

ISCHL, *May.*

I have been in Ischl a week and I thought I had written to tell you so ; I also thought I had been more explicit about

Widmann.   After thanking you most heartily for your letter
and card, then, I will explain matters to you more plainly.
He did not wander into the stowage room, but the chain bearing the baggage threatened to pull him down there and would
have done so if, as luck would have it, one of his feet had not
got caught in some way and held him fast, so that he was
ultimately released from his perilous position in the air.   The
foot which he had already broken once, was broken again.
We remained with him in Naples, and took turns to keep his
bandages constantly changed (making most delightful excursions in between) until he was able to travel with his leg in
plaster of Paris.   Hegar went with him as far as Berne, but
Freund and I, who could be of no further use, went to Venice.
We all went off together on the afternoon of the 7th.   In case
you should care to send him a note, his address is simply
J.B.W., Editor of the *Bund*, Berne.

It is really too kind and friendly of you to offer me some
of the MSS.   But thank God the temptation is out of my way,
and so it only remains to thank you.   As for the medal, surely
it is a very simple matter ?   I do not take nearly so much
care of such things as you do ; they lie about in open cupboards, and I only keep my MSS. and letters under lock and
key.

I am tempted to have a short pianoforte piece [1] copied for
you, as I should very much like to know how you get on with
it.   It teems with discords.   These may be all right and quite
explicable, but you may not perhaps like them, in which case
I might wish that they were less right but more pleasing and
more to your taste.   It is exceptionally melancholy, and to
say—" to be played very slowly " is not sufficient.   Every
bar and every note must be played as if *ritardando* were indi-
cated, and one wished to draw the melancholy out of each
one of them, and voluptuous joy and comfort out of the discords.   My God, how this description will whet your appetite !

I had a letter to-day from Baroness Heldburg from whom
I had not heard for a long time.   She is going back to Meiningen, which is certainly a good sign.   Enough for to-day, with
heartiest greetings, Your JOHANNES.

[1] Op. 119.

CLARA *to* BRAHMS.

FRANKFORT A/M., *June* 8.

You must have known how enthusiastic I should be when you were copying out that bitter-sweet piece which, for all its discords, is so wonderful. Nay, one actually revels in the discords, and, when playing them, wonders how the composer ever brought them to birth. Thank you for this new, magnificent gift ! It is a topsy-turvy world ; instead of my giving you something, as I should so much like to have done for your birthday, you send me a present. But I could never have sent you one like that !

We have been through troublesome times. There is scarlet fever at the Sommerhoffs, but thank God things are taking their normal course and only one of the children has had it. But we have been very anxious. I have not yet been able to find time to write to poor Widmann, because I have been very busy with correspondence once more about Ferdinand's boys. All this means much annoyance and one is not in the mood for anything. . . . I think Widmann's poem enchanting. Thank you for that and no less for your kind letter. . . . If only heaven would allow me to hear a little music next winter ! But unfortunately my infirmity does not improve. Let us have a sign of life soon. Your old and faithful friend CLARA.

I have not yet received the medal. I am very curious to see it.

BRAHMS *to* CLARA.
(*Postcard.*)

June.

I must write a line at once to tell you how glad I am that my little piece has pleased you. I really had not expected that it would, and now shall be able to enjoy it in peace and calm at my own piano as if I had a licence to do so from the head of the police. I have begged Widmann to send you the descriptions he is publishing in the *Bund* of our travels in Sicily. This is instead of the letters which I never wrote, and a little better. Most affectionately yours, JOH.

BRAHMS *to* CLARA.

ISCHL, *June*.

It is so tempting to be able to give you some small pleasure, and as I have just finished a little piece which will at least suit your fingers, I am copying it [1] out for you as neatly as possible. If this neatness should prevent you from being able to read it, you will at least see that I meant well. Meanwhile the empty space has lured me to write another piece, but do not plague yourself with the handwriting, I really cannot do it any better. The fact that such copies are for your hands alone and must on no account get into anybody else's goes without saying. And so with most affectionate greetings to you and Marie, I beg most courteously to take my leave [2] as Your JOHANNES.

CLARA *to* BRAHMS.

FRANKFORT, *June* 24.

I almost require a treasure-chest to keep all the jewels I have received from you, and now comes this further exquisite addition. They are pearls. The one in B minor [3] which I received the other day is a grey pearl. Do you know them ? They look as if they were veiled and are very precious. The new pieces are once more enchanting, and most interesting. I cannot get them out of my mind, and I play them over several times every day. I am always trying to discover which I like best, but can arrive at no conclusion, for I really love all three. Thank you very much indeed for the sunshine which you introduce into my life. Our hearts have been very sad of late. We have had many worries (not financial), but probably worse. . . . Now Ferdinand will probably change over to music as he has no gifts whatsoever for a business career. His is a dreamy nature more suited to a musician than to a business-man. . . . I think he might make an excellent teacher, for he has plenty of talent, but it is too late now for him ever to be a pianist. All I can hope is that he will some day find a good position either in America or Eng-

---

[1] Op. 119.

[2] Here a snapshot was stuck in of Brahms walking away as if going out of the letter. Hence his expression " take my leave."

[3] Op. 119, No. 1.

land ; he will certainly not do so here.   But it is terribly hard to have to settle such vital questions and I feel the responsi- bility very much. . . .

I think we shall leave on the 30th, but we have not yet found rooms in Schlangenbad.   Once more many thanks.   No one, of course, will get the pieces out of me, they are carefully put away, and soon I shall have my little treasure-chest made so that I can put in it everything I have ever had from you. The full-length portrait pleased me very much.   It is you to the life.   I almost thought I could see you coming in through the door.   With a hearty hand-shake, Your CLARA.

BRAHMS *to* CLARA.

ISCHL, *June* 28.

Only yesterday I was thinking that I had to thank you again and express my joy over your own and my little pieces. (Others would not go on such a small sheet of paper and would not suit your dear and delicate fingers either.)   Now, however, I must write to you about something else, and beg you most urgently to send me a card by return on which I hope noth- ing but a short yes will be necessary.   You remember that at the time the final volume was in contemplation I suggested that it should include a certain duet.[1]   I could not find my copy of it and asked Härtels to send me one.   But they sent it to you, and you wrote to me saying how disinclined you felt to see it in the volume.

Now yesterday Mandyczewsky sent me the duet and I find that my memory had not played me false.   It certainly ought to go in and can and must not be left out.   I do not like to contradict you, and at the time I could not do so, because I had not got the piece before me ; nor did I require it, for I did not think at that time that my name would be mentioned as editor.   In accordance with your express wishes, however, this is now to be the case.   I have signed the preface with my own name, and am therefore responsible not only for the contents of the volume but also for anything that has been left out.   Now the duet is a genuine and very good example of Schumann, and you allowed yourself to be led astray by a few details and particularly by a very ugly note which is

[1] *Sommerruh von Schad.*

unquestionably a misprint, although it is one which was not recognized as such by the last editor. Do you really think that Schumann ever wrote more beautiful duets than this ? If so, how many songs would you not exclude because more beautiful ones are to be found in the Eichendorff series ?

If you examine it a little more closely you will find that the best verse—aye, the only beautiful one, is by your husband (the third). So do please say yes ! It will of course delay the publication, but I will ask Härtels to send you the preface in case you may think of something you would like to have mentioned.

With best wishes for your journey and above all hoping you will find nice rooms where you will be as comfortable as I am here in my little diggings, affectionately yours, JOH.

CLARA *to* BRAHMS.
(*Postcard.*)

FRANKFORT, *June* 30.

Your letter came just as we were on the point of leaving for Schlangenbad. So in great haste let me just say that whatever you think is right I shall agree to. You understand these things better than I do, so let the duet be included. My address in Schlangenbad is Villa Concordia. Farewell for to-day. In great haste, Your CLARA.

BRAHMS *to* CLARA.

ISCHL, *July* 2.

I cannot resist the temptation of trying my new paper in writing to your new address. I am sending you a piece which although it is not really difficult is unfortunately not suited to your fingers ? I expect to see you smile over a round dozen of the bars (which are they ?). But otherwise the piece will seem to you rough and crude enough. I don't suppose you are rid of your troubles, but it seems to me that it is always a good thing and that they disturb one less when they assume a definite form. However, I hope things will go well with you. With affectionate greetings to you and Marie from Your JOHANNES.

CLARA *to* BRAHMS.

SCHLANGENBAD, VILLA CONCORDIA, *July* 13.

Here I am contemplating your remarkable piece but quite unable to read eight bars in succession, for the music in my head is so loud that it drowns everything else. If only I could try it on a piano, but where ? I can never be alone in the pump room, and I don't know where else to go. I am feeling very miserable about it. At first sight the piece strikes me as being quite remarkable. How original the 4–1 and the 3–2 time are ! In a fortnight, however, I shall be at the Vonder Mühlls in Bâle, and then my first thought will be to seat myself at the piano with my new treasure. I feel sure that I shall very soon find the dozen bars which you mention, and many more that will please me. So please accept my hearty thanks meanwhile for your kind thought and for the pleasant surprise which you have again given me.

It is very charming here, but I find the heat very trying and long for Switzerland where the air, in spite of the heat, is certainly less oppressive.

Widmann was kind enough to send me his reminiscences, which I have read with great interest, and which have conjured up the old longing with a vengeance. And now farewell. I heard from Ilona that you are all very happy in Ischl. Here we have no distractions. With most affectionate greetings, Your old friend CLARA.

BRAHMS *to* CLARA.

ISCHL, *July*.

I had hoped and believed that you had to a certain extent got rid of your head trouble and much regret to hear that this is not so. I cannot understand, however, why, when you go away for a fairly long time you do not give yourself the luxury of a piano in your rooms. Anybody would be glad to let you have one and, if you preferred it, you could keep it for a very small sum. Aren't you going to have one in Interlaken either ? The question interests me because it would greatly stimulate my industry as a copyist if I knew that it would give you a quarter of an hour's pleasure. Surely you will only be passing through Bâle ? But if any manuscript compositions from me would give you any pleasure (perhaps

in Interlaken) just let me have a note on a postcard. There
is one which is at your disposal which is not always so brutal
as the last. . . .

But I am very anxious to have good news of you. I hope
they are on their way from snug little Switzerland where you
are always so happy. With affectionate greetings, Your
obedient copyist, J. B.

CLARA *to* BRAHMS.

INTERLAKEN,[1] HOTEL OBER, *Aug.* 10.

At last I have succeeded in getting to know your wonderfully original piece, only imperfectly, it is true, for I still
continue to be distracted by the terrible humming in my ears
and it takes a long time before I understand complicated
harmonies and progressions. I shall have to study the piece
thoroughly before I can hear everything correctly. You probably do not understand my condition and how hard it is to
bear, and how miserable it makes me to be prevented from
enjoying what was once so easy to me. It is true, however,
that when once I have grasped everything clearly I enjoy it,
and your wonderful piece is the first thing I shall study when
I have a piano again. But this will not happen during the
summer, as I am supposed during that time to have a complete rest from music. And even if we were to make the most
strenuous efforts to procure an instrument here, for instance,
we should not succeed. Marie and Eugenie go every day
for a couple of hours to the schoolmaster, who has a small
untuned upright piano. But now to return to the allegro,
how powerful the first motif is and how original, and I suppose Hungarian, owing to the five-bar phrases. It is strange,
but otherwise this five-bar arrangement does not disturb me
here at all—it just has to be so. Then how remarkable are
the third and second bars. The A Flat major is charming,
as is also the passage with the triplets. In fact there is not a
bar which does not carry one away. But I must study the
piece well in order to be able to grasp it thoroughly, and I
look forward to that with great joy. Let me thank you once
again, dear composer.

Everything is heavenly here again. The weather is wonder-

[1] Clara had gone to Interlaken on August 2.

ful and the Jungfrau magically beautiful at all times of the day; we even saw it once in the Alpine glow. . . . On our return journey I propose to go through Berne and to visit Herr Widmann who has very kindly invited me; this is always supposing that it is not possible to return *via* the Brünig and that we do not stay a week in Lucerne, which is certainly a very attractive proposition. . . . But now I must close, and again beg you to send me a word to tell me how you are, etc., etc. With most affectionate greetings from Marie, Eugenie and myself, Your old friend CLARA.

CLARA *to* BRAHMS.
                    INTERLAKEN, HOTEL OBER, *Aug.* 23.
Thanks to Herr Widmann's kindness we have at last received an upright piano from Berne which we have installed in a small peasant's house, and thus I have to-day for the first time diligently studied your allegro and it stands revealed in all its glory before my soul. In its passion, energy and grace, it is a wonderful piece. How enchanting is the A Flat major, the transition back to it, and then the organ-point! Surely this is the passage at which you hinted in your last letter to me? And now that I have a piano you can start sending me things again!!! But the piece is difficult—though I am learning it notwithstanding. Widmann has just left me—he visited me twice and was very friendly—he is walking remarkably well again. . . . So let me send you my heartiest greetings, dear musical scribe, and let us have some more of the fruits of your industry, Your audacious but most grateful CLARA.

CLARA *to* BRAHMS.
(*Postcard.*)
                              INTERLAKEN, *Aug.* 24.
Yesterday I forgot to ask you in what year your *Kinderlieder* were composed. The musical critic of *The Times* has asked Eugenie to let him have the information at once. Please let me know on a card. It was surely in the year when we were at Göttingen, but I cannot be certain about it. So please send me the year on a postcard. Most affectionately yours, CL.

BRAHMS *to* CLARA.

ISCHL, *Aug.*

I can satisfy neither your inquisitive Englishman nor, to my much greater regret, Frl. Eugenie either. The *Kinder-lieder* [1] are much older than you imagine. But of anything else about them, and particularly their date I have not the remotest notion. Hard luck for the next volume of the history of the world! I did not know that you had been prescribed the very bitter medicine of doing without music in the summer. But I often think that one has to resign oneself to a good deal in the course of years, and my next thought is, that I hope I may be allowed to enjoy my books, my music, and nature to the full as usual! But you have retained your sense of appreciation for all these things, and the fact that you are disobeying the prohibition bodes well for your present condition, I hope.

Unfortunately the charming people who come to you there are not so easily lured here to me. The only thing to be said is that on the whole the accessories to the landscape are more pleasant. Instead of Swiss people and Englishmen I have Austrians.

As chance would have it your Ilona was here yesterday and because she is yours and your letter had just arrived I played some of the pieces to her.

Herewith I send you another little piece and shall write more to-morrow. Please let me know if you think it is not quite happy. The organ-point in the E Flat major piece was of course the passage at which I felt sure your face would break into smiles. I know your old weakness for organ-points! Incidentally the middle movement in A Flat major is badly written. From the fifth bar onwards the arpeggio should be from above downwards :—

But now I must finish copying out the little piece and send my letter off (it is Sunday to-day and the post will probably

[1] The *Volkskinderlieder,* dedicated to Robert and Clara Schumann's children, appeared without any Opus number in 1858.

close early). With heartiest greetings to all three of you and
the same to the Engel- Haus- and Widmanns, Yours ever,
JOHANNES.

CLARA *to* BRAHMS.

INTERLAKEN, HOTEL OBER, *Sept.* 2.

What treasures I am collecting ! It is really quite amazing
to get a glimpse at the inner workings of your mind, to see
it all gushing, sparkling, surging, and yet thrilling one by the
greatness and depth of its thoughts. It sweeps me off my
feet and makes me think with longing of my piano at home
—a small and perpetually out-of-tune upright piano like the
one here is ghastly. With what enthusiasm shall I not study
when I return home ! Heaven grant that my infirmity will
not wholly prevent me. I have a genuine, consuming dread
of this. In the short piece, with its "not quickly but with
passion," what strikes me as remarkable is the amount of
feeling you are able to express in the smallest compass, not
to mention the longer pieces "*Andante teneramente*" and
"*Andante largo et mesto*" which are so wonderfully interesting
(what does *mesto* mean ?) Are not the last two sonata movements ? And is not the *Allegro resoluto* the same ? I should
so much like to say more but I can hardly find words to express
my feelings. But you know how much joy your parcels give
me and how I absorb your music and thoroughly grasp it.

The inquisitive Englishman is incidentally a big bug. He is
Fuller Maitland, *The Times* critic. I am surprised to hear
that the *Kinderlieder* are so much older than I thought.

A day or two ago Widmann sent me his play [1] and we shall
read it as soon as we have finished a biography of Mrs. Harriet
Becher Stowe (the author of *Uncle Tom's Cabin*) which is
very interesting. It was really most kind of him. He has
also paid me a second visit. Herzogenberg sent me a pressing
invitation to go to Heiden, and I accepted it. But I now
hear that it is very bleak there in the autumn and it might
possibly do me harm. So it must depend upon the weather.
We shall probably go to Baden-Baden after all about the 15th
or 16th of September. You are quite right about the people
of Switzerland. . . . We notice it every moment. There is

[1] *Jenseits von Gut und Böse.*

no news. And so with my heartiest thanks, I am ever Your devoted CLARA.

BRAHMS *to* CLARA.

ISCHL, *Sept.* 7.

The enclosed is a small offering for the 13th. It comes early because it would fain be read in peace, which would not be possible on the day itself. Many thanks for your kind letter. But my thanks would be doubled if only you would write—" E Flat minor monotonous, F Sharp major detestable, G major insignificant," etc. *Mesto* means sad. You would not have played the piece in a lively manner, even without this instruction—but it is not " sad " in any other sense ? We have had a number of visitors here. Stockhausen and his wife were at the Billroths, and Joachim is staying with the Queen.[1] I was also her guest yesterday, and was delighted with the friendly, cheerful and dignified old lady and the demure and charming Princess Mary. . . . Other pleasant and lively guests were such strangers as Sembrich, Nikisch, the musical conductor, and his wife, etc. You would take a greater interest in Widmann's very fine play if you knew more about philosophy and Nietzsche and his influence. Perhaps your daughters may be able to tell you something about it. Now wishing you a very happy birthday, and greetings to you, Marie and Eugenie, most affectionately yours, JOHANNES.

CLARA *to* BRAHMS.

BERNE, *Sept.* 19.

I have not yet thanked you for your charming birthday greeting. How original the two pieces are once more ; I like the second one particularly. Unfortunately I could only play them over once or twice as the room in which the piano stands gets very little sun and I caught a bad chill in it and was not allowed to go in it again. This will certainly sound faint-hearted to you, but what can we do when the flesh is no longer willing ? It is very sad. We left on Sunday, with the intention of exploring Berne thoroughly for once, which we did yesterday. I was also able to visit Widmann, which

[1] The Queen of Hanover.

was a great pleasure to me. To-day, however, I have to keep to the sofa though I am longing to be out. We had planned a walk, but I can hardly move for rheumatic pains. The weather is simply perfect—what a wonderful city Berne is! We see it lying before us from our hotel window. And Widmann lives in a charming house. How homely and comfortable it is! We have read his play again and again with the greatest interest.

To-morrow we hope to go to Baden, although I leave Switzerland with a heavy heart. Who knows—it may be the last time I shall be here? Above all, then, my heartiest thanks, my dear Johannes, and with most affectionate greetings from us all, Your old friend CLARA.

BRAHMS *to* CLARA.
(*Postcard.*)

ISCHL, *Sept.* 27.

I hope you will reach home safely to-day, as I hope to do to-morrow. I should like to have been with you on your return journey through Berne and Baden and would also have begged leave for Herzogenberg to join us, for he has surely come off badly. I hope that you will settle down comfortably at home now—and also at the piano—for that is a *sine quâ non*. I like to think of all the happiness you had on the 13th—but shrink with horror at the thought of what followed and the quantities of notepaper it demanded!!! With most affectionate greetings, Your JOHANNES.

CLARA *to* BRAHMS.

FRANKFORT A/M., *Oct.* 25.

Every day my most beautiful hour is the one I owe to you, and I feel I must tell you that it is only now after I have been seriously studying them that I have learnt fully to appreciate the treasure you have given me in your new pieces.[1] They now constitute my only musical joy. Can I say which I love best? I hardly know! The E Flat major, the E Flat minor, how magnificent each of them is in its own way. The A major, the F major and the G minor, each of them equally wonderful. And then there is the A major, and its middle movement in

[1] Op. 118.

F Sharp minor, with its lovely medley of melodies, and the F
Sharp part in chords, how full of profound feeling and how
dreamy it all is ; and the F major piece with its extremely
original middle movement—so how can one make a choice ?
It is an inexhaustible treasure house ! You tell me that I
ought to pick holes, but I can't. The most I could say would
be that the F Sharp minor piece pleases me least, and yet I find
it so interesting that it rivets my attention. If only I could
practise a little more ; but half an hour twice a day is the
utmost that I can allow myself. Each of the pieces is difficult
in its way and I fret with impatience because I have not yet
mastered them completely. The E Flat major is very difficult
and gives me a lot of work, but I shall manage it.

I was very pleased to find your dear card on my return. I
certainly feel very happy to be home again. If only I felt
better ! But in addition to the persistent trouble in my head,
I am racked with neuritis which depresses me horribly. It
also makes me feel sorry for Marie, for although I complain as
little as possible, she cannot help noticing it when the pains
are particularly acute. She requires all the buoyancy and
good spirits possible for her manifold duties, and yet she has
so many anxieties.

There is little news, and in any case I seldom hear anything.
The new conductors naturally give us much food for conversation. Rottenberg produced the *Leonora Overture* quite well
the other day, but it lacked fire, for in contrast to the other
conductors he is inclined to go to the other extreme and to take
it too slowly. I certainly do not like the Presto of this Overture, but his tempo was too much of a good thing.

But I must close, for in spite of a month's work there are
still about twenty letters remaining which I must answer. Let
me hear from you again soon, my dear Johannes, and with a
hearty handshake, I am, Your old friend CLARA.

Marie sends you greetings, Eugenie is in London.

BRAHMS *to* CLARA.

VIENNA, *Nov.* 7.

The best, in fact the only sensible thing I can write about
is to send you my hearty thanks for your kind letter concerning yourself and me. For what could be more pleasing to me

than your friendly and tender relationship to my pieces, and what could I be more pleased to hear than that you are feeling tolerably well, that you can play, and that you remain so young in heart and soul ?

You are still suffering from your birthday and the letters it entails. But let me warn you about the next, which will be an even more terrible and solemn affair—your seventy-fifth !

Like myself you will probably have been receiving applications for contributions to special numbers of various musical newspapers. It is as well that you should know that this sort of thing may increase enormously and that you ought to be on your guard against it now—that is to say, make it an invariable rule always to dictate a curt refusal and not to allow yourself to be tempted by the more or less earnest or enthusiastic nature of the appeals to enter into further correspondence. Such things are certainly not worth while, and to make any exception would be very dangerous. All the papers want is something sensational ; they think some rubbish that has never been printed more important than the best work—about which they don't know what to say.

On the other hand, how pleasant and gratifying it is when an intelligent man writes about his own life as Hanslick is doing now. If you have not read them already make sure to get numbers six, seven and eight of the *Rundschau* of last year, and number two (and the following numbers) of this year. (I believe I saw the *Rundschau* lying about at the Sommerhoffs.) It will be the most pleasant reading you have had for a long time, and from the very start, when he talks about his father, your whole heart will be in it. I regard Hanslick as an exceptionally " good " man, and I think that you too will be compelled to feel and to believe this when you read his reminiscences.

Please send me Eugenie's address some time. I should like to send her the pianoforte pieces when they are printed— without being reminded to do so. When I write to you I always have the feeling that I am taking some small share in the pleasure of sitting at your breakfast table, but it is really only a " small share," for talking is better than quill-scratching.

You too will be enjoying the remarkably warm weather which is lasting right into November. An overcoat is quite unnecessary here, and even at night one can sit in the open air quite comfortably. And now with heartiest greetings, Your JOHANNES.

CLARA *to* BRAHMS.

FRANKFORT A/M., Dec. 16.

Heartiest thanks for having sent me your new pieces [1] through Simrock, although it is always difficult for me to part with the MSS. But I suppose I must do so if I wish to play the pieces to anybody else, for musicians always look so covetously at MSS. and I am still too uncertain to play them by heart. But I will not conceal from you the fact that I am a little bit shocked by the production. What an incompetent fellow Simrock must have given Op. 118 to. It is incredible ! In the Ballad he prints page 7 with narrow spacing, and in the same piece he prints page 10 quite broad. Then the middle movement in the E Flat minor Adagio is hardly legible. This cannot be because the publishers wanted to economize, for Op. 119 is printed with broad spacing—I cannot get it out of my head. . . .

I have promised a few musicians to play the pieces to them to-morrow. I can now also manage the Rhapsody in E Flat major. You can send the pieces for Eugenie through me. She will be with us at Christmas and I will put them among her Christmas presents. And now at last let me thank you for your dear letter. I was astonished at your warning about my seventy-fifth birthday. I did not think that was ever honoured with special celebrations. I have certainly received a few letters from journalists with requests for all kinds of things, but I had no idea what they meant. I refused everything. I always do that, and never enter into any correspondence with them.

I had already read some of Hanslick's charming reminiscences in Interlaken, but had no idea that they were being continued. So I had them given to me as a present and have read them with great joy, as I read everything he writes. He is always so appreciative of you and I have kept many of the passages in which he mentions you. Now farewell, dear joy-giver. Oh, if only I could find words to express what the new pieces mean to me, what a cordial they are to my soul ! You have my

<hr>

[1] Op. 118, 119.

heartiest wishes for Christmas which you will probably spend at the Fellingers. Think of me sometimes if you do. Your old friend CLARA.

BRAHMS *to* CLARA.

Dec. 22.

Since I last wrote you will have received the pleasant and melodious *Uebungen* [1] (exercises), many of which you have already known for some time. But do not allow yourself to be tempted to play or practise them. Also warn your pupils to be cautious in their dealings with them. They are very apt to cause all kinds of harm and damage to the hands (sensitive hands !).

If you want to be kind to me and my publisher you have only to say all sorts of nice things about the new pianoforte pieces. Just have a look at pianoforte pieces by Grieg, Kirchner, etc. and you will see how eight bars which appear on the first page are repeated on the second and then have the goodness to think what we, in this part of the world, get for our money. Don't think only of the difference as regards beautiful content, but also as regards quantity and mass. I agree that the E Flat minor piece has been too closely spaced. But if we had had the thing engraved again we should have had to add a single sheet, which once more would have found favour neither with you nor with our esteemed public. Bearing all this in mind, examine the exercises with friendly eyes and note how cleverly and economically they have been arranged. . . .

But I had quite forgotten to excuse or defend the passage in the E minor piece. But it could not be attacked in a court of law, it is theoretically unimpeachable. Perhaps it is only out of consideration for the esteemed public that the whole thing is not given *da capo*, and if this alteration does not please you here you can, for the time being, play it simply *d.c.*

I hope you may spend a pleasant Christmas in pleasant surroundings. As for myself I shall be quite satisfied if people would only leave me contentedly at home. With heartiest greetings to you all, and wishing I could join the party round your Christmas tree, Your JOHANNES.

[1] 51 *Uebungen*, two Vols. without any Opus number.

CLARA *to* BRAHMS.

FRANKFORT A/M., *Dec.* 23.

. . . I have already been right through the studies and have marked with an x all those which my pupils can play.   But how they will be attacked by the pianists !   I have just glanced with pleasure at the more difficult ones.   I do not require them for your newer things, but I was delighted with the various intricacies and harmonies.   I had already realized that the passage in the E minor piece was theoretically unimpeachable. Nevertheless, I take the liberty of abiding by the first version. I shall play the pieces again once or twice during the holidays. They give me great joy.

. . . To-morrow we three shall be all alone.   Julie and Ferdinand are in Gera with their mother.   The Sommerhoffs are with their children.   So farewell, and with my best wishes for the New Year also, Your old friend CLARA.

1894

Vienna, *Jan.* 4.

Dear Clara,

I think our letters must have crossed, and I was therefore amused to hear that you had examined the exercises carefully both for yourself and your pupils, as I advised you to do, and had even marked those your pupils might or might not play. I was glad to see, moreover, that, regarded in the proper perspective, they had pleased you. . . .

I have just had a most pleasant surprise in a " *Brahms Fantasie* " by the painter Max Klinger, and I wish you could have shared the pleasure with me. It consists of forty-one drawings and etchings based upon songs by me, particularly the *Schicksalslied*. But they are not really illustrations in the ordinary sense, but magnificent and wonderful fantasies inspired by my texts. Without assistance (without any explanation) you would certainly often miss the sense and the connection with the text. How much I should like to look them through with you and show you how profoundly he has grasped the subject and to what heights his understanding and imagination soar. But without this you would certainly be able to admire only a few.

Let me know whether you will be able to get the book (which will appear shortly). Perhaps some friend of art in your part of the world will buy it (is Herr Sommerhoff one of these ?). I should then endeavour to write you something about them. I hardly like to give it to you, because I am too much afraid that you will not get the full measure of enjoyment out of it. But I could certainly bring it to you, because then I could be your interpreter and share the pleasure it would give you. Finally with heartiest greetings to all the trio, Your Johannes.

Brahms *to* Clara.

VIENNA, *Jan.* 30.

Dr. Cl.

If you have anybody to whom you can dictate, I beg you most urgently to let me have more precise details about Margarethe Stockhausen and her death. The news has affected me deeply, because I cannot help thinking or suspecting that there was something particularly gruesome or sad about it. At all events poor Stockhausen seems to have had some hard knocks from Fate, for when on the top of it all I remember his eye trouble, I cannot think how he carries on.

I had heard that Margarethe had been suffering with her hands, but it surely was not on that account that she went to Freiburg ? I should be grateful to you for a little news and I hope you will be able to add to it that you are extremely well yourself. With affectionate greetings, J. B.

Clara *to* Brahms.

FRANKFORT, *Feb.* 1.

Thank God, my arms are giving me less trouble than ever so I can report to you at once myself. The poor Stockhausens have been very sorely tried of late and yet what you fear has not been the case. Gretchen had been in Freiburg for about two years at a school of glass-painting, where she had already attained to the position of directress, for she was very clever and gifted at the work. She did not get on with her mother at home and wanted to have her own sphere of influence. But Frau Stockhausen did not wish to let the power go out of her own hands, as she is herself still vigorous and a great support to him in everything. As a poor musician's daughter Gretchen had no standing among the families here, and she therefore decided to go in for glass-painting. At the beginning of October she had the misfortune to run a rusty nail on an easel into her finger and by the following morning the wound was so bad that she had to go to hospital. It took some months for the finger to heal, but it remained stiff and she could do nothing with her right hand. The doctor said that if she wished to take up her work again she must have her middle finger (the one that had been poisoned) amputated, a step to which she heroically consented. Unfortunately, however, suppuration again set in in the hand, and it looked as if the blood were still diseased. Then suddenly she contracted diphtheria from which she died in a few days. Her parents were with her but could only see her for a few minutes each day owing to fear of infection. But she constantly made signs to them (she was unable to speak and wrote everything that she wanted to say with her left hand). He, the poor man, who is now almost blind, is said to be quite beside himself, but I found her full of fortitude and composure. She said to me that if she did not pull herself together she did not know what would become of her husband in all his helplessness. At Christmas he went into hospital for a preliminary operation, and the main operation will take place at the end of February. In addition to all this not only has Frau Stockhausen herself been very ill for some months but news arrived that Imanuel had become engaged to an actress in Berlin, which made her very unhappy, as altogether it was most unsuitable. But Imanuel insisted upon going through with it and the marriage was fixed for the 28th—the very day on which Gretchen was to be buried. Apparently the fiancée behaved in a heartless manner at this time (his parents did not know her), and now the son has just come to inform his parents that he has broken off with her. So they have at least been spared this trouble, but what they are going through is really too much. If only the operation is successful ! . . . [Frau Stockhausen] has certainly some very good points and is a faithful support to her husband and has brought up her children very well. I don't suppose she has always found things too easy. You can well imagine how much we have been affected by all her troubles. And this is not all, for we have been upset by another sad business, young Scholz's divorce. . . .

But we have also had some pleasures, particularly through la Duse,[1] whom I was unfortunately only able to see once, and who interested me enormously, although she cannot compare with Wolter. We also had Joachim with us for an evening and he played me a quartet by Robert and then played your third sonata with me. That was such a joy as one seldom has. In the first movement with its surging harmonies melting into each other I constantly had the feeling that I was floating on

[1] In *La Dame aux Camelias*.

the clouds. I cannot tell you how I love this sonata, every movement of it—who knows whether it is not the last time I shall ever play it!

You have probably heard that Siegfried Wagner is going to conduct the next concert at the Opera House ! ! ! . . .

I have heard that you have been asked by the theatre people here to come and conduct a concert, but much as it would please me to see you, I don't like to think of you as a travelling musical conductor. If you came with a new orchestral work it would be another matter. I have heard nothing more about it ! ?

I feel it is rather bold of me to dare to say anything about a new symphony when you have already showered such precious treasures upon us this year.—In London they are writing very searching criticisms about the new pieces which Ilona has played. Much of what they say is very good, although it is hardly possible, after only one hearing (particularly in a large hall) to understand all the subtlety, depth and greatness of them. Moreover, between ourselves, I do not believe that Ilona understands them as they need to be understood. She goes too quickly over everything. But this strictly between ourselves.

We were much interested in Hanslick's essay on you and Wagner. He is really a most splendid judge and has courage. Finally, as regards myself, I may say that although I am not well (the trouble in my head is alone sufficiently upsetting) I feel strong enough for work in moderation. Farewell, dear friend, Your old CLARA.

A year ago to-day we were together at the Sommerhoffs.

CLARA *to* BRAHMS.

FRANKFORT A/M., *Feb.* 8.

I feel compelled to write you a few words, as I can well imagine how deeply you must have been shaken by Billroth's death. You have lost a great deal in him—how well he understood you and how thoroughly devoted he was to you! Oh, how hard it is when such people are taken away!

I was at the Stockhausens yesterday and found him a little more composed. They were both deeply touched by a kind letter they had received from you. While I was sitting with

them in the evening Marie was at the Opera House witnessing
Siegfried Wagner's first appearance there, and thus a well-
schooled orchestra had to play under the direction of a wholly
unschooled conductor merely because he happened to be Wagner's son. He had the pieces drummed into him for a year in
Heidelberg and made his appearance with them here. He
seems to have carried it off fairly well with all the customary
tricks, but Marie says that never in her life has she heard anything more tedious than the first part of the concert. Apparently the public also remained cold, but then gave Rottenberg
a very warm reception in the second half. Nevertheless I fear
we shall not keep him long. He does not seem to be particularly
suited to the post of a theatre conductor. He asked to be
allowed to resign a little while ago, but the Director would not
accept his resignation. And now with most affectionate greetings, ever your faithful old friend CLARA.

Everybody is asking me whether you are not coming ?

BRAHMS *to* CLARA.

VIENNA, *Feb.* 8.

My heartiest thanks for the great pleasure your last letter
gave me. What particularly pleased me was the splendid and
kindly proof it gave of how much your arm trouble had improved for you to be able to write so easily. And I was also
pleased to hear about dear Margarethe, concerning whose death
I had feared to hear worse.

You must just have been reading Hanslick on Billroth when
you heard of his death ? Those words were Billroth's last joy,
and I am sure that they went to your heart too. I was deeply
moved in reading them and thought that it would be impossible to describe a friendship more beautifully and with
greater feeling. Quite unintentionally the account proved
to be an obituary notice written during the lifetime of its subject. The grief over Billroth's death is extraordinarily wide-
spread, but you cannot possibly have any idea how unique is
the manifestation of sympathy in all circles here. His death
had long been expected and for his sake was to be desired. He
had never really recovered properly from his severe illness
and during the last few years, as he himself used to say, every
hour of his life was a gift.

I should like to discuss many more points in your letter, but in any case I must say how delighted I am when you write as kindly about my music as you have this time about my third violin sonata, and I went straight away and took it up tenderly and played it to myself. Your theatre certainly invited me, and by way of a change I actually wrote to them refusing.

Have you made any plans about going away in the spring ? Are you not tempted to go to Heidelberg, Baden or the Italian Lakes ? If you have I should be inclined (as in the case of the sonata) to enthuse with you. The Scholz affair is most unedifying—but I feel deeply for Stockhausen and often think sympathetically about his poor wife, who is not having an easy time now and certainly never has had with him ! ! ! With most affectionate greetings, Your JOHANNES.

CLARA *to* BRAHMS.

FRANKFORT, *March* 19.

What a long time I have been in debt to you for your last very kind letter. But so much has happened. . . . We now have so many family disputes that I am completely shattered by them. Think of it, Ferdinand has just come to us, after three years' apprenticeship with a chemist—in order to study music. We shall certainly have a try, but three years lost— how galling ! Besides which, in this matter, Marie and I are acting entirely against the wishes both of his guardian and Eugenie. But the lad has absolutely no practical gifts whatsoever, is quite useless in business, and thinks only of music. He says he would prefer to hold the most insignificant position as a musician than to spend his life as a chemist. What struggles it has meant and what scenes there have been before we got as far as this !

I am terribly sorry about poor Stockhausen. It is still impossible to have the operation because his eyes are always inflamed. This is probably due chiefly to Gretchen's death because he has wept so much. Now he can do nothing. It really is dreadful. How long the day must seem to him ! The Scholz affair too seems to be endless. . . . What the poor woman is putting up with is indescribable. . . . But she is showing admirable energy. We are all trying to help her as much as we can.

What plans have you made for the summer ? Ischl again ?
A few days ago Woldemar paid us a visit. He is on his way to
Italy in order to get over an attack of influenza. I can give
you no musical news as I have heard nothing, but there is very
little which I regret not having heard. Frau Joachim gave
two concerts with Mariechen, but they were not very full and
Mariechen did not meet with much favour. Apparently she
has quite ruined her high notes with Wagner. Now wishing
you a happy holiday and with greetings to the Fellingers, with
whom you will probably spend it ! ? waiting to hear from you
soon, Your old CLARA.

BRAHMS *to* CLARA.

VIENNA, *Beginning of April.*

Even if the holiday from which you have just returned was
not a particularly jolly one, I hope that it cheered your spirits,
and that you were able to enjoy seeing your old friends again
without being worried. I suppose Frau Bendemann is still
alive and continues to live in Düsseldorf ? Thank you very
much indeed for your kind letter, but I have to make a great
effort to conjure up before my mind all the amenities of your
comfortable home when I wish that many of your troubles
might vanish from it. As a matter of fact I could, or would
like to try, to introduce a little sunshine into your room. I
might, for instance, (in about a week) send you a whole heap of
beautiful old songs,[1] which I am tempted to publish arranged
for the piano by myself.

The question now arises whether you have the time, the
desire and the strength to devote a few hours every day to the
casual reading and playing of these pieces ? I am thinking
that you will take pleasure in all sorts of subtleties in the piano
part, but almost fear that the magnificent words and melodies
will not appeal to you immediately as much as they have to me.
For this reason I would beg you not to examine them with too
much care or gravity, but only enjoy one or two of them in a
casual way—just as you might the above-mentioned ray of
sunshine. If you would like me to send them to you just let
me have a short " yes " on a postcard. My copyist was here a

---

[1] *Deutsche Volkslieder* without Opus number.

moment ago, and I could send them in a few days' time, but unfortunately only for 3, 4–8 days ! ?

Write and tell me quite frankly whether you would like this little distraction.   With affectionate greetings, Your ladybird [1] JOHANNES.

CLARA *to* BRAHMS.
(*Postcard.*)

DÜSSELDORF, *April* 4.

I have just received your kind letter here, but we return home to-day.   Please send me the songs, but let me keep them for a week so that I do not have to hurry over playing them through.   I am much looking forward to them.   Your ears must have burned a good deal all this time for I have been playing your pieces so often.   The other day I played them to Grimm and his wife who, to my great delight, paid me a visit. Ade !   Your CLARA.

BRAHMS *to* CLARA.

Beginning of April.

In order that I may not press you too much I have sent the music to Berlin first, and Herr Spitta will forward it to you in the course of the week.   But you will be alarmed at the flood of letters that is breaking over your head and which is supposed to represent my little ray of sunshine.   Once more I beg you, take it easily, nibble at them a little at a time quite casually and light-heartedly.   I also entreat you most earnestly to begin with the song on page 75 (! ! ! ! !) and then to continue playing the short things with choruses.   I think you will find them quite easy, and then you might see whether you are successful with the rest.   I don't suppose the texts will always please you.   But you will certainly be interested or stirred by one or two ;   for instance, by *Schwesterlein*, if you can imagine the situation of the poor jealous girl.   In regard to Gunhilde and the story on page six, think of the *Peri* and of the meaning of the tears of repentance.   The nun and wife of the knight are

---

[1] This word "ladybird" was not written, but was represented by a little image of the insect.   This was supposed to stand at the head of the notepaper, but Brahms had turned the sheet upside down so that it came at the bottom.

leading a suspicious existence, but as they repent and do penance, the lilies bow their heads and an angel prays for the sinner. Well—and so it goes on.

I do not wish you to examine the stories too closely. Besides, they are often imperfect and therefore not comprehensible. . . .

With affectionate greetings, and hoping that you may approach the Viennese songs in good health and spirits, Your JOHANNES.[1]

BRAHMS *to* CLARA.

VIENNA, *April* 15.

Early yesterday Simrock was to send my collection of songs to Spitta and in the afternoon I heard from Joachim that Spitta was dead. I was not a little shaken by this news. It seemed as if I were speaking to him and received that as an answer. But in other respects, the loss of this friend is a very painful one to me, and I see nothing to replace his science and his school.

I have now begged Simrock to send my things to you. I could complete them from here, but you will have enough with those. . . . With affectionate greetings, and hoping that you are keeping well, Wholly yours, JOH.

CLARA *to* BRAHMS.

FRANKFORT A/M., *April* 26.

Just a note to-day to tell you that I am in the midst of your treasury of songs and am greatly enjoying them. I am not yet through with them, but only take three or four a day, and of course play them several times so that I can make myself familiar with each at once. I still cannot tell which I like best. Would have any objection to my showing the songs with choruses to Stockhausen some time ?—that is to say, he would have to let me sing and play them to him. Let me have yes or no on a postcard. I shall quite understand if it is no and beg you to answer me without reserve.

Otherwise there is nothing to tell you.—I had a good deal of sunshine through Eugenie's three weeks here. We had a lot

---

[1] Beneath his signature he stuck two photographs, on the left one of Hamburg, 1833, on the right one of Salzburgerstrasse, Ischl, 1851.

of music together, chiefly, of course, Brahms ! Another hearty handshake for the new joys you have given me, Your old friend CLARA.

Are you going to Ischl soon ?

BRAHMS *to* CLARA.

VIENNA, *April* 28.

I am extremely glad that the songs are not unpleasing to you, and as they have since undergone a good deal of valuable correction, and one or two of the best are missing from your lot, I may hope that they will be even more of a pleasure to you when you see them again in print. I don't like to press you, but—I really do want them rather badly. I would therefore most humbly beg, as the figure shows,

[a grasshopper on its knees]

that you will not delay on Stockhausen's account to send them at once. For as things are he would not get much out of them and it will not be long before he will be able to see the music with his own eyes, I hope, and sing them himself if you play them to him. I have been having a lot of visitors lately. Every day a different married couple arrives. I would have gone to Ischl already but am waiting for the songs which I should like to send to Simrock before I go. And this I must do from here on account of the texts, for which I require all sorts of books. So thanking you in advance and regretting that you always give yourself so much trouble with the packing, with heartiest greetings from Your JOHANNES.

CLARA *to* BRAHMS.

FRANKFORT A/M., *May* 1.

That was really a Job's post—I had already marked all my favourites and was hoping to lead a very agreeable existence with them ! In order to be able to find them again at once (seeing that I have very little memory for texts) I had marked them with little xx. But these xx I have not removed. They are not in the way and will show you my favourites. But it is nice to hear that they will soon be published and I have sent them off to you to-day after a short delay owing to the fact that we had no postal forms in the house. So once more, many thanks, dear joy-giver. A few days ago Dr. Hans Müller and his wife called upon me and told me a good deal about Spitta's impressive obsequies. It is a terrible loss for the Hochschule and they are apparently at their wits' end about it. Herzogenberg's name has been mentioned, but he is surely not strong enough for such a post. If you should be going to Ischl in the course of the next few days please let me know (also about the receipt of the songs). I am always a little bit uneasy about such things. Frau Faber writes about a photograph of you which is very fine, but I have not yet received it ! And now farewell, and give us another sign of life soon, Your old CLARA.

BRAHMS *to* CLARA.

VIENNA, *May* 6.

Your parcel has arrived safely. I was much touched to see what trouble you had taken with it, and then highly delighted with the many crosses and double crosses. As I may readily assume that the other ones would all have received a double cross as well, I am very much looking forward to the time when you will see them again beautifully printed.

Hausmann and Mühlfeld are here and we are getting a good deal of distraction. As to what music we are having the others will give you more detailed accounts. Instead of doing this myself I will correct the songs and greet you most affectionately, Your JOHANNES.

BRAHMS *to* CLARA.

ISCHL, *June*.

I no longer dare to thank you for your birthday greeting.[1] And so please forgive me (among other things) for not having written. But I should like to send you a greeting from my beloved Ischl, and to tell you that every day I am expecting the proofs of the forty-nine (!) songs. It is probably the first time that I have been looking forward with so much pleasure to a set of proofs and to the publication of one of my works,—not to mention the prospect of your putting many crosses and double crosses against them when they come to you again ! But may I really send the thick bundle to Interlaken, be-

[1] On the 6th of May Clara had as usual sent him a birthday greeting, but owing to a bad headache from which she was suffering at the time, the letter was short and contained nothing except her good wishes.—TR.

cause it can certainly wait till then ?   To my great astonishment I heard from Frau Franz that you intended taking your
maids and everything with you and running your own house
there ! ?   I cannot think such a thing possible in Switzerland
and particularly in Interlaken—in the first place because of
the very marked repugnance that the Swiss feel towards strangers.   You ought really to see some time how the people here
(I mean all of them, even those unconnected with the house one
is in) rejoice and are grateful when their visitors are happy.
So it is either quite untrue or else you have looked into the
matter more closely and thought over it more thoroughly than
I have had reason to do.   At all events I hope that it will be
quite pleasant and comfortable for you there—just as it is for
me here in Ischl !   As I have just been interrupted I will
merely add my most affectionate greetings and best wishes for
Interlaken, Wholly yours, JOHANNES.

CLARA *to* BRAHMS.
                    INTERLAKEN, CHÂLET STERCHI, *July* 4.
    Your dear letter has been lying by me for a long time and I
have only just found time to thank you for it.   We have now
thoroughly settled down and although it was rather hard work
for Marie until the house was in running order, we never had
to complain in any way about lack of friendliness on the part of
the people.   We have a nice little flat with a balcony on which,
as it is fairly roomy, we almost live, and at breakfast particularly
we always enjoy the view of the Jungfrau.   We also have a
piano, and yesterday we at last managed to secure a tuner from
Berne for twenty francs ! ! !   So now, if you will send them to
the above address, I can get on with the songs.   I am writing
under difficulties because I am in the midst of the woods
whither I go every morning.   But as the ground is damp until
midday I sit in my bathchair and read and write.   If only I
had in me some of that contemplative spirit which belongs to
age, but unfortunately I cannot yet attain to it.   I still have
too much life in me and yet I am so often tired of life.   Oh, it
frightens me ; but I will not send you a song of woe, though when
one has so little to relate one is apt to descend to trifles.   We
have Julie and Ferdinand with us now, the latter in order that
he may not interrupt his musical studies which have hardly

begun.. And so he is diligently practising in his attic on a very dilapidated upright piano which we found in the house here (I hired it for him). This would have been impossible in an hotel. Every day Marie gives him lessons at the piano in theory and both children French lessons, etc. . . .

He does exercises daily, is learning to swim in the lake, which is very easy for him here, and from five o'clock till eight every day, he goes out for a walk and a run ; occasionally also we go out for the whole day. In three weeks' time Eugenie will come, and then Julie will go to her mother. Eugenie is getting on very well in London, and strange to say her health is improving visibly. I attended the Beethoven festival in Bâle, but it is true I hardly heard anything. I had, however, such a magnificent impression of the whole in Münster that it has never faded from my memory. Apparently the whole thing went wonderfully well and the violin concerto was, as it were, transfigured—the softest note is said to have been heard quite plainly. But Joachim's appearance distressed me greatly, and Frau von Beulwitz, who had come with him from Berlin, told me that he was quite beside himself because his wife was again moving to Berlin and had taken a place where he had to go to her once a day. . . . And now let me entreat you once more to send me the songs and to add a kind word. Farewell, and enjoy yourself as you so well know how to. It is a magnificent gift which heaven has given you in addition to so many others. Marie sends you affectionate greetings. She is very happy here in our charming " home." In faithful friendship, Yours, CLARA.

BRAHMS *to* CLARA.

ISCHL, *July* 6.

" This letter was found lying on the ground in the gardens of the Rugen and was posted in Interlaken by the finder ! "
I was very much tempted to telegraph to you yesterday, and I do not think it at all nice of me to be satisfied only with writing, unless I am prompted by the secret desire of getting a second letter by this means ? ! But now let me thank you heartily for the frail lost one, your very dear letter. I am so glad to hear that you are so happy and comfortable where you are, and that both as regards Ferdinand and Eugenie every-

thing is going as you wish.   What with sitting in the woods to write letters and contemplating the Jungfrau at breakfast—your summer promises to be a very beautiful one.

I try to avoid both in thought and in person to spend too much time with Joachim.   To think that he deliberately went to great pains to bring this comfortless and muddled existence on himself, without any real grounds for doing so !   Surely in such circumstances it is better to be alone as I am ?

My *Volkslieder* will probably be sent off to you and to me in the course of the next few days.   I think with joy that very few of them can possibly be unsympathetic to you, and that probably there are many that will seem ever more beautiful and more dear the more closely you study them and the more deeply you go into them.   How often the profoundest things are expressed by a word or a note and every feeling drained to the dregs !

It has just occurred to me—does the beginning of my letter require any explanation ?   You must have noticed that you had lost your letter.   I got it with the words quoted written on the back of the envelope, and was very grateful to the kind finder. . . .

With most affectionate greetings to you all, and hoping that the dear *Volkslieder* will be a great joy to you, as also Interlaken and everything else, Yours ever, JOHANNES.

CLARA *to* BRAHMS.

INTERLAKEN, CHÂLET STERCHI, *July* 25.

I have the beautiful songs once more and am delighted.   The way they have been produced also pleases me very much.   I shall drop the crosses, for I love almost all of them.   If only I had a singer who could sing them to me !   But first of all let me thank you for them, dear Johannes.

You can imagine how astounded I was by the beginning of your last letter.   I had not missed the one in question nor had I lost it, but Ferdinand, who had taken it to the post with two others had left yours in the pocket of his jacket ; and when he was out walking he was caught in a shower of rain, and throwing his jacket over his arm, the letter fell out. . . .   You can imagine how horrified he was.   But what a good thing the finder went to the pains of putting the letter in the post. . . .

We are expecting Frl. Wendt, the faithful old creature, in the course of the next few days ! Her brother is surely in Ischl again ? Greet him warmly for me, and also Ilona, and tell her that she should recuperate and recover her strength. We are all very well so far and quite comfortable in the flat, and I have at last been able to get my piano tuned, although it cost me thirty-five francs. One tuner put it more out of tune than ever, the other one made it at least usable. Both of them came from Berne.

In a fortnight's time Stockhausen is at last going to have his operation. If only it could be successful ! I have felt great pity for him. He has really borne his infirmity admirably. And now, dear friend, with most affectionate greetings, in which Marie and Eugenie join—the latter is constantly casting covetous eyes on the songs and I believe would be only too glad to take them to London ! Always your old friend, CLARA.

Widmann has sent me a very nice volume consisting of his new stories—it is charming of him. I have not written to him to say we are here as I didn't want to put him to any inconvenience.

BRAHMS *to* CLARA.

ISCHL, *Aug.* 3.

I hope I have provided adequately for the covetous eyes of Frl. Eugenie. . . . But was it not a good thing that I should have explained the beginning of my letter the other day ? My first thought was to telegraph to you as I imagined you would be at your wit's end about your lost letter. Herr Wendt intended to arrive yesterday evening—when he comes shall we exchange so that you get the Goethe scholar and I the ladies ? . . . Your excessive consideration for Widmann will hardly be appreciated by him—he will certainly not regard it in the light you do and will be inclined to feel that less delicacy would be more friendly ! If it doesn't please him to visit you he need not do so, but he can't think that he will be welcome if he is not invited at all ? ! Even if he is not entitled, like myself, to assume that his productions are more pleasant to get on with than himself ! By this I do not mean to cast any aspersions upon his last two novels in verse which I think quite charming, and which you will also certainly enjoy very much. But if you should see him, greet him warmly from me. In any case you will see many of my friends there. I do not see them here. Germans do not seem to come to Austria much. If you should have news of Stockhausen please let me have a short note.

With affectionate greetings to all, Your JOH.

CLARA *to* BRAHMS.

INTERLAKEN, *Aug.* 6.

. . . You have given Eugenie a great joy and she will write to you herself in a few days. She practises your studies every day, and I always have to warn her about the too complicated ones. But I greatly enjoy her playing. She plays with such musical refinement. What a pity it is that in her youth she was not as strong as she is now, for she ought to have practised more. We are also revelling in the songs. No one could have adapted the melodies so well as you ; it is wonderful !

It has occurred to me that in number 17, page eight, system three, first bar, there is a ♮ before the G, ought it not to be a ♭, preparing the way for the G Flat in the second bar ? It sounds to me very good ? Then in number 49, page 18, system 3, bar 1, that should surely be an A in the base, as in the following bar ? . . .

So adieu for to-day. I prefer to leave the Goethe scholar to you rather than the ladies who, by the by, greet you enthusiastically. Ever most affectionately, Your old friend CLARA.

CLARA *to* BRAHMS.

INTERLAKEN, CHÂLET STERCHI, *Aug.* 17.

. . . We have a friend here now, Frau Vonder Mühll from Bâle, who is singing your *Volkslieder* a good deal. She has a delightful voice. So we are at last able to hear them, and how different they sound from when they are hummed ! . . .

Now let me ask you something I have long been wanting to. Can't you induce Simrock to place his caution about copying, etc., somewhere else than on the first place just opposite the first song ? It is really too depressing to find it precisely there where in the flush of enthusiasm one throws open the volume. It really is a too detestable piece of prose !

At last we are having fine weather and very hot into the bargain. Ferdinand is seizing the opportunity to go for long walks, and so is Marie, and then Eugenie and I remain wistfully behind. I have got a magnificent grand piano which really makes one long to play. Frau Viardot will soon be coming. It is such a long time since we have met that we shall hardly recognize each other !

There is really no news. I only meant this as a letter of thanks. Farewell ! Give an occasional thought to Your CLARA.

BRAHMS *to* CLARA.

ISCHL, *Aug.*

I hope Frl. Eugenie did me the credit of believing that I would have written to her at once and exhaustively if I had been able to say anything about how to learn transposing. I regard it chiefly as a matter of practice and habit. Anybody who has to accompany singers every day soon learns it, and I would therefore recommend this above all. Then let her try her hand at waltzes and easy Haydn Symphonies for four hands and things of that sort. The principal thing seems to me to be to treat the matter lightly and with skill. Of course a thorough knowledge of harmony is also very useful for that sort of thing (but how anyone can give lessons in harmony for years I have never been able to understand). That you continue to study my beloved songs is a great joy to me. . . .

Has it ever occurred to you that the last of the songs comes in my Opus I, and did anything strike you in this connection ? It really ought to mean something. It ought to represent the snake which bites its own tail, that is to say, to express symbolically that the tale is told, the circle closed. But I know what good resolutions are, and I only think of them and don't say them aloud to myself. At present, now that my sixtieth year has passed, I should like to be as sensible as I was at twenty. At that time the publishers of Frankfort tempted me in vain to have something printed. In vain did Kranz offer me all the money which I as a poor young man had such difficulty in earning. Why this was so, it is not so easy to explain. At sixty it is probably high time to stop, but again without any particular reason ! !

But in any case I am going to give myself a treat very shortly, I am expecting the visit of the clarinet player Mühlfeld, and will try two sonatas [1] with him, so it is possible that we may celebrate your birthday with music. I don't say solemnize! I wish you could be with us, for he plays very beautifully. If you could extemporize a little in F minor and E Flat major you would probably chance on the two sonatas. I would send them to you because you could play them quite comfortably, but the clarinet would have to be transposed and that would spoil your pleasure. Thus in this letter I have managed successfully to come back to where it started, and so I will close, with most affectionate greetings to you all, Wholly yours, JOHANNES.

CLARA *to* BRAHMS.
       INTERLAKEN, CHÂLET STERCHI, MATTEN, *Sept.* 8.
(*Dictated.*)

In the first place let me thank you, on Eugenie's behalf also, for your kind letter. I was particularly pleased to hear that you had not remained true to your resolutions and that we might expect something glorious from you again. We must set the clarinet player in gold. I am very glad about your celebration of the 13th, but I should be even better pleased if I could listen to you in more than spirit.

I cannot write to you myself to-day, because I have had a very peculiar mishap which might very easily have been a disaster. Frau Vonder Mühll, Eugenie and I were forced by an incompetent rider on a frisky horse to jump down a bank, which, although it was fortunately not high, was very steep. I got badly bruised in the arm and shoulder and had violent pains the whole week. The others came off more lightly because they rolled down the bank more easily than I did. It will take a few weeks longer before I can use my arm again—a very sad prospect for me.

I think we shall stay here until about the 18th of September, but what then, I do not yet know. When one feels so poorly one has little enterprise. Farewell, and with renewed thanks, Your faithful old friend CLARA.

[1] Op. 120.

BRAHMS *to* CLARA.

ISCHL, *Sept.* 11.

The enclosed photograph, which has been taken quite recently, is of a gentleman who comes to present you with his heartiest greetings and best wishes. Try to pick out the best of the letters you have received to-day and imagine that he is singing *unisono* with it and an octave higher into the bargain ! A second picture also finds its way into the letter. It will perhaps amuse you to see the first gentleman by the side of Johann Strauss of beautiful Blue Danube fame.

The music on your birthday has come to nothing, and there will be no more at Ischl either. As, however, Mühlfeld is anxious to hear the two sonatas, he will probably come to Vienna to try them. I wish I could make the matter simpler for him. Perhaps there may be a town nearer his home to which I would also gladly go, where someone could offer us a room and a piano for our attempt ? ! Perhaps Hanau (the Landgrave ?) or Frankfort (the lady Professor in the Savigny strasse) ? [1] Or somebody and somewhere else ? ! That would be very nice—meanwhile, perhaps it is better for me to remain at home with the sonatas.

At present we are not having very good autumn weather and if you are not getting it any better where you are, you will, like myself, be thinking of returning home pretty soon. But you will still be there for the 13th and I hope you will spend the day as cheerfully and happily as could possibly be wished. With affectionate greetings and rejoicing with you, Your JOHANNES.

BRAHMS *to* CLARA.
(*Postcard.*)

ISCHL, *Sept.* 16.

Just a line in great haste to say that I have decided to leave here on Tuesday to spend a few days in Berchtesgaden, and shall go to Vienna about Saturday. My last letter (with the very unnecessary photographs) has, I hope, reached you safely. Thank you for yours, and I hope that the distressing accident is now completely and utterly forgotten. The hateful part of it is that it makes you nervous instead of merely cautious.

[1] Where Stockhausen lived.

With affectionate greetings and hoping that there will soon be letters between Frankfort and Vienna, Your JOH.

CLARA *to* BRAHMS.

INTERLAKEN, *Sept.* 17.

(*Dictated.*)

Just a word of thanks for the many charming surprises you have given us and above all for the request that the sonatas should be tried at Myliusstrasse. Any time after the end of October will suit me, but not before, because our visitor's room will be occupied until then by various lady friends. You can well understand that my birthday did not go off so cheerfully as it would have done if I had been quite well. But I am now better and we want to leave at the end of the week for Thun, Baden-Baden, and on the 28th we shall be back in Frankfort. This is not the letter I should like to have written to you. But I have got such a mass of letters and inquiries to deal with that I don't know which way to turn, and in addition I cannot use one of my arms. So we shall hope to see you again soon and also have news of you. Remember me to Ilona and tell her everything. I cannot possibly write to her, and I have already had to express my thanks for all the letters from Frankfort through the Press. On account of my accident my work has been doubled this time. How pleased the reporters are when they have any little misfortune like this to talk about. It is terrible! [In her own hand] Ade! Ever your faithful CLARA.

BRAHMS *to* CLARA.

VIENNA, *Oct.* 17.

Would you kindly let me know by return whether it would be convenient to you if Mühlfeld and I were to play the sonatas to you on November the 12th? I should be tremendously pleased if you were to write me a kind "yes." Joachim is playing in Frankfort on the 9th and the 11th, and will have time to be one of the audience on the 12th. We might play the pieces to you on the preceding days so that you could thoroughly appreciate them on the day itself. You will have had enough to disturb you in your house and I propose at first only to stay in the town (I am thinking of coming as

early as the 8th) ; but to come to you on the 12th, and if
you like, to bring Mühlfeld with me, whom I shall ask whether
the time suits him. You will have heard from Frau Franz
that in any case you will have been spared the doubtful pleasure of a first rehearsal, as we have already practised the
sonatas diligently in Berchtesgaden. Anxiously awaiting to
hear whether you can have us, and hoping you will let me
have word soon, with most affectionate greetings, Your
JOHANNES.

CLARA *to* BRAHMS.

FRANKFORT A/M., *Oct.* 19.

I was pleasantly surprised when I received your note yesterday promising me such an enjoyable time.—As far as all the
other arrangements are concerned I shall of course fall in with
anything you may decide, and the oftener I hear the sonatas
the better pleased I shall be. I should be particularly grateful
if you could send them to me at once, so that I could have a
look at them beforehand, for with the wretched trouble in
my head, I am obliged to play very slowly at first anything
which contains a frequent change of harmony, as for instance
developments of all kinds, which are quite new to me. Only
when I have done this can I follow everything in a room.

I gather from your letter that this time you wish to stay
in the town, which I can quite well understand as you would
perhaps feel freer with regard to Mühlfeld and the other musicians. But I cannot agree to your reason that you would
put me out, for your room is, of course, always ready for you
whenever you like to come. With affectionate greetings,
Your old CLARA.

BRAHMS *to* CLARA.

End of October.

Well, this is excellent ! I thank you most heartily, and
look forward to the time [1] as merrily as a cockchafer,[2] that is
to say, quite marvellously, for I haven't the faintest notion
how such a creature behaves when it is merry. I thought of

---

[1] Concerning the time, see Clara's letter to Rosalie Leser of the 17th
of November, 1894, in *Life*, Vol. II, pp. 427–428.

[2] A picture of this creature adorned the sheet of notepaper.

coming early on the 9th, and naturally, if convenient, to come to you. I should have hated to look for an hotel! Mühlfeld has a concert on the 9th, and will come on the afternoon of the 10th, so you could try before supper to see how one or other of the pieces appeals to you.

And now I have to tell you about something which will cause us both a little annoyance. Mühlfeld will be sending you his tuning fork, so that the grand piano to which he is to play may be tuned to it. His clarinet only allows him to yield very little to other instruments. In case your piano differs very much in pitch and you do not wish to use it for this purpose, perhaps Marie will sacrifice herself and allow her grand piano or her upright piano to be tuned to Mühlfeld's fork ? ! I do not really like sending the sonatas (but I shall do so in a day or two). I believe that they may well occupy you for a few hours, but as it is you will have done with them and had all the pleasure out of them by the time we want to start on the 10th !

I have heard vague rumours about a Stockhausen concert or jubilee ? Could you please let me know briefly on a card what, and particularly when, it will be ? He is well again, isn't he ? With affectionate greetings, Your JOHANNES.

CLARA *to* BRAHMS.
(*Postcard.*)

FRANKFORT, *Oct.* 25.

In the first place, thank you for the sonatas just received— I have already exchanged amorous glances with the F minor. How beautiful the clarinet must sound in the first bars, particularly in the second, and again in the fourth ! Many thanks.— I can find out nothing about a jubilee concert for Stockhausen. In any case it cannot be for his fiftieth year. So we may expect you on the morning of the 9th ? May heaven grant that I shall be well enough to enjoy your visit. With affectionate greetings, Your CL.

CLARA *to* BRAHMS.

FRANKFORT, *Nov.* 16.

Shortly after your departure on Wednesday Klinger's work arrived, and I should not like to miss thanking you once more for the beautiful (and all too costly) present. We have already plunged into it once or twice and admired his vigorous imagination, particularly in the plates dealing with the *Shicksalslied*, as well as many details in the execution. But we cannot reconcile ourselves to some of his realistic touches, which strike one all the more in association with such magnificent conceptions. You will know what I mean, and we shall soon, I suppose, be able to discuss it by word of mouth.

My mind is still full of the sonatas and I hope soon to be able to study them, for only then shall I feel that I know them thoroughly. Dear Frau Franz was with us yesterday. It was a real delight to see her. I hope, my dear Johannes, that you did not misunderstand my frequent fits of depression. They were due chiefly to the trouble in my head, which so cruelly marred the great joys that I might have had. Farewell! I am so glad to be able to say *au revoir*! With greetings from Marie and myself, Your old CLARA.

BRAHMS *to* CLARA.

SCHLOSS ALTENSTEIN, *Nov.* 17.

Day follows day here so smoothly and beautifully that it is hard to tear oneself away. Moreover, our Frankfort revelry is continued here. Champagne every day and all sorts of other splendours! It is difficult to describe how charming the family is, but how easy and delightful to enjoy their company! The dear Conductor [1] was also invited to meet us. Young Wüllner was here yesterday and will return to-morrow. Besides being an excellent actor, he plays the violin beautifully and sings equally well. You could not hear my *Volkslieder* sung better than he sings them, for it is not for nothing that he is also a good philologist!

I wish (and the family also wish) that you could sit here at my window, or go out on to my verandah and thence into the glorious park and woods. The most beautiful pheasants, stags and hinds wander about by the dozen before you, and in addition the weather is mild and the company delightful. You would be very happy here.

On Wednesday morning I think of having a few of Bach's orchestra concertos played to me in Meiningen, and a clarinet

[1] Steinbach.

concerto by Weber, and anything else beautiful and rare that may be available. On Thursday I shall probably be in Vienna, and then I shall look back gratefully—above all and most cordially to you and the lovely days I had with you.

Looking forward to seeing you again, I hope, in February, with affectionate greetings, Your JOHANNES.

BRAHMS *to* CLARA.

VIENNA, *Dec.* 23.

A Christmas tree stands in my room for my hostess's two dear boys, and reminds me of the pleasant festival and of those for whom I wish it to be bright and merry. And this I wish you with a warm and—light heart. For although you may have much to complain about, for which age is responsible, you are fundamentally cheerful and are just as able as you were in the prime of your youth, to enjoy all that is beautiful and good.

Allgeyer's fine book [1] was awaiting me also in Altenstein, and to my great joy I found a copy of it here sent to me by the author himself. I hope he will have reason to be pleased with the reception of this excellent work, and this is all the more to be desired seeing that, as you probably do not know, Frau Feuerbach, whom he held in such high respect, has recently become completely estranged from him. In the case of a woman, however excellent she may be, there is no need to inquire into the reason, although she happened to be particularly sorely tried.

Your friend Humperdinck leaves here to-day with his wife after having had a most enjoyable time, as he always does everywhere. His opera was wonderfully produced and has pleased everybody immensely. Even you have enjoyed the piece. I did not pay much attention to what you said at the time, because I had not been particularly pleased with the piano arrangement of it, and had certainly not expected such a pleasant evening. We ought to be all the more glad of his success, seeing that he will certainly not have many more chances. I do not mean because of certain other reasons, but because there is exactly the same light in his eyes as Hermann Götz had.

[1] The Life of Anselm Feuerbach. See *Life*, Vol. II, p. 428.

I must go to Leipsic at the end of January and—show your indignation !—conduct my two concertos for d'Albert on the same evening. I don't think it is in very good taste, but the programme is fixed and, in a good mood, I thought it would be better to give myself the pleasure—which would certainly be none to Reinecke.

The only thing about your Christmas which does not altogether please me is that I shall only be coming in February when Frl. Eugenie will be back in England. With affectionate greetings to you all, Your JOHANNES.

CLARA *to* BRAHMS.

FRANKFORT A/M., *Dec.* 23.

Our last letters must have crossed, and meanwhile Christmas has come upon us and so I will send you my hearty greetings together with my sincerest wishes for the New Year. I wish you every conceivable kind of happiness, health above all.

I must also thank you to-day for the dear letter from Altenstein. How glorious your days there and in Meiningen must have been ! Oh, to have had such an experience for once !

It is nice to think that the New Year will bring you to us so soon again. With such a prospect in view one does not feel the parting so much as when one has only uncertainty to look forward to. The death of Rubenstein was after all somewhat of a shock. It came so suddenly and calls up so many memories. He sacrificed ten or more years of his life to his reputation as a composer, left no stone unturned, never rested and never cried halt. And now he is dead, and probably not a single work of his will survive. It really makes one feel quite sad. How different it is with you ! Everything and everybody, even those who don't want to, stand lost in admiration. You are honoured in every land and it goes on and on. What a magnificent feeling it must be for you ! . . .

Hanslick appears to have written a very fine obituary notice of R. Do you think I might have it some time ?

I often have a look at Klinger, and would so much like to appreciate him without reserve, as the book was a gift from you. But I really cannot ! In spite of all the power of his imagination I cannot get over some of his more prosaic touches.

I feel more inclined to like the bits of landscape ; for instance, the sketches in the margin, and one or two of the plates. I am very anxious to have a good deal explained to me by you.

But now I must close. I should like best of all to think of you on Christmas Eve at the Fellingers ! With most affectionate greetings from the girls and myself, Your old CLARA.

1895

VIENNA, *Beginning of February.*

DEAR CLARA,

It is always a real *gaudium* to you to hear your beloved Leipsic praised whole-heartedly. So let me tell you about my week there, and this pleasure will be yours. It was really one of the most pleasant concert adventures that I have ever had, and the whole visit was so successful that it is difficult to point to anything in particular. First of all, there was the weather, which although it is not often enjoyable in Leipsic, gave me fresh enjoyment every day. Then there was the fact that Herr Kraft (Hôtel-de-Prusse) treated me like a prince but charged me as he would a poor peasant. Thus one thing followed on another, each one better than the last—the orchestra, the quartet, d'Albert, Mühlfeld, the public, the Directors, and, in addition the Museum, Klinger and all the rest. A proof that others were also pleased with the way things went you may see from the following—that d'Albert received 200 marks more than he usually gets from the Directors, and that I who had only counted on a round sum for my travelling expenses received 2,000 marks ! Moreover, the Directors gave a big gala dinner (160 guests) in my hotel, which was so lively and animated that it quite put into the shade the function you and I once attended at Limburger's.

You will not find it easy to imagine two pianoforte concertos following hard upon each other, nor would the idea appeal to you. But everything both in the rehearsal and in the concert itself went so smoothly and perfectly that you would have put up with it. At the final Overture I waited in vain to see whether anybody would get up and go. You will marvel at the intermediate items, but even these were quite right, chiefly owing to the fact that the singer was a really most delightful young girl who sang them excellently (she is a pupil of Frl. Orgeni, whom I happened to see again on this occasion). At this point my gossipy letter strikes me as very poor, but it is impossible to improve it owing to the mass of correspondence that is lying before me. But you have good reason to be pleased with your Leipsic and incidentally with the glorious time it gave me.

On the 14th there is to be a rehearsal of the quintet with clarinet in Frankfort. Could this not take place at your house so that you might listen to it in comfort ? [1] On the 15th I am at Mannheim, on the 16th at Frankfort, on the 17th at Rüdesheim-Beckerath, and on the 18th perhaps I hope I may be allowed to wish you farewell ? With most affectionate greetings, Your JOHANNES.

BRAHMS *to* CLARA.

VIENNA, *Feb.* 6.

DEAR CLARA,

If only you could understand and believe that my pleasure over Frankfort could not be either diminished or enhanced by anything unconnected with you. The mere thought of seeing you for a few days makes me happy. I don't mind seeing in addition any number of musicians and pretty girls —or even the Landgrave and anyone else. As far as I am concerned you can invite him every day and, if at any time he becomes inconvenient, your age and everything associated with it will be sufficient excuse. For he certainly won't be in our way at the rehearsal and we shall only have the pleasure of his hearty appreciation of music.

I was never any good at dates, but I fancy that our days are as follows—13th rehearsal, 14th Mannheim, 15th Frankfort, quartet—17th popular concert (where Mühlfeld will play his clarinet), 18th Rüdesheim. Afterwards I ought really to go on to Meiningen where, among other things, they are giving *Fidelio* and *Les Noces de Figaro*, to which Hanslick and his wife are invited. He would like to go too, but his three-score years and ten make it somewhat doubtful and he cannot make up his mind. But what I should like best of all would be to go straight back home after a last quiet day with you. We

[1] See Diary for February 8, 1895, *Life*, Vol. II, p. 429.

shall see, and above all we shall see each other, with or without the Landgrave, and always with the same pleasure. With affectionate greetings, always your JOHANNES.

CLARA *to* BRAHMS.
(*Postcard.*)

FRANKFORT, *Feb.* 10.

I have just heard that on Wednesday there is to be a subscription concert at the theatre and that Dr. Rottenberg is to produce one of your symphonies. I am writing to tell you this so that you can make arrangements if possible not to arrive here on Wednesday—it would be too much for you after a night in the train and possibly arriving in a snowstorm into the bargain. So come on Tuesday so that you may be fresh and lively on Wednesday. With hearty greetings, Your CL.

BRAHMS *to* CLARA.
(*Postcard.*)

VIENNA, *Feb.*

So I think of leaving here Tuesday evening and reaching you on Wednesday before you sit down to table. If the rehearsal of the quintet should have taken place in the morning the afternoon will be all the more peaceful. But even if it hasn't, the quintet would not upset me. It would not even prevent me from taking a nap. Your card has just come. If I should manage to leave on Monday I shall telegraph in the morning, otherwise I shall look forward to seeing you on Wednesday, Your JOH.

CLARA *to* BRAHMS.

FRANKFORT A/M., *March* 7.

How is it that I have no news of you, for you promised to send me a card from Vienna as soon as you returned ? What a difference, first the lovely week [1] and then your complete silence—it seems so hard to me ! Here everything is very wretched. There is illness everywhere, and deaths among our nearest acquaintances. Stockhausen's child has again been

[1] Concerning Brahms' visit to Frankfort, see Clara's Diary, *Life*, pp. 430-431.

lying for weeks between life and death. It is really difficult to bear up with so much misery all round one. I implore you to let me have a sign of life. You have so much to tell me about. I have heard nothing about Meiningen, *Fidelio*—how my thoughts were with you during the whole of your stay there !

The cold continues and I cannot get out, so sit and brood within my four walls. Let me hear from you soon, Your old CLARA.

BRAHMS *to* CLARA.

March 10.

So by way of return I will sit down at once to my desk and talk to you a little. I should have done so immediately upon my return here—if I could have chatted to you and enthused about Frankfort. Incidentally, if the many letters I found awaiting me here prevented me, the good will to answer them at least made it impossible to write intimately. *Fidelio* was very beautiful. I had not intended to be present on all three evenings, but I did not miss a single bar and literally sucked in the magnificent work with ever-increasing gusto. The performance was in every respect excellent and Frl. Ternina in particular, as Fidelio, was extremely sympathetic (at least for so small a stage). I often wished that you might have been in my seat in a dark box quite close to the stage alone with the Baroness.

Occasionally, when I had a morning free, I used to give myself the pleasure of letting the orchestra play me symphonies by Méhul, Bach and other things which are rarely heard. Sometimes of an evening we would have some chamber music and crack all kinds of most lively musical jokes at a jolly supper table. Half-way through my stay we once went to Merseburg. The enclosed will show you that the people there had some right to see me once in person. All your friends here are, as usual, quite well, except Frau Fellinger who is not in such good health as she usually is. She has to lie down a lot so that I have not yet seen her. To-morrow (Monday) Frau Soldat-Röger with her three colleagues are giving their first ladies' quartet !—Haydn, Schumann, D minor Trio, and Mendelssohn (Ignaz Brüll instead of Frl. Baumair, who has fallen ill).

I love to recall your circle of charming people and musicians. You ought certainly to give yourself and them the pleasure of meeting and talking without restraint more often. To be together is in itself a pleasure (to you as well ?), and you must not think that any special effort is always necessary. I am very, very sorry for Stockhausen. I don't expect to hear the worst yet, for the illness has already lasted so long. Give him my heartiest greetings, as also to others in the town, until at last you come back to Myliusstrasse, where in thought there gladly dwells Your JOHANNES.

CLARA *to* BRAHMS.

FRANKFORT, *May* 6.

Once more a year has gone by on which both you and we can look back with pleasure. To you it has brought much splendid recognition, and to us it has brought you twice. May all the good things of last year be repeated this year. Nowadays I can only look to the immediate future and prefer to let my thoughts dwell on the past. May heaven preserve your wonderful health of body and spirit, this is my greatest wish for you, for all other blessings follow in its train. Unfortunately I missed the Fritschens who visited you a little while ago and could have brought me later news of you. So I do not even know whether you are going to Italy ! And my greeting may not find you in Vienna after all. . . . I know you will be glad to hear a piece of local gossip ; to me it is more than that, for I was delighted to hear it. You know that young Frau Scholz put up a fight to keep her eldest son (ten years old). The divorce was made absolute a few months ago, but she was not allowed the custody of this boy, and was only allowed the two youngest children. Now Scholz has recently married an American (a widow with three children) and the boy in question ought to have gone to his step-mother. But lo, his mother, who had him with her for the Easter holidays has now fled with him and the other children no one knows whither, but it is believed that she has gone to Norway or England ! She was terrified that her husband would go to America and take the boy with him. . . . I marvel at Frau Scholz's spirit but can quite understand it.

A great many of the people here have already gone to the

country, but we must wait until the middle of June, and have taken rooms in Interlaken again. Interlaken suits me so perfectly in every respect. But now enough of this chatter! Farewell and be happy, dear Johannes, and sometimes give a thought to Your old friend CLARA.

BRAHMS *to* CLARA.

VIENNA, *May.*

Your kind greeting reached me here and I might say " unfortunately " in a twofold sense. I should have been glad to have received it on my return from Italy, for that would have meant that I had gone. I am sorry to say I was prevented from doing so for a very lamentable reason. Widmann who has long been deaf in one ear is now threatened in the other. There had been some talk of an Italian watering place which would have been very convenient to me as headquarters for excursions. But he had to remain in Berne to be further mauled about and can only think of travelling now.

Everything else, as far as we are concerned, is in keeping with the spring weather and seems propitious ; the only shadow across our path is poor Rheinthaler.[1] You know that he had a stroke some time ago. His wife once wrote to me that if he had another she would prefer it to be the end. But now she herself, his faithful nurse and companion, is dead, and he must be in a very sad plight.

But, as I say, everything else is all right and they even wanted to invite you here, as you are believed to be already in Munich. So you did not come as far after all. But I am glad about Interlaken and I hope you will be as pleased as you were last year. Shall we go to the musical festival in Zurich together in the autumn ? I was highly delighted by your account of young Frau Scholz. . . .

I am thinking of going to Ischl the day after to-morrow, but all sorts of things have been hindering me, last of all, Frl. Barbi. But the spring is beautiful here too and the Prater quite pleasant.

Now I hope you will be happy in your garden until the greater beauties of Interlaken claim you. With affectionate greetings to you all, Your JOHANNES.

[1] This appears to be meant for Reinthaler.

CLARA *to* BRAHMS.

FRANKFORT A/M., *June* 12.

Yesterday your sonatas arrived and I so much enjoyed seeing them at last so beautifully printed. But just imagine, I have got to let them go to-day ! Eugenie has begged me most urgently to send them to her at once, as she wants to play them to Davies and would like to learn them thoroughly first, because she will then be able to enjoy them more. I do not like to refuse her, and so am writing to you to ask you to get Simrock to send me another copy which I can take with me to Interlaken. Is that very presumptuous on my part ? But you have so often been good enough to let us have two copies that I am emboldened to ask you. But Simrock would have to send them to me at once because we are leaving in the middle of next week (the 19th or 20th).

We were in Düsseldorf the other day and while we were there Kufferath was at the musical festival at Cologne and I did not know it. It really was hard lines ! . . .

This morning I saw the young Rottenberg couple and gave them greetings for you. They want to stay six weeks in Ischl. I know that you like him, so that perhaps if you get to like her when you know her better, it may be very pleasant for you to have them there. They have a horrible custom here —a newly married couple have to give a public reception at their parents' when the bride is on view for the benefit of the most casual acquaintances. I can well imagine what an ordeal this is for a simple man like him.

. . . I am very sorry for poor Rheinthaler.[1] It is terrible. Has he not one of his children with him ? A daughter ? I wonder what you think of Rubenstein's *Christ* ? The reports seem so enthusiastic, but I cannot believe that the music is any good. And now finally to come to what I ought to have said at first, let me thank you for your last kind letter. I wish we were comfortably settled down in Interlaken—there is so much misfortune all round that one becomes quite nervous.

Please greet Ilona for me and tell her what you know, and add how pleased I am to hear of her fine prospects in England next season. Marie sends you heartiest greetings and I hope that you will occasionally give a thought to Your old friend CLARA.

[1] This appears to be meant for Reinthaler.

BRAHMS *to* CLARA.

ISCHL, *June.*

My heartiest good wishes go out to you for your visit to Interlaken where I hope you will again be very happy. What a pity it is that your liking for I. did not happen to coincide with the three years that I was in Thun. How often I used to go over in those days, and how much more often would I not have done so if you had been there! . . . Rheinthaler [1] is full of praise of his youngest daughter who is with him. Rottenberg is still in the offing. . . .

Concerning Rubenstein's *Christ* you need not worry your head any more than the rest of the world! Its notes re-echoed for the last time in Bremen, and it can now rest in the grave of oblivion by the side of its predecessor, *Moses.* The fact that the production was possible at all is due chiefly to speculation supported by the newspapers. Bulthaupt is just the sort of man who can get money out of stockbrokers' pockets and induce newspapers to write articles. With *Moses* they only got as far as a scenic rehearsal (in honour of R. in Prague). One prefers to remember his earlier oratorios rather than these two last and greatest—i.e. longest works. The same applies to other people too. . . .

Bruch has just published a *Moses*, and Herzogenberg has followed up a Mass and a Requiem with a sort of " Birth of Christ." If only one could feel a spark of joy over all these things! They are in every respect weaker and more hopeless than the earlier works of their authors. The only pleasant feature about it all is if one can, as I think I can, thank God for having saved one from the sin, the vice, or the bad habit, of merely covering paper with notes. But in this connection I cannot help again praising your circle of young musicians.

A publication is now appearing in Frankfort called *Der Musikführer*, which though of course very poor and often quite bad, contains essays by Ivan Knorr (about my work too) which cannot help pleasing you. They are as sincere and penetrating as the nature of the publication allows, and—as is so rarely the case to-day and therefore all the more praiseworthy—written with liveliness and vigour. But you must

[1] This apparently is meant for Reinthaler.

surely know them—the bad ones into the bargain, if you have not overlooked the good ones in all the rubbish.

With heartiest greetings to you and Marie and begging you to remember me warmly to Widmann in Berne, Your JOHANNES.

CLARA *to* BRAHMS.

INTERLAKEN, *Aug.* 2.
DR. AEMMER, LINDENGARTEN.

In the first place, belated thanks for your last letter. These were only delayed because I wished to send my Sketches [1] at the same time. You promised me you would look through the Sketches. I had not been able to do so myself, as I had no piano. At last yesterday the Steinweg semi-grand arrived, and so I am able to send them off to you to-day. You were kind enough to promise me your help in this matter, and the thought of it relieves me greatly, for what I regard as most important in these Sketches (which any artist can really arrange for himself) is that they should be as easy and convenient to play as possible. . . . Please, dear Johannes, tell me quite frankly if there is anything you do not like in them. I am not afraid of any amount of trouble, for it would be dreadful if there were any mistakes in them. Eugenie has sold them to Novello to whom I have promised to send them at the end of this month. You will perhaps not agree to the somewhat chaotic method of writing in certain places, but I was thinking more particularly of amateurs to whom I wished to make the voice-progression clear. Then, ought I to give instructions for the use of the pedal everywhere or only here and there where it is absolutely necessary ? So please, please, give me your kind advice ! Ought I to use German or Italian signs of expression ?

We are now quite at home again here and very comfortable in our fine quarters. As usual Marie is looking after everything. If only one did not keep on hearing of so many sad things which haunt one all day. Various kind friends of mine on the Rhine [2] have died, and every week I have to write letters of condolence. And now we are in the middle of a tragedy

---

[1] Clara's arrangement for two pianos of her husband's pedal pieces. They were published by Novello in London.

[2] Among others her old friend Lida Bendemann in Düsseldorf.

which affects us very much. A nephew of Wachs', the son of Mendelssohn's eldest daughter, went for a tour with a friend but without a guide, and they never returned. This was three weeks ago. The father and mother came from England and have had a thorough search made everywhere for the last fortnight. But all in vain! What a terrible thing for the poor parents! . . . Now let me thank you once more for your last letter which greatly interested and amused me. Farewell, do not be angry with me for giving you so much trouble, and for asking you to send me back the Sketches. I hope you will have someone there who will pack them for you. With most affectionate greetings from the three of us, Your old CLARA.

BRAHMS *to* CLARA.

ISCHL, *Aug.* 10.

In the first place the material as it stands is good enough for the engraver and you need not have any of it copied, or try to make anything clearer (or ink over the pencil marks). But I am rather afraid of sending the things back to you! In my first enthusiasm I made a lot of corrections which are certainly wanted, but now I have added all sorts of modifications which I hope you will allow to stand, though I cannot take it for granted that you will. Your work reveals such splendid and loving industry that I can assure you I did not mark it for the sake of doing so. If only you will be able to understand it all and agree with me! ? ! Many thanks for your letter and may I beg you to let me have a short account of how the sad Mendelssohn affair ends. Perhaps you will be able to send me a newspaper describing it. I am sorry for Reinecke (we have his successor here). But the same thing is happening to him as has happened to almost everybody whom I have seen grow old. It affects some people worse, as, for instance, Verhulst and Rheinthaler [1] among others. Rottenberg and his young wife were a real joy. . . . (Mühlfeld and Steinbach have just announced that they are coming for the afternoon.) Widmann has written to tell me what delightful quarters you have. And now with heartiest greetings to the whole of the round table, Your JOHANNES.

[1] This apparently is meant for Reinthaler.

CLARA *to* BRAHMS.

INTERLAKEN, *Aug.* 17.

How can I thank you enough for the pains you have taken with the things I sent you.[1] What a lot of trouble you must have had with so amateurish a MS. as mine, how many sheets were missing, how many false strokes there must have been and how many signs of all kinds lacking. If only I could do you some really great favour in return !

Of course I cannot do anything else but agree to all your alterations, and have naturally left them just as you made them. I am not quite sure what the title ought to be and don't like to leave it to the publisher. Shall I call it : "Selections from the Studies (Sketches) for Pedal-piano. Op. 56, 58, by Robert Sch., arranged by Cl. Sch." ? To mention the numbers in the title seems wrong somehow. Please help me about this too. You are so used to these things. Just send me the title as it should be on a postcard, do not trouble about a letter, for you have so many to write.

The sad affair about young Benecke remains shrouded in mystery. He was last seen climbing one of the less known paths up the Jungfrau. He was a member of the Alpine Club and may perhaps have been wishing to find a new road. In a paper in which the reward of 500 francs for the recovery of the body is offered by the parents, it is also announced that the young people probably had a good deal of money on them which would become the property of the finder. But this makes one begin to wonder whether they were not perhaps waylaid and robbed ? They had no guide with them. It is dreadful. Of course nothing more will be heard of them.

We have had almost three whole weeks of bad weather. We ought now to be able to hope for something better. To-morrow I expect Widmann and his wife and I am much looking forward to it. Yes, if only you were in Thun as you used to be, how nice it would be for you to come over whenever the weather was fine ! Now let me thank you once more, my dearest Johannes, very heartily and please let me know the title on a card !—My greetings to Ilona. Thank her for her letter. She writes so gratefully about your kindness and

[1] See Clara's Diary for the 13th of August, *Life*, Vol. II, p. 432.

affability to her. Everybody, including myself, sends you
greetings. Your faithful old friend CLARA.

BRAHMS *to* CLARA.

ISCHL, *Second half of August.*

That you should think that everything I sent you was
right has given me the greatest pleasure. I should not object
and the publisher could only be pleased if the individual
pieces were mentioned in the title, with key (and price). One
or two of them are sure to be particularly liked and in demand.
So I suggest something of this sort, " Selections from the
Studies and Sketches for Pedal-piano by R. Sch. Op. ? (now
do not forget) Piano-arrangement for two hands by Cl. Sch.

Studies.			Sketches.		
No. 1.	A minor.	50 Pf. [6d.]	No. 1.	C minor.	40 Pf. [4½d.]
No. 2.	A Flat major		No. 2.	F minor	
No. 3.	B minor		No. 3.	D Flat major	
No. 4.	B major "				

So you have had three weeks' bad weather ? I don't remember ever having had such an exemplarily fine summer. It has
seldom been too hot to be comfortable and although the sky
was often overcast most of our heavy rain has come at night.
We have a large company of very nice jolly people here and
have a lot of music—Mühlfeld was also here, so we had the
clarinet quintet and sonatas. Yes, in Thun I should certainly
have had the most delightful and pleasant things to do—on
Sundays ; but for the more numerous days of the week Austrians are after all more pleasant company than the cosmo-
politan crew you get over there. Greet Widmann heartily
for me. Does he ever send you his newspaper ? You might
also ask him for an essay about Allgeyer's Feuerbach which
is well worth reading and noting.

Will you be so kind as to let me know when you intend to
go on your travels again. I ought really to be at the Meiningen
musical festival at the end of September (ditto in Zurich,
middle of October). I have given Frl. Eibenschütz your
greetings. Thank God, lady pianists are modest in their
demands and readily think me amiable ! When the time
comes why don't you simply send the proofs of the pedal-

piano pieces to me ? I think you will give yourself more
trouble with them than is necessary. With most affectionate
greetings to you all, Your JOHANNES.

BRAHMS *to* CLARA.

ISCHL, *Aug.* 27.

. . . You surely don't think it possible that I shall attend
the festival,[1] a notice of which I enclose. I don't like talking
about it and shall not do so. But I don't know what to do.
It is no good protesting and if I stay away I shall offend a
number of very worthy people. On the 11th of September
Hanslick will celebrate his seventieth birthday at a friend's
house in Gmunden. If you want to do him the pleasure of
sending him a line of congratulation let me have your note a
few days beforehand. I cannot help it, but I know few men
for whom I feel such a hearty attachment as I do for him.
To be as simple, good, benevolent, honourable, serious and
modest and everything else, as I know him to be, I regard
as something very beautiful and rare. How often has it not
been my privilege to find with joyful emotion that he was all
these things ! And I am all the more entitled to proclaim his
immense ability in his own sphere, seeing that we each have
such very different points of view. Nevertheless, where he is
concerned, I entertain no illegitimate expectations or demands.

But now let your English gold pieces be forwarded to you
and quaff your champagne merrily every evening in Interlaken, and may they outlast your stay. With hearty greetings to the beloved trio, Your JOHANNES.

BRAHMS *to* CLARA.

ISCHL, *Sept.* 10.

It is in September that one realizes what a lucky number
thirteen is and how unjustly it is maligned. For very special
stars must have gleamed—anno 19—, and what is the good
of other beautiful months (May, for instance), and the most
sacred of numbers (seven, for instance) ; nothing much good
ever came out of them ! May we all celebrate this beloved
thirteenth often and right merrily, feeling grateful to the

[1] The Saxe-Meiningen Music Festival, conducted by Fritz Steinbach,
from September the 27th to the 29th.

auspicious stars—you for all the beauty and joy your life has brought you, and we—because they brought us you.

Things are progressing splendidly with regard to my visit. The Duke is suffering with such severe ear trouble that he is not allowed to listen to any music at all, so he will not be able to be present at the festival and I have to pay him a visit at Schloss Altenburg. So I shall be able to reach you precisely at the right time and see Frl. Eugenie come to the breakfast table—a little bit later than the rest. I cannot help feeling in my heart of hearts that so soon after your own return home a visitor will be a little premature! I propose to go to Vienna on Monday the 16th. To-night I am going to Gmunden and Joachim is also coming there to-morrow. The Fellingers left the other day for Aussee on a short visit. The weather continues to be extraordinarily fine, and this is very pleasant, especially for people with short holidays. Wendt who left yesterday has never known it so fine. . . .

But now turn to your other letters for correspondence will be your lot these days. With affectionate greetings to you all, Your JOHANNES.

BRAHMS *to* CLARA.
(*Postcard.*)

ISCHL, *Sept.* 13.

The 13th is a wonderful mild grey day, admirably suited to allowing one to send out friendly thoughts to a certain person. Your little note pleased H.[1] immensely, particularly the ending! He was wonderfully lively and well disposed and thoroughly enjoyed the two days (on the eve of his birthday there were fireworks, etc.). I wrote and told you that Joachim was coming too, and that I was leaving on Monday. And so with best greetings for to-day and all the days that may follow, Your JOHANNES.

CLARA *to* BRAHMS.

INTERLAKEN, *Sept.* 17.

Your letter and the card that followed pleased me very

---

[1] In response to Brahms' request, Clara agreed to write to Hanslick, and in a letter dated August 29th she says: "I have the greatest respect for him, and even if I had not, your high opinion of him would be enough to make me write."—TR.

much. Many thanks. We spent the day quite pleasantly. The weather was not fine, but it was cheerful enough indoors, thanks to the love of my daughters, and the kind thoughts of my friends, whose total number was almost alarming. I had over a hundred letters, not counting telegrams and cards. This time I decided to answer about half of them with a few printed lines. I suppose we shall hear before the end of the month when you are coming. We shall probably return about the 28th or 29th inst. as the lessons begin on the 1st of October. Your room will be ready from the 2nd of October onwards. I hope you will not mind if things do not go quite smoothly, as we are a servant short and shall have to find one. All news when we see you, which the trio are heartily looking forward to. CLARA, MARIE, EUGENIE.

I am so glad Hanslick was pleased with my letter. I have really forgotten what I said at the end. Widmann has written beautifully about him and must certainly have sent you the article. . . .

BRAHMS *to* CLARA.

VIENNA, *Nov.* 4.

I have not forgotten that you wanted to have news of my journey. Well, it was a successful and very pleasant one, particularly that part of it from Zürich on the Arlberg railway. Unfortunately you could not do the journey or enjoy it because it is often rather adventurous and dangerous. But it is magnificent, notwithstanding, and I enjoyed it in the finest possible weather after a cheerful and pleasant time in Zürich. You will have received the programme, and you do not require to be told that the people of Zürich are a jolly crowd who delight in giving themselves a little extra amusement by playing with theatricals, wreaths and speeches. But on this occasion they had selected an exceptionally beautiful and gifted girl who appeared wreathed for a speech. She was the daughter of Baechtold, the biographer of Gottfried Keller, and the festive performance was also by a highly gifted poetess (Ricardo Huch).

Robert Schumann's *Nachtlied* is a particular favourite of Hegar's and of the people of Zürich. On this occasion, however, there was an amusing intermezzo as far as we were con-

cerned, though it was not amusing for him.   After the eternal
ff in the *Triumphlied* and the Ninth Symphony, the chorus
could not, at the general rehearsal on the following morning,
accustom itself to the p and the pp of this delicate piece.
Hegar was not at all happy, but in the evening it went perfectly.

To set your mind at rest I must tell you that my journey
from Frankfort here was very beautiful.   The first prerequisite
of a journey, if it is to be pleasant, is that one should have
enjoyable things to look back upon and to look forward to.
Consequently I looked back—and forward to my next visit
to you.   You ought really to give one evening a week to the
charming young folk around you.   Such a delightful circle of
people is not easy to find, and for you as well as for them it
would be a genuine pleasure.   You too will find the beautiful
mild weather very agreeable.   In Zürich I went about without an overcoat, and I am still doing so here.   Wishing you
farewell, and with most affectionate greetings to you and Marie,
Your JOHANNES.

CLARA *to* BRAHMS.

FRANKFORT, *Nov.* 28.

I have not yet thanked you for your last letter, but there
was no news to write to you about here, except that things
are looking rather wretched, so that it was better to be silent.
But to-day I am writing to ask you to be good enough to look
at the Novello things (proofs) for me.   I corrected the Studies
weeks ago, but not the Sketches, which I have only just
received.   I feel so unwell, however, that I am sending the
whole batch to you at once, as you so kindly promised to
do it for me.

I have heard a lot about Zürich.   It must have been very
fine.   Marie has been in bed for a month with sciatica.   It is a
great trial of patience for her, because she is otherwise quite
well and is only unable to use her legs.   For the last few days
she has been giving her lessons from a couch and is quieter
now.   It was a terrible thing for her to have to leave her pupils
without their lessons, because the courses are arranged and
she has to make up for lost time.   I was able to take a little off
her hands, but it was not enough.   I am still far from well.

I only see those who come to me and only live for the poor patient. With most affectionate greetings, dear Johannes, Your old friend CLARA.

BRAHMS *to* CLARA.
(*Postcard.*)

VIENNA, *Dec.* 1.

Probably through an oversight on the part of the publisher I have only received the first page of each of the four Studies, i.e. four pages in all. The simplest thing would be for the publisher to send me complete proofs of the Studies. I would then send the whole back to you. The things, however, seem to be excellent and free from faults. I am very sorry about Marie's illness of which I had already heard. It is to be hoped that the most inconvenient stage will soon be over, and that you will be able to look forward with all the greater joy to the coming festival. Hoping that this may be so, and with affectionate greetings to you both, Your JOH.

CLARA *to* BRAHMS.

FRANKFORT A/M., *Dec.* 2.

How shocked I am to find that my carelessness should have given you so much trouble. I had already corrected the Studies and sent them back at once, but the main point is I felt so ill, that after merely glancing at the title pages of the proofs, I sent them on to you. If I had calmly waited a day or two this would not have happened. (Forgive the drop of water.) I have written off at once to Eugenie to ask her to inform Novello, etc., etc. You will now be sure to receive the proofs direct.

Things still look very sad here. For a month now Marie has practically been in bed the whole time, but, to our great relief, is now giving her lessons again, although, of course, she can still only lie beside the piano. As for me, I have been suffering from stomach trouble all through the autumn. This has given me rather a bad time, and, in addition, I have been frightfully depressed by Marie's illness. In such circumstances one has to make a real effort to keep going. In this respect the lessons are a godsend to me, for they prevent me from being idle, and my thoughts are diverted from my own troubles.

Farewell, be indulgent, and think kindly occasionally of Your old CLARA.

CLARA *to* BRAHMS.
FRANKFORT A/M., *Dec.* 7.

I am quite desperate, for to-day I found in a pigeon-hole, where I put all important papers requiring attention, my first proofs of the Studies. Owing to my anxiety about Marie, which unfortunately is not yet over, I had forgotten that I wished to keep these proofs back until Novello sent me proofs of the Sketches. So I am sending them to you at once, and would be glad if you would kindly look at them to see whether by any chance there are not some further corrections which might be made in the final proof. I know very well that nothing escapes you. But I think it better to send them to you all the same. Forgive me for giving you this extra trouble. It is terrible to have so much on one's shoulders, and to be ill oneself into the bargain ! Send me a word of comfort soon, dear Johannes, and be lenient with Your most distressed friend CLARA.

BRAHMS *to* CLARA.
VIENNA, *Dec.* 11.

Your revised proofs are going off to-day, and I hope and pray that you will be content just to look through and glance at my numerous corrections without giving yourself the trouble to search for further mistakes. You will see that in the case of a loving proof reader like myself a quite sufficient number of them have been found, and I hope you will think this is enough.

If you are afraid that everything has not been carefully and properly seen to, let Novello be asked to send either to Frl. Eugenie or to me a set of revises ; but they must enclose my corrected proofs with them. Then all that we (Frl. E. or I) will have to do will be to glance through them to see that all my corrections have been put in. But what a lot of trouble you always give yourself ! Once again I have been touched by it and perhaps faintly annoyed too. If I can be of service to you, I regard every crescendo in the trouble you give me as most welcome. And fancy your having copied three of the Sketches and three of the Studies over again ! It almost

tempts me to play a little trick on you.   But I will confess it
to you beforehand—it tempts me to put these things in our
archives by the side of the venerable MSS. of our old Caldara,
Fux, Haydn and Mozart!   They would really do very well as
gifts for kind friends and good pupils, but you would never
think them neat and clean enough for that!   If you want
them for this purpose, just drop me a line.

I hope your sky will at last clear.   There is nothing I would
like to hear more!   Your JOHANNES.

CLARA *to* BRAHMS.

FRANKFORT, *Dec.* 13.

I am quite horrified at the number of mistakes you have
been able to find.   I could not resist looking through the
pieces, for after all I am very much interested in them.   Of
course Novello will have to send revises, but I shall not trouble
you with them again.

What's all this about my stuff that you want to send to the
Library?   Those MSS. were not written by me!   You must
have kept some of them back.   Even if they were my MSS.,
however, I should think it far too conceited and undignified
to present them to the library.   Your intention can surely
only be flattering to me.   Please send me a card about it, as I
don't understand at all.   Neither outwardly nor inwardly is the
sky clearing, and I really don't know what to talk to you
about.   So once more many thanks for all you have done, and
with most affectionate greetings, Your old friend CLARA.

Marie also sends her kindest greetings.   Eugenie is coming
on the 17th, and that will be our Christmas treat.

BRAHMS *to* CLARA.
(*Postcard.*)

VIENNA, *Dec.* 16.

You can't get out of it now—in your last parcel you enclosed
by mistake three studies and three sketches in your own very
best handwriting, in addition to the copies for the printer.
Don't forget that the revises must have my corrected proofs
with them in order that you may see that all corrections have
been embodied and can, moreover, look for other mistakes
yourself!   It would be much simpler if you would leave the

whole thing to me ! ! ! But how delightful that Frl. Eugenie is coming for Christmas ! Your sky will most certainly have to clear and become bright before then. With hearty greetings, Your JOH.

CLARA *to* BRAHMS.

FRANKFORT A/M., *Dec.* 19.

How I came to send you the old MS. again with the other things, I have not the faintest idea !—probably because it was so dreadful that I had it copied again. So let me implore you to allow one of your zealous disciples to pack the MS. up and to send it to me. It will greatly relieve my mind, because I am thoroughly ashamed of such badly written music. Don't be angry with me for the trouble I have given you about this matter, but I shall feel so much relieved when I have got it again—but not to present it to anyone !

To-day I received the last proofs, but could only look at the first few pages, and found everything all right. Thank you once more. And now wishing you a happy Christmas, and myself your kind thoughts, Your old CLARA.

Everything is just the same with us. But we have a Christmas treat in our Eugenie, who arrived yesterday and who with Marie sends you heartiest greetings.

BRAHMS *to* CLARA.

Dec.

Praise be to Eugenie whose arrival will certainly work miracles and turn the coming holiday into a real festival for you. In addition I should like to think of a few dear jolly girl pupils round the brightly gleaming Christmas tree.

On the 10th of January I have got to conduct my two concertos in Berlin for d'Albert. Unfortunately it is announced in the papers and I am now being pestered with invitations to and from all corners of the globe. Has Widmann ever sent you his new volume of stories [1] and particularly a little poem called " *Bin der Schwärmer* " [2] ? If he hasn't I will give it to you, as a belated Christmas present. It is extremely charming ! In any case I would like to give you something for

[1] *Die Weltverbesserer und andere Geschichten,* 1896.
[2] Idyll, 1896.

Christmas if only I knew what ! All rooms, cases and caskets are full—and I prefer to have the best books lent rather than given to me. . . .

And now with best wishes for the New Year and affectionate greetings, I am, Your JOHANNES.

1896

CLARA *to* BRAHMS.

FRANKFORT A/M., *Jan.* 21.

DEAR JOHANNES,

I have not written to you for a long time, have not even sent you my good wishes for your journey, and yet I have thought so much about it. But I have been too much depressed. We still have so much to worry us and cause us anxiety. Marie is better. She can come downstairs for half the day again, but a great trouble which has been occupying us for the last week has made us feel very miserable. About a week ago Louis [1] had a stroke when he was out hunting. It is true that the doctors say that it is only a slight one, but it is serious enough nevertheless. Elise went to him at once, with how heavy a heart you may well imagine. He is lying in a gamekeeper's cottage about eight hours' distance from here, and everything had to be fetched from Reydt, which is two hours away. Night and day the doctors have been with him, and although they entertain every hope of his recovery he hasn't got back his speech yet, which makes him desperate— he is quite conscious. His son Robert has just arrived to tell us he is going there to-morrow and that his father will be brought here on Friday. But we are naturally very anxious, for the utmost care will be necessary to prevent another stroke. Poor Elise ! What calamities we poor mortals have to endure !

You have had another magnificent reception—I followed it with the same old faithful heart ; you know that, although I have been silent. I myself have not been at all well,[2] and must

[1] Sommerhoff, her son-in-law.

[2] In spite of this she played the piano to the pupils on the 23rd of January at the end of a so-called *Vorspielstunde* (demonstration lesson), and selected for the purpose some of the sketches she had arranged for the piano. " She played with wonderful power and freshness, as also with her own peculiar rhythm. It was the first time this winter that

therefore close. With most affectionate greetings, Your old
CLARA.

BRAHMS *to* CLARA.

VIENNA, *Jan.* 26.

DEAR CLARA,

I cannot get your unexpected bad news out of my head. I
suppose Elise will at least have the unfortunate invalid at home
by now. I wish you could let me have a card to tell me that
she has less cause for anxiety, or that she has at least no reason
to fear more serious developments.

It is a beautiful thing to have a family and to live in close
relationship with people who not only belong to us through
ties of blood but who are dear and precious to us on their own
account. In the course of a long life you have had your full
measure of such joys, but with how much anxiety and pain
are they not all too often paid for ? And this also you have
experienced to the full and continue to do so. At such moments one is apt to forget for a while that the best in life has
always to be paid for by such suffering. You would not like
to change places with some anchorite who can no longer go
through such things. If only this time it may not be too hard !
But unfortunately some anxiety and trouble must needs remain.

I do not feel as if I could begin to discuss other matters to-
day, not even my journey, the greatest joy of which to me was
Menzel and his wonderful pictures. I hope soon to receive a
card from you which will relieve my mind a little. Give Elise
my heartiest sympathy and accept my most affectionate greetings for Marie and yourself, Your JOHANNES.

CLARA *to* BRAHMS.

FRANKFORT A/M., *Jan.* 30.

Many thanks for your extremely friendly and sympathetic
letter. True as all you say undoubtedly is, I find it very hard
to derive comfort from what is past, when really the only
thing that truly comforts one is hope and this is ever more and
more denied to old age. But you will naturally have realized

she had played before anybody." From a letter of Marie Schumann's
to Rosalie Leser. See *Life*, Vol. II, p. 434.

that, just as you happened to be in Berlin I was in the midst of all my trouble, and I kept completely silent, although I often thought of you. My heart was much too depressed, I could certainly think longingly but I could not write about anything that stirred me.

Louis is a little better, but it is so little that it is hardly perceptible. He cannot speak yet, which is very painful to him, and he cannot even think coherently. To-day he is to sit up in bed for the first time, but his head will have to be supported all the while. Some comfort may be derived from the fact that the doctors believe him to be a thoroughly healthy man and that they venture to prophesy a complete recovery. Marie is better and is once more a living guardian angel at my side. I am so pleased about it. If only I could feel better! But, after all, although they give me so much pain, mine are only small infirmities.

I was very much surprised by your remark about Menzel. Is he really such a great artist? I hardly know anything of his. If you have any time to spare, do write and tell me something about him. And now with most affectionate greetings from Marie and myself, as ever, Your old CLARA.

Were you satisfied with Leipsic? Do you know an author of the name of Prof. Rudolf Künhel-Engelsberg in Vienna?

BRAHMS *to* CLARA.

Feb. 4.

First of all let me say that I happened to find myself in the company of Hanslick and other members of his craft, but no one knew the name of your Viennese author. So spare your scruples this time and—remain silent, as I do in such cases (true, I don't know what it is all about!?).

I wanted to have a shot at talking to you a little about Menzel, the great artist (probably the greatest of our time), and the splendid man as well. But it has occurred to me that it would be simpler to send you the accompanying volume. If you care to look through it, it would tell you much more than any letter could. What I like about him more particularly is that he is the only one of our famous men who lives in the most humble bourgeois circumstances. His rooms are not half as high or as big as yours, and you have never seen a studio furnished with such supreme simplicity.   The vitality and *joie de vivre* of this little octogenarian would certainly amuse you.   When I am in Berlin he always comes towards midnight to my tavern or wherever else I happen to be—Joachim and others would like to do the same !

It was very fine in Leipsic.   Nikisch is an extraordinarily gifted conductor.   When he is dealing with things about which he is enthusiastic (and my symphonies are among these) he does his work perfectly.   The other day he gave the fourth. It is impossible to hear it better done.   I sincerely hope and believe that Sommerhoff will steadily improve and ultimately be quite well.   If only the critical period might soon be over ! Heartiest greetings to Elise and to your living, and, I hope, now twice happy guardian angel from Your JOHANNES.

CLARA *to* BRAHMS.
(*Postcard.*)

Feb. 10.

I want to thank you, if only on a card, for the interesting volume which you have sent me.   Unfortunately I am feeling so poorly that I cannot write a letter.   I hope I shall soon be better.   Louis is improving slowly step by step.

I have been diligently reading about Menzel and had no idea that he was so important.   And now thanking you once more, Your CLARA.

CLARA *to* BRAHMS.
(*Postcard.*)

Feb. 25.

Please do me the favour of adding the address to the enclosed card and putting it in the post.   I cannot write to you as well as I should like because I am very poorly.   The northeast wind which you, lucky creature, hardly notice, tells on me very much although I do not leave my room.   The poor Fabers !   Most affectionately yours, CLARA.

BRAHMS *to* CLARA.

Feb.

. . . It pleases me and does me good to tell you something about young Röntgen.   Yesterday he gave his second concert

with Messchaert, and will return in a few days for a third and
fourth. They have both made a very good impression and
have had the greatest success. Messchaert, whose voice really
has no particular charm, sings so simply and with such warmth
of feeling that it is a real joy. Yesterday the *Dichterliebe* [1] was
quite exquisite, particularly as far as R.'s performance was
concerned. Every note and every chord came out as if it were
struck with peculiar love. But he is in any case quite a unique
and exceptionally lovable man. He has remained a child, quite
innocent, pure, open and enthusiastic, and you have long been
familiar with his extremely comic, naïf and nervous manner-
isms. He is so careless in his demeanour that many people
asked me whether he was really to be taken seriously. And yet
one can and ought to take him seriously. I have not got so
much enjoyment out of a man for a long time.

Our weather here is almost always glorious—I certainly
never trouble to inquire whether the wind is north-east or south-
west. After the concert and lunch to-day I am thinking of
going with Röntgen to Schönbrunn. A poor concert-giver
like him is never able to see anything ! Next time he is going
to bring his sister from Leipsic and hopes to have a few quiet
days. I hope Elise's affairs are straightening out and that
you and Marie are well. With affectionate greetings, Your
JOHANNES.

BRAHMS *to* MARIE SCHUMANN.

VIENNA, *April.*

What a fright your dear mother has given us. [2] Fortunately
other comforting news has come, besides your letter, so that
for the time being I suppose I may feel reassured.

You know you have my heartiest sympathy, but although
at a time like this I should like to do everything possible to
spare your feelings, it can't be helped, and with a heavy heart
I must ask you, if you think the worst is to be expected, to be
so good as to let me know, so that I may come while those dear
eyes are still open ; for when they close so much will end
for me !

[1] By Rob. Schumann.
[2] After having felt very ill for the whole of the month, Clara had had
a slight stroke on the 26th of March. See *Life*, Vol. II, p. 346.

Forgive me, for I sincerely hope that my anxiety is unfounded. But just think how gladly I would make the unnecessary journey and with what joy I would return if she, who is above all things dear to us, were still left to us. So I implore you as urgently as I can, and Ferdinand I am sure will be good enough to send me a short telegram, which I still hope will be reassuring and comforting ! Affectionately yours, J. BRAHMS.

BRAHMS *to* MARIE SCHUMANN.

April.

How can I thank you heartily enough for your letter ? . . . The first painful news arrived on the day on which I wished to go to Meran. The journey never took place and ever since then I have daily felt the temptation to come to Frankfort, chiefly, of course, on your mother's account, but also because my heart yearned to see you and your dear sisters and to prove, as far as I was able, how much attached I am to you. But as far as you were concerned I was afraid I might only be an inconvenience, although as regards your mother your fears were also my fears. But the latter could not have been more completely and more comfortingly confirmed and at the same time dispelled than they were by your dear letter.[1]

The Berlin Academy Festivals (to which I am not going) can be given to your mother as a pretext for my dropping in at Frankfort during the course of the next few weeks,—as it were on my way there and back. How glad I should be to see her and to be able to tell all three of you how deeply I feel for you. Your most devoted J. BRAHMS.

CLARA *to* BRAHMS.

May 7.[2]

Heartiest good wishes from your affectionate and devoted CLARA SCHUMANN.

I cannot very well do any more yet, but or soon Your ——

[1] From the 3rd of April onwards Clara's condition seemed to improve, and the improvement lasted for about five weeks.

[2] On the evening of the 7th Clara's grandchild, Ferdinand, reminded her of Brahms' birthday. She immediately took a pencil and wrote in bed these not very legible and not very lucid lines.

BRAHMS *to* CLARA.

May 8.

" The last was the best "—never has this maxim been brought home to me more beautifully than it has to-day when the dearest thing of all, your wishes for the 7th, arrived. A thousand thanks and may you have as happy a surprise quite soon—above all, of course, the exquisite feeling of returning health.

I understand that you intend going to Baden-Baden. If so I must beg you to let me know when and for how long you think of going. For quite apart from your visit I always feel a sort of longing for Baden ; but would be so glad to take advantage of this opportunity in order to see that long-loved landscape— and friend again.

But you certainly cannot be allowed to read more than this, nor do I wish to write about anything else. But it would be selfish of me to be the only one to send you greetings, you can have no idea how much you are in the thoughts of numberless people here ! At all events I hope you will believe that none of them send you heartier greetings than Your JOHANNES.

BRAHMS *to* MARIE SCHUMANN.

VIENNA, *May* 8.

I thank you from the bottom of my heart that you did not keep back your dear mother's greetings to me and that you sent such a dear kind letter of your own with them. Just as your mother's greetings were the last, there was one that came from Grimm in Münster on the 6th which was the first.

You know, of course, what sad experiences the poor man has had and how hard it has been for him. But he has fortunately risen above it all and finds his son and daughter, who are living with him, the greatest comfort.

May I be allowed to repeat my request that you will let me know if and when you are going to Baden,[1] and with most

---

[1] On the very day that Brahms wrote his last words to Clara she felt so much better that she allowed herself to be taken out into her garden full of flowers in her wheeled chair. But on the night of the 10th she had another and more severe stroke, and on the 20th of May, at twenty-one minutes past four in the afternoon, she breathed her last. At half-past six the sad news was telegraphed to Brahms as follows : " Our

affectionate greetings to all, and the best and heartiest wishes,
Your J. B.

BRAHMS *to* MARIE *and* EUGENIE SCHUMANN.

June 12.

I feel I must tell you once more how constantly and with what
feelings of deep sympathy my thoughts are with you.   You
have a number of real friends who cling to you faithfully and
are wholly devoted to you—many more than you think, for of
the best you will hear least.   But what I am thinking is that
the loss of your beloved mother has not only given you untold
pain but has radically altered your position and your circumstances and made them in many respects very difficult.   What
great and valuable possessions has not her full long life left
behind for you !   Regarding many things you may be at your
wits' end to know what to do, or may be troubled by this or
that difficulty (how can I tell ?).

Forgive me for these few vague words.   What they really
wish to convey is simply this, that I am a good and true friend
to you, that I am in every respect quite independent and that
I can think of no greater pleasure than to be able to serve, to
advise, or to help you in any way.   I cannot unfortunately add
that I am a very practical man !   But—after all you know me,
and I hope that with all this I am telling you nothing you do
not expect.

I hope that Herr Sommerhoff will continue to improve so
that you may find your best support in your sister Elise.

With most affectionate greetings to you all, Your deeply and
truly devoted J. BRAHMS.

BRAHMS *to* MARIE SCHUMANN.

July 7.

What I was really thinking of when I spoke of the things
that might be perplexing you, was above all the diaries, letters
and such things.

Unfortunately, for the time being I know of only one word—
Caution !   In the first place be careful to make arrangements

mother fell gently asleep to-day.   Marie Schumann.''   Regarding the
funeral ceremonies at Frankfort and Bonn, where Brahms walked behind
the coffin at the head of Clara's old friends, see *Life*, Vol. II, pp. 438–439.

that in any circumstances (or circumstance) these things shall only leave your possession in order to be transferred with full rights to the second daughter, i.e. Elise.   Then I implore you not to allow anything to leave your hands and to go to anybody else without first consulting me or some other friend in whom you have complete and unbounded confidence.   Regarding all this I may some time have a good deal more to say.   But at all events I am ready to come to Frankfort at any moment if you have any questions to ask or wishes to be carried out.

I cannot accustom myself to the thought that you are leaving your house and putting it up for sale.   But I do not ask you to send me any details about this, as I feel certain you have considered the matter thoroughly.   But, as you still possess it, I can only entreat you to think the matter over quite dispassionately.   You will certainly find a good tenant for part of the house, and even if you may live a little more expensively than necessary, think of what compensations you will have.   On the other hand, if you move, and have occasion to change about again, which is not improbable, think what a lot of trouble and expense you will be involved in.

Now just one thing more.   If you should receive a volume of " serious songs " in a few days' time, do not misunderstand it. Quite apart from my dear old habit of always writing your name first in such cases, these songs really concern you very closely.   I wrote them in the first week of May.   Some such words as these have long been in my mind, and I did not think that worse news about your mother was to be expected—but deep in the heart of man something often whispers and stirs, quite unconsciously perhaps, which in time may ring out in the form of poetry or music.   You will not be able to play the songs yet, because the words would affect you too much, but I beg you to regard them and to lay them aside merely as a death offering to the memory of your dear mother.

I must thank you most heartily for your kind offer to send me some memento of her—but I want nothing.   Men are wont to desire some outward token of remembrance, and the smallest trifle would suffice for me,—but I possess the most beautiful of all !   With most affectionate greetings to you all, Your wholly devoted J. BRAHMS.

INDEX